UNDER THE TABLE

UNDER THE TABLE

SAUCY TALES FROM CULINARY SCHOOL

KATHERINE DARLING

ATRIA BOOKS
New York London Toronto Sydney

ATRIA BOOKS

A Division of Simon & Schuster, Inc.
1230 Avenue of the Americas
New York, NY 10020

First Atria Books hardcover edition April 2009

ATRIA BOOKS and colophon are trademarks of Simon & Schuster, Inc.

For information about special discounts for bulk purchases, please contact Simon & Schuster Special Sales at 1-866-506-1949 or business@simonandschuster.com.

The Simon & Schuster Speakers Bureau can bring authors to your live event. For more information or to book an event contact the Simon & Schuster Speakers Bureau at 1-866-248-3049 or visit our website at www.simonspeakers.com.

Designed by Nancy Singer

Manufactured in the United States of America

10 9 8 7 6 5 4 3 2 1

Library of Congress Cataloging-in-Publication Data

Darling, Katherine.
Under the table : saucy tales from culinary school / Katherine Darling.
    p. cm.
  1. Darling, Katherine—Anecdotes.   2. French Culinary Institute (New York, N.Y.).   3. Cookery.   4. Cooks—Anecdotes.   I. Title.
TX652.D332 2009
641.5—dc22   2008053566
ISBN-13: 978-1-4165-6527-7
ISBN-10:   1-4165-6527-2

For Annabelle

A SHORT NOTE ON RECIPES
AND INGREDIENTS

You certainly do not need to have any special equipment or expertise to conquer the recipes in this book. A few basic pots and pans, a mixing bowl or two, a whisk, and a good knife and wooden spoon will see you through almost everything. Where special equipment is mentioned, I have also given a substitute method or explained the absolute necessity of it to the recipe. Really, all you need is a desire to make, and eat, good food.

Unless otherwise indicated, all the eggs should be large and as fresh as possible. Organic ingredients really do make better food, in my opinion, so do try to use them whenever possible. I prefer to use coarse kosher salt for savory dishes and fine sea salt for baking, but feel free to use whatever tastes better to you. Likewise, I prefer freshly ground black pepper in general, unless the flecks of pepper will look unsightly in the final product, like mayonnaise. Use white pepper if you like, but the difference is purely aesthetic. All the butter should be unsalted, and like the eggs, organic and as fresh as possible.

AUTHOR'S NOTE

THE NAMES OF CLASSMATES AND PROFESSORS
HAVE BEEN CHANGED TO PROTECT THE GUILTY—
THERE ARE NO INNOCENTS IN CHEF SCHOOL.

LEVEL 1

ENTRE NOUS

The night before chef school began, I dreamt I ate Jacques Pépin. I woke in a sweat. He didn't taste very good. Like a slice of liver, well done. Somehow I was expecting seared foie gras.

Everyone is anxious before the first day of school. However, most people do not dream about eating the teacher. I put it down to nerves. I was giving up a promising career in the publishing industry to pursue my dreams of glory as a chef. I wasn't sure I was making the right decision, but it was too late to back out now. I was due at orientation in a little under five hours.

I had tried to ready myself for my plunge into the culinary underbelly. I really thought that I was finished with life in my fishbowl cubicle, and ready to surrender the neat piles of paper fortifying my in-tray for a set of razor-sharp chef's knives. While I loved my job working at a literary agency, book publishing hadn't turned out to be quite as glamorous as I thought. I realized that I was spending more and more of my time browsing recipe Web sites and fantasizing about what to make for dinner than reading through the mountains of manuscripts that came in the mail every day. I needed to do something more with my life, but what was it?

I come from a long line of women who can cook. My mother, in the long-ago mists of time before she had children, had taken classes at L'Academie de Cuisine near Washington, D.C. While she had not become a professional chef, she had made, from scratch, almost every single meal I ate in childhood. Not for her family would there be frozen dinners or Pizza Hut delivery. We ate real food, from omelets to *fricassée aux champignons,* calf's liver (yuck!) to

Châteaubriand (my birthday request, every year). It was a wonderful way to live and eat, and as soon as I was old enough to stand on a chair and wield a wooden spoon, I was my mother's eager assistant, graduating from bottle washer to vegetable peeler to sous chef.

The memories of the meals that had sustained my childhood—from the piles of warm doughnuts dusted with powdered sugar and herbes de Provence that Mom made on snow days, to the taste of tomatoes from my grandmother's garden, still warm from the heat of a July afternoon, sprinkled with crunchy gray sea salt and a few coarse grinds of pepper, to the airy richness of my first taste of cheese soufflé, made by my father to soothe a sore throat—these were the memories of love, of home, of a place where I belonged. As I left my cramped apartment each morning, joining the endless throng of commuters on the crowded subway platform to jam myself into a cramped, sweaty subway car, I felt alone, disconnected from this tidal wave of humanity. At work, I wrestled with the piles of paper flooding my desk every day, an endless stream of manuscripts that would never be published. With every sad rejection letter I would type in response, I knew, deep down, I wanted to do something else, something that held all the comfort of those memories, something that would give that comfort to other people. As I struggled to make my place in the city, to make a life I loved with people I loved, I knew that food was the key.

What if I went to chef school? At first the idea seemed silly—is this really what I was going to do with all that education? But gradually, it seemed to make more and more sense, a natural progression from passionate amateur to professional. I would be doing something I loved—how many people could say the same? I was at home in Virginia, cooking Easter dinner and bossing everyone around the kitchen, when I decided to take the plunge and see what my family thought. I cooked all the time, and had held down a job at a winery in summers home from college, preparing plates of runny, creamy Camembert and snowy white goat cheese with spicy *pâté maison* or fat, juicy rounds of venison sausage, toasting crusty baguettes to go with the cold, crisp glasses of seyval and robust cabernet franc wines made from the vines that trailed down the purple slopes of the Blue Ridge Mountains. I had the desire, the drive, the ambition. As I rubbed racks of lamb with a wonderfully pungent paste of lemons, garlic cloves, rosemary, olive oil, and coarse sea salt, I thought again about the possibilities. Could I chuck my nice, steady job for a future behind the stove? I pressed chilled pastry dough into a deep tart pan and covered it in a shaggy layer of grated Gruyère cheese before tipping a panful of sweetly caramelized onions on top. As I slipped the heavy copper roasting pan filled with new potatoes, spears of baby carrots, and branches of fresh herbs into the oven, I thought about what to say.

Hours later, as plates full of food were passed back and forth across the vast expanse of tablecloth and family silver, and the usual Darling family banter went on around me, I was still thinking. Judging by the clean plates coming back for seconds of the rack of lamb and three-onion tart, I had a little talent (inherited from my mother, no doubt). I couldn't love cooking any more if I tried—I thought about it all the time, doodling plating ideas in the margins of manuscripts at work, dreaming about new flavor combinations at night. Apparently, I had even woken up my boyfriend, Michael, several times to tell him about some new food idea I had, only to drift back to sleep again, leaving him awake, and hungry, for hours.

Still, I wasn't sure if I was ready to leave the security of my job at the literary agency to go back to school. And then what? I dreamed about owning my own little bistro: a tiny place full of fresh flowers, old silver, and mismatched Wedgwood china, cooking a simple (but spectacular, of course!) menu for a handful of rabidly devoted regulars. Even more scintillating, I fantasized about landing a job in front of the cameras at the Food Network, suddenly able to coach millions of foodie followers through my delicious recipes, maybe even endorsing a special line of cookware Le Creuset made just for me. So my daydreams about chef school were a little pie-in-the-sky. But, I thought, if I can't have champagne wishes and caviar dreams about my future in food, why take the risk?

I was still undecided, but as the long meal drew to a close over one more crispy stalk of oven-roasted asparagus and a final morsel of my mother's heavenly homemade bread rolls smeared with butter, I told my family what I was thinking. Holiday dinners in my family are always a no-holds-barred, lively forum of ideas, and everyone always has an opinion. I think of them as good-natured discussions, but after his first encounter with a Darling family dinner, Michael had asked me plaintively, "Why do you guys fight all the time?" As I served the lemon génoise roulade cake with lemon curd and raspberry coulis, I brought up my idea. For once, there was total silence at the table. I couldn't tell if it was because the cake was a hit or because everyone was too appalled to speak. Michael knew that I had been thinking about doing something different for a little while, but to leave a nine-to-five job and plunge myself (deeply) into debt to go into food full-time? It was lunacy, surely.

My older brother, Eben, looked surprised but was probably relieved that at least I wouldn't be going to grad school with him. We had both gotten undergraduate degrees in history (he from Dartmouth, me from Williams a year later), and I knew he hadn't forgiven me for getting a degree in English as well, one-upping him. Eben and I had spent our entire childhood competing with each other in school, on the swim team, everywhere. Eb had never figured out that I wanted to do everything he did because I considered him the coolest person on earth. Recently he had decided to go to graduate school at Georgetown University to get a master's degree in business. Cool my big brother undoubtedly was, but I drew the line at endlessly crunching numbers; I would far rather dice carrots.

My grandfather was the first one to speak, though he kept sneaking pieces of cake as he talked, popping in a raspberry or two in between sentences. "Well," he said, pausing for a morsel of whipped cream, "I think it is a wonderful idea. I know we were all worried about you moving to New York, although I'm sure it's gotten better than when I was there." Pop-Pop had worked as a proofreader for Condé Nast for forty years. He could do the *New York Times* crossword puzzle backward and forward, and could pick out a misspelling in a thousand words of text in a split second. It was generally agreed in the family that this was where I had gotten my love of words. "After all, you've managed to find yourself a nice young man . . ." Here again Pop-Pop paused for another quick bite of cake and to cast a big, sunny smile at Michael. Everyone in the family loved Michael. "And if going to school will make your wonderful cooking any better, watch out, Rachael Ray, here comes Katydid!" Pop-Pop had obviously been watching the Food Network, too. I smiled at the use of my family's long-standing pet name for me, though I secretly shuddered at the thought that my future classmates might one day find out about my dorky nickname.

With my family firmly behind me, I decided to research my options. I looked at chef schools across the country and beyond. After a brutal assessment of my financial situation (grim, verging on dire), I reluctantly put aside thoughts of going to Le Cordon Bleu in Paris. It would be the chance of a lifetime, but I wasn't positive my French was up to it. (All I could remember from four years of high school French was watching *Delicatessen* with subtitles. A French movie poking fun at cannibalism didn't seem like the best preparation for French chef school.) So I confined my search to the States, looking for schools with great reputations and good financial aid programs. I found both at the Culinary Institute of America. Unfortunately, the CIA is located near Poughkeepsie, the armpit of upstate New York. I applied, telling myself that I could take the train every morning and evening, shuttling back and forth from SoHo, capital of hipsters and Eurotrash, to Hyde Park, capital of white trash. Not so much. The train fare alone would cost more than my monthly paycheck, and the commute would leave me no time to study, see Michael, or work a part-time job—a necessity even with financial aid. I started looking at schools in Manhattan, programs that would fit the life that I was carving out for myself.

I found it at The French Culinary Institute. Their culinary arts program consisted of nine hundred hours of work in the kitchens spread out over six months (nine if you enrolled in the night program) with small class sizes and a comprehensive and challenging curriculum. We would gradually build up our skills and repertoire of recipes through four levels, going from utter beginners in Level 1, learning how to chop and dice, to making the classic dishes of the *cuisine bourgeoise* for the chef-instructors in Level 2, to actually cooking for the school's reputable restaurant, L'Ecole, in Levels 3 and 4. Their roster of chef-instructors and deans read like a who's who of culinary titans—everyone from Alain Sailhac to Jacques Torres to André Soltner to Jacques Pépin was on the list. The Institute was also housed in a beautiful facility five blocks away from my apartment. As I went on a tour of the school, I took in the spacious kitchens—one each for Levels 1 and 2, and a huge combined kitchen for Levels 3 and 4, in addition to a gorgeous bread kitchen and a separate set of kitchens for the pastry students—all the shiny appliances on hand, and the blur of white uniforms as students prepared for the lunch rush. I felt like I was at home. This was the life I had been looking for, the excitement and activity that was missing from my usual routine of faxing and filing. And all the students were busy creating, making something delicious for someone else to enjoy. I was hooked. One month after taking the plunge and applying, I was accepted for the class beginning in June.

It was harder than I thought to quit my job at the agency—not only was I leaving my friends and coworkers, but I was also leaving the safety of the office environment. I was trading chats by the coffee machine and office birthday parties and getting off early on Fridays in the summer, not to mention the constant comfort and distraction of the Internet and e-mail, for something completely unknown.

Still, the night before orientation, as I lay wide awake after my dream about Jacques Pépin, listening to the night noises of Manhattan, I couldn't help but wonder if I was making the right decision. I was taking a pretty big leap of faith. I loved to cook, but did I have what it took to become one of the best? There was only one way to find out.

Later that morning, as the commuters began their daily spill from the subways and filtered through SoHo's cobbled streets to spacious loft offices, I stood at the corner of Broadway and Broome Street, looking at the plate glass windows of L'Ecole, The Institute's restaurant. For the next six months of my life, I would be making my way from the small apartment I shared with Michael and our cat, Spankie, through the streets of SoHo, to work in the kitchens of The Institute. One day soon, the diners I had watched many times enjoying their lunches would be eating something I made. I tried not to let that thought terrify me.

I pushed through the double doors etched with The Institute's tasteful logo and wound my way through a series of hallways until I found myself standing outside a small but immaculately appointed auditorium, complete with a chef's demonstration station: a Vulcan range, a bank of wall ovens, even a marble-topped pastry station. It was more like a television studio than a school auditorium, and some of the top chefs from all over the world had demonstrated their signature dishes on that stage. We would be having our orientation inside in a few minutes.

I was so nervous I could barely keep my hands from shaking as I pinned my name tag to my dress. I had agonized over what I should wear to orientation, wanting to strike just the right note with my future classmates and the chef-instructors I would be meeting for the very first time. I ransacked the tiny closet I shared with Michael, creating a blizzard of clothes all over the bed, the nightstand, and the floor. Michael had laughed as I tried on first one outfit and then another, demanding his opinion of each one. No matter what he said, I tore off the outfit and began rooting through the piles of clothes for something else. My entire wardrobe was made up of things I could wear to work at the literary agency. Skirts, dresses, sweaters, blouses, jackets: nothing too revealing or casual, but nothing too dressy, either. When did my fashion sense shrink to business casual? In defeat I finally put on my old interview outfit, the one I had bought in college to wear to my job interviews in the city. Even though it was a few years old and made from some sort of fabric guaranteed not to show sweat, the black knee-length dress looked passable, and I jazzed it up by exchanging the jacket (too structured, too desperate, too polyester) with a tissue-thin gray sweater flung over my shoulders and a pair of jazzy red strappy sandals. I grabbed my oversize red bag and headed off to school. As I stood outside the auditorium, shifting my weight from foot to foot to keep those three-inch heels from cutting into my tender flesh, I could catch an occasional glimpse of one of the imposing chef-instructors as he stalked across the stage. It made me so nervous I wanted to throw up. I tried to calm myself down by picturing what I would make for dinner. The thought of chopping vegetables and sautéing immediately made me feel more calm. At last we were invited in to sit down; I took a seat and began to case my future classmates.

There were twenty-four of us in all, twelve men and twelve women, and as students filtered into the auditorium, I wasn't the only one checking everybody out. I was one of the only people wearing something other than jeans, and I was definitely the only one in high heels. Most of the male members of my class were wearing jeans and T-shirts, and not in the Euro, artfully disheveled way I was familiar with, but in the I-just-rolled-out-of-bed-and-put-this-on way, like they might be late for a monster truck convention somewhere. The girls were all wearing jeans or skirts with tops in varying degrees of trendiness. One girl was rocking the whole seventies thing—Dr. Scholl's, polo shirt, Farrah Fawcett waves. She looked cool. Another was wearing a loose knee-length skirt with a surfer tee and hemp bracelets—total West Coast laid-back chic. I was the only one who seemed to be trying so hard that even my clothes were embarrassed.

I knew I should be paying more attention to the instructions we were being given in this lecture, the first in our three-hour orientation session before classes were slated to begin. But I was still nervous, and feeling more uncertain that I had made the right decision quitting my job to pursue my dream. But I definitely wasn't the only twenty-something here—most of the class looked like they were in their late twenties or thirties, probably looking to do something a little bit different than the nine-to-five grind they had been doing since college. That made me feel a little better—I was being daring and following a different path, but here were a bunch of other people just like me. There were a few people who were older than the rest of us, and a couple of students looked like they were fresh out of high school. Well, if my dreams of being a chef didn't work out, at least I could fall back on my actual college degree. I wondered what these youngsters would do if there was a chef recession, but I guess no matter what, people need to eat.

I tried to focus on what was being said from the podium onstage. There were directives on what could and could not be worn underneath our school-issued uniforms and on personal grooming. Men were expected to shave every day, and women were expected to keep their hair up and out of harm's way at all times—not just to keep it out of the food, but also to keep it from becoming tangled in the industrial-grade machinery we would be working with. I thought of getting sucked into the chomping jaws of some giant sausage grinder and shuddered. I brushed my own long blond bangs out of my eyes and wondered whether I should just lop it off for the duration. Hands and fingers should always be scrupulously clean; no jewelry would be permitted—not even wedding rings.

No problem there, I thought to myself. I had never been the sort of person to wear a lot of jewelry, and while Michael and I were perfectly happy, I didn't think wedding bells were going to be in our future anytime soon. Maybe ever. Michael was in his late thirties, never married, and hadn't ever had a really serious girlfriend before I moseyed into the picture. I had always vowed that I would wind up a little old spinster with lots of cats, tending a huge vegetable garden and canning my own jam.

For a few minutes I was so lost in my thoughts, mapping out my heirloom tomato patch and refining my recipe for tomato jam—perhaps some balsamic vinegar for zing, and a vanilla bean for comforting spice—I forgot to listen to the lecture. I came back to earth with a thud, just in time to catch the rest of the instructions about proper grooming. The nails should be trimmed very short and always be free from dirt and grime. There could be no polish on the nails, either. It was too prone to flaking and falling into the food. What a disgusting thought. Well, I had no fears on that front—my nails had always been woefully short, despite my attempts to pamper them with rich moisturizers and the occasional manicure.

There was one more thing: absolutely no perfume or cologne could be worn in the kitchens at any time. This last restriction seemed a trifle strange—who cared what we smelled like as long as we smelled good? But after some thought, it made sense. We were going to be learning to be classically trained chefs, and true chefs use all five of their senses to cook with. Perfume merely blunts the sense of smell of the wearer and those around her, without adding anything to the food. I thought wistfully of my bottle of Chanel No. 5 perched on the dresser at home. I would pass it on to my mom, who always seemed to smell better in it anyway.

I had been making conscientious notes throughout our lecture, more out of habit than a real need to remember the things being said—we had received a large orientation packet with copious quantities of paper, most of which was a straight regurgitation of what was being said, word for word. I could hear some of the students in the rows behind me whispering back and forth. A few of them obviously must have known one another already, and I cursed myself for giving in to my good-girl tendencies and sitting in the front row—I was already missing out! After several firm, very intimidating lectures from various chef-instructors warning us that the next six months would be harder than we had ever imagined (my highly active imagination automatically kicked into overdrive, dreaming up visions of finger amputations, grueling trials by fire—literally—failing the practical exam, and other horrific situations that might be in store), we were given a bit of a breather by Rose, head liaison between the students and the rest of the support staff and chefs. One by one, she called us to the front of the room, where we each received a large black duffel bag containing our new uniforms: two side towels, two neckerchiefs, two pairs of checked chef's pants, and two chef's jackets embroidered with our names and The Institute's logo over the breast pocket.

Back at our seats, the sporadic whispering broke into an excited buzz as we eagerly dug into our duffels and ran our hands over the nifty things inside—it was even better than Christmas, and even though everyone's uniform was identical, we enthusiastically held up our own jackets and oohed and aahed over each other's. I whipped around to see everybody else with identical grins—the same one that was no doubt plastered all over my own face. They were giving us real chef's jackets; it was almost like we were real chefs! (Little did we know.) While I couldn't say I was superexcited about wearing pleated-front polyester blend pants every day for the next six months, I was thrilled with my chef's jackets. There it was, in black and white: my name, in tasteful block embroidery. There really was no going back now—I was going to be a chef like my heroes: Jacques, Julia, Mario, Alice.

The awe and wonder of the voyage we were all embarking on lasted another half hour. We had one more intimidating lecture about the consequences for not obeying various school regulations. I hoped they were joking about being disemboweled with a boning knife and fed through the industrial Cuisinart, or being boiled alive in one of the schools fifty-gallon stockpots, but even a day's suspension from school and automatic ineligibility for class honors was enough to scare me. (My good-girl tendencies again.) Then we were released to find our way down to the small reception held in our honor in the school's restaurant. Burdened by our bulky duffel bags, we herded together in several large groups, sticking close to the walls and trying to stay as far away from the instructors as possible. One of the instructors, a very handsome, very tan ringer for a young Johnny Depp, wearing the most gorgeously starched and snowy white uniform I had ever seen, brought a tray of hors d'oeuvres over to the group of frightened students I was currently clinging to. *Helllooo there,* I thought to myself, before remembering my darling Michael and the school's strict regulations against fraternizing with the instructors.

Offering the tray around, the chef introduced himself as Chef Paul. He would be our pastry chef in Levels 3 and 4. I was suffering from a major attack of shyness and looked everywhere around the room instead of directly at him. Chef Paul seemed to sense the nervousness in all of us and he laughed gently at us.

"Don't worry about me," he said. "I'm a total pussycat. Worry about some of them over there." He gesticulated toward a group of chefs clumped together by the bar. They looked like a malevolent cloud bank—all puffy white shirtfronts and frowns.

"Here, have a cheese puff." Chef Paul pushed the platter under my nose. "You'll be making thousands of these little goodies soon enough. Enjoy them while you have the chance."

I detected a definite twinkle in his eye, so I took one. "Good," he said. "Now go brave that bar and get yourself a glass of wine. The other chefs won't bite."

I took a deep breath and heeded his advice, putting down my bag and making a beeline to the row of red and white wine bottles lined along the polished wood of the bar, hoping to snag a glass of white before I could attract the attention of the chefs lurking far too close for comfort.

I was soon joined by my future classmates. Once we had managed to get a glass each of the very nice Chablis (not too dry, with a hint of crispness, just what I needed to quench my nervous thirst), we started to get to know each other, peering at each other's name tags and discussing where we lived and what we had done before chef school.

While there were plenty of people from New York, many students had come from distant parts of the country and even the world to attend class here. Imogene, a petite brunette in a stylish outfit, was a suburban mother from just outside the beltway loop of Washington, D.C. Despite her youthful appearance, Imogene's two girls were almost grown, and at a little past forty, Imo had decided that for her next career, she would become a professional chef.

Philip was a native New Yorker from Long Island, and had recently quit his job as a very successful bond trader on Wall Street. His office had been in the World Financial Center, and as Philip watched the events of September 11 unfold from his window, he realized he wanted to spend the rest of his life doing a job he loved, not one he loathed. I would have pegged him as a fellow New Yorker—his Levi's were Capital E brand, and I thought I detected that his artfully scuffed loafers were Prada. His plain white T-shirt looked softer than my precious 500-thread-count sheets and definitely didn't come in a three-pack from Fruit of the Loom.

Before I could get to know Philip any better, he was enveloped by an exotic foreign woman whose long black hair and pouty lips set off a flawless café au lait complexion. Her makeup was perfect, but I noticed a faint fan of lines around her eyes, and while she was swathed in the smallest pair of Paige Premium Denim jeans I had ever seen, something about her stance proclaimed she had been around the block a few times and was probably closer to forty than thirty. The enormous Kelly bag she hitched casually over her arm was real, and I salivated over its vintage gorgeousness even as she used it to expertly elbow me out of the conversation. Who knew vintage bags packed such a wallop? That was definitely going to leave a mark—I would have a couture bruise. I caught her name as she coyly whispered it to Philip's chiseled pecs, " . . . call me Mimi. *So* pleased to meet another student with a bit of class." I guess my outfit (and all the agonizing I had done over it) hadn't cut the mustard!

Amanda, the girl with the surfer tee and hemp bracelets, was indeed from Southern California and had the trademark laid-back lifestyle and speech pattern. Working in public relations had been "a total downer" for her, and she had decided to try living on the East Coast and making a go of her hobby of cooking before she turned thirty. "I mean, one meal at Chez Panisse and I was like totally blown away. It's like *beyond food* food."

Angelo was a New Jersey native, and had graduated from the Fashion Institute of Technology with a degree in graphic design. After an unfulfilling stint at an ad agency, Angelo realized his creativity needed a different outlet, and had turned to food, interning at several well-known restaurants in the city before deciding to get his culinary degree. His tight T-shirt didn't quite cover what looked like a massive tribal tattoo, encircling one massive bicep (more like a whole *jamón serrano* than an appendage), and the ring through his nose heavily accentuated his bull-like physique—his neck was as wide as my waist—with his heavy Jersey accent making him seem even more like a tough guy. Fashion was definitely not what I would have expected from such a tough customer, but his blue eyes were very kind, and he swirled the wine around in his glass with a practiced motion of his massive, meaty paws. It turned out he had gone to high school with the retro seventies chick—her name was Jackie. Her long brown hair, big brown eyes, and the way she absolutely rocked her super-low-cut jeans made me think I had just met the class bombshell. When she mentioned that she used to work for the Yankees and still got tickets from the organization, I was certain.

Jackie was a total man magnet. This was her second round of food education: she had recently completed a course in food styling at the Institute for Culinary Education and was doing an internship in the prop department at the Food Network—the Holy Grail for the rest of us.

Off in a corner, a middle-aged biddy had managed to corral Dean Jacques Pépin and seemed to be asking for his autograph. Her flat midwestern vowels were making mincemeat of the melodic French syllables he uttered, and I clearly heard her referring to her "world-famous green bean casserole Franceeese." (Apparently, canned pearl onions provided the "Franceeese-ness.") I tried not to stare openly. My hero Jacques Pépin was being mauled by a future classmate of mine. I wondered if she had dreamed about eating him, too—it looked like she was trying her best to gobble him up right now.

I looked around at the other students populating the room. Most of them had stowed their duffels and detached themselves from the walls to mingle, have a glass or two of wine, and corner the quickly disappearing noshes. They certainly seemed to come from all walks of life. Where was I going to fit in? I sipped the rest of my wine, thought about the office job I had so recently left behind, with all the comforts of the cubicle life—limitless Internet, endless coffee, and free paper clips. I hoped I had made the right decision. I saddled myself with my duffel bag, suddenly heavy with uncertainty in addition to uniforms that would have to be hemmed and dry-cleaned, and headed out into the June afternoon in downtown Manhattan.

TUCKER

While it was mere chance that I ended up across the table from Tucker on our very first day of chef school, it was no accident that we became such good friends and partners.

We couldn't have been more different. Tucker was a proud product of the absolute middle of the Midwest. Michigan born and bred, he had never left the state but once or twice, when he traveled to Chicago to eat at Charlie Trotter's restaurants. Tucker went straight from high school to a job on the assembly line cranking out car parts, and buying a house in the small suburb he grew up in.

Tucker came from a long line of autoworkers. His entire family—parents, grandparents, aunts, uncles, cousins, and siblings—were employed by General Motors at one time or another, before the industry took a dive and layoffs became more common than paychecks. When Tucker was laid off himself, he went into the repo business, reclaiming the cars, trucks, refrigerators, televisions, even the bedroom furniture of people who believed the economy would be golden forever, or at least until they caught up on their payments. It was nasty work, and Tucker disliked having to tow away the hopes and dreams of his neighbors. But it wasn't until he stumbled upon the Food Network one day after work that he began to dream of doing something different.

Mesmerized by the antics of Emeril Lagasse, and finding a hero in the macho posturings of Bobby Flay (an alum of our alma mater), Tucker began to believe that his hobby of fixing elaborate meals for his friends and family could be a career. He got a job slinging hash in a restaurant at night for the necessary restaurant experience while he saved up money from his day job until he was accepted at The Institute.

By the time Tucker came east, he had a wife who worked in a GE refrigerator plant, and two kids under the age of three. Tucker was a man with a lot of responsibilities, and he was taking a gamble that school and the six months he would be out of work would eventually pay off. But Tucker loved to cook and he dreamed big, and those things, more than anything else, were what we had in common.

I'd attended a small liberal arts college in Massachusetts before settling down in New York and finding work in publishing. I had a nice apartment and a lovely, not to mention very handsome, boyfriend, but I wasn't ready for the sort of responsibility Tucker handled—forget kids, it was enough for me to share ownership of our cat, Spankie.

It was 8:00 AM sharp on our very first day of class, and as I walked into the large room that was dazzlingly bright with the glow of many overhead fluorescent lights bouncing off the stainless steel workstations, ovens, pots, pans, sinks, and even the tools of my classmates, I saw that Tucker had taken up a spot at the front of the room, closest to our chef-instructor's dark green marble–topped lecture station. While I had been hoping for that spot myself, I was content to take the open spot across from him, determined that the foot that separated us, and put him closer to Chef, would not hinder my learning curve. And my parents thought I was too competitive. If I were competitive, I would have created a diversion and just snatched his spot when he was momentarily distracted. Okay, maybe I was a little bit competitive, but as it turned out, so was Tucker.

We eyed each other warily for a moment or two, and then I decided to introduce myself.

"Hi, I'm Katie, nice to meet you," I said as I juggled my toolbox, knife kit, neckerchief, notebook, and textbook from one hand to the other, trying to get a hand free to shake with.

"Pleasure, ma'am," said Tucker, as he grabbed a few things from my failing grasp, setting them gently on the table, before he shook my hand. He had large hands that ended in blunt fingers, I noticed, and they were well scarred from doing manual labor. Despite their size, Tucker was not a tall man, and I looked him right in the eye as we shook hands. They were nice eyes, their corners upturned in a way that made him look almost elfin, and he had the beginnings of smile lines fanning out toward his temples. He was a few years older than I, it seemed, probably in his thirties, and it looked like he had been hard at work for most of his adult life. His small nose was garnished with a spray of freckles, and his face was balanced by a wide mouth, just now flashing a big grin. I realized I was staring, and tried to cover my awkwardness with conversation.

"So, how do you tie this stupid thing?" I asked, waving my neckerchief at him. I noticed his was perfectly aligned and the tails were neatly tucked out of view under the mandarin collar of his spanking new chef's jacket. He was obviously already well ahead of me in the sartorial aspect of class. Taking the large, itchy bit of cloth from my grip, Tucker smoothed out the wrinkles I had managed to crimp into it and folded it in neat little accordion pleats from a large triangle to a flat rope almost an inch wide. Tucking the triangular end under, he deftly flipped the length of polyester over my head, tails dangling down either side of my neck. Undoing his own pristine knot, he then led me through the steps—something about a rabbit going around a tree twice, then ducking under to pop up again. Somehow, from all that nonsense, Tucker managed to turn my mess into a perfect knot, complete with two even tails. These I tucked into my jacket, and Tucker and I smiled at each other.

Things were going well—it seemed like I was making at least one new friend. Together, we took a moment to check out the rest of the class that was rapidly arriving and milling about the room. It was a confusion of students in various states of dress—everyone had managed the jacket and pants, but most were having the same trouble with their neckerchiefs that I had. There were two dozen large red toolboxes scattered throughout the room—one for every student—and the bulky three-ring binders that were our new textbooks littered every flat surface. The babble of many nervous voices raised in conversation made further interaction with my new friend almost impossible.

I made my way to the quickly emptying coffeepot in one corner of the vast room and snagged two cups of the very dark brew. I threw some cream and sugar in Tucker's cup and brought it back to him as a thank-you for helping me. As I delivered it, I asked Tucker if he knew any of the other students milling about. We almost had to shout to hear each other over the sound of chatter bouncing off the gleaming white-tiled walls and orangey red-tiled floors. Because Tucker was in the school-sponsored housing on Roosevelt Island, he actually knew several of the dozen male members of the class, and was able to point to several women as fellow boarders. In fact, one of the other guys sharing our kitchen island was Tucker's roommate, a tall, gangly fellow with a name at least twice as big as he was. Before I could commit the many multisyllables to memory, Tucker said not to bother, that everyone was already calling him Junior.

Further discussion of our classmates was forestalled by the arrival of Chef-Instructor Jean and Assistant Chef Cyndee. Chef Jean was an impressive figure in his crisp chef's whites, complete with a tall chef's toque set at a jaunty angle on his curly black hair. His round glasses flashed in the overhead lights, and something about his sharp nose and wide mouth reminded me of a benevolent amphibian, like Mr. Toad in the children's classic *Wind in the Willows*. He seemed very nice, smiling good-naturedly at us all, and I immediately began to lose some of my first-day nerves. Assistant Chef Cyndee, on the other hand, scowled at all of us before barking sharply at us to sit down and shut up.

We were quickly brought to order and our first lecture began. Chef explained how this first level would work—every day, five days a week, we would report to our classroom and set out chairs for our morning lecture, where Chef Jean would explain the culinary concept for the day and guide us through the basic recipes we would be preparing. After lecture we would break into teams and prepare two recipes before lunch. Sometimes we would get to eat our morning's efforts for lunch, if we were making *poulet au sauce chasseur,* for instance, or a *blanquette de veau à l'ancienne.* If we were making only salad dressings, mayonnaise, and veal stock, we would eat family meal—a hot lunch made by the students in Level 2 for all the students and staff of the school. After lunch we would make one or two more recipes, taste and critique each other's efforts, clean the kitchen until everything sparkled, and then we would be dismissed for the day at 3:00 PM sharp. This would be repeated every day, with weekly written exams and the occasional pop quiz, for six weeks. Then we would be passed on to the next chef-instructor for Level 2.

An hour later, after Chef had lectured us about everything from proper attire and footwear (again!) to the correct way to wash our hands and prepare vegetables, we were at last ready to begin working. We stacked away the chairs we used for lecture and resumed our places at the six large kitchen islands spaced around the class. Chef Jean then announced that for the rest of our first term of classes with him we would be learning and cooking with a partner. Not too surprising—pairing us off would be a good way for us to learn teamwork and cooperation in a fast-paced, physically demanding setting. I wondered how we were going to be paired off, as I looked nervously around at my possible mates. It didn't take long to find out. Chef Jean merely surveyed the class and said, "Take a look at the person standing across from you. Say '*Bonjour*' and play nicely with them. They will be your partner for the next six weeks." I smiled at Tucker, and he smiled back. While I wasn't quite prepared to say it was the beginning of a beautiful friendship, it did have promise.

Tucker and I were well matched, it turned out. Both of us had lots of amateur kitchen experience, a bit of professional drudge work under our belts, and a burning passion to do well in class and beyond. While it wasn't always easy to divide the work evenly—we both wanted to do the challenging part of every recipe to show off our chops, and neither one of us wanted to just sit around, washing pots and waiting for water to boil—we were amicable about things. Tucker almost always beat me into the classroom, and he would set up both of our places with cutting boards, pots, pans, and anything else we might need for the day's recipes. For my part, on my way to class, I would stop and pick up coffee for Tucker: extra cream, extra sugar.

As the days passed and our routine took shape, I found myself relying on Tucker's steadying influence—when I worried that we were falling behind and rushed to turn up the heat under our pot of vegetables, it was Tucker's steady hand that turned the flame down before I could burn things. I looked forward to our study sessions when Tucker would ask for my help translating some of the French in our recipes to "plain talking." We seemed to fit together, better than most of the other teams in Level 1, and soon we were working as one unit, a coordinated machine that peeled and prepped our recipes with increasing speed and accuracy. Chef Jean didn't compliment our efforts, but we had escaped the harsh criticism other teams suffered—so far.

While I couldn't understand the fact that Tucker wore acid-washed jeans and plaid shirts (occasionally with the sleeves removed) and smoked White Owl cigars he bought for a buck at the deli, he couldn't understand why I went to all the trouble of wearing a skirt or a dress to and from classes and why I would ever want to live in this filthy city in the first place. We loved to tease each other. Everything was fair game, from Tucker's Aqua Velva aftershave (he'd douse himself with it in the locker room after class was over for the day) to my unswerving devotion to coffee drinks that cost as much as a Big Mac. We also got to know each other very well—Tucker told me about what it was like to fish the Great Lakes around Michigan, and I told him about growing up on a farm in Virginia. He brought me pickled bologna to try—a local specialty where he came from—and I brought him corn bread soaked in melted butter and dark buckwheat honey. We bonded over the comfort foods of our radically different worlds.

TAKING STOCK

Michael was keenly interested in my new daily routine. We had gone from working down the hall from each other all day (we met in the elevator of the office building where we both worked), with frequent e-mail exchanges back and forth, to a rushed kiss hello/good-bye before I headed off to school and he headed off to the office. To earn some much-needed money—already monthly bills were coming in the mail for my student loan—I had found a job tutoring private school kids in everything from biology and algebra to Latin and medieval history, and often I would only make it home from the posh Upper East Side apartments of the little monsters after ten o'clock at night. That left enough time to make dinner, usually a rendition of whatever recipe I had prepared in class that day with varying levels of success, study the next day's recipes, and collapse into bed before doing the whole thing again.

I spent a lot of time describing Chef Jean and the other students to Michael, and at first he was jealous of all the time I would be spending at school. Despite my assurances that school was hot, sweaty, and *work*, not fun, I couldn't put his fears to rest until the night during that first week when I showed him my uniform. I was so proud of myself—checked chef's pants, white chef's jacket, I looked *exactly* like a chef!—I was eager to show off for Michael. I put on the pants. They came only in men's sizes, so I could either order one with an elastic waistband (Mom always warned me away from clothes with elastic. We both felt that it was a small step from that to lying around the house all day, eating store-bought frosting straight from the tub.) or guess what size pants to order. The woman in charge of uniforms wasn't helpful. She insisted that all the female students in school had always made do with the elastic pants. Besides, she said, the elastic might come in handy. Chef school could be hard on the waistline. With that comment, I was determined to get the regular pleated men's pants. I ordered the smallest size they had and had them tailored to fit. I also ordered the smallest chef's jacket they had—I was little, and the jacket was a loose fit on me.

I was anxious to show Michael how professional I looked, how cool, and so on my uniform went, down to the Hanes wifebeater-style tank top I wore under my jacket and the Doc Martens on my feet. We were allowed the choice of combat boots or chef's clogs, both in black leather. No athletic shoes allowed. I debated buying a pair of clogs, but the Dansko ones all the celebrity chefs wore cost more than a hundred bucks. I had a pair of Docs left over from college (they kept out the piles of snow wonderfully, even if they lacked sex appeal), so I wore them, though after the first day of class, my feet hurt so bad from standing up all day, I had to hobble home in my most comfortable flip-flops. I bought some cushy insoles that made the long hours of standing a little easier, but my feet, used to tripping around town on stilettos, were having a hard time adjusting to their new utilitarian home. I tied my neckerchief around my neck and even tied one of my school aprons around my waist. All that I was lacking was the little absorbent paper hat we wore to keep our hair (and the sweat that poured off our brow) from getting in the food.

With a flourish, I swept into the living room, swishing my apron around me, and even doing a little runway strut—*work it, Chef Katie, you sexy* saucier, *you.* Michael burst out laughing, and kept laughing until tears rolled down his face. This was not the effect I was going for. I was totally dismayed and angry. For the first time, I considered resorting to violence—beaning my beloved on his noggin with a cast-iron sauté pan, for starters.

"Oh, ha ha ha. Oh, I'm sorry." Michael was actually wheezing with laughter. "Oh, you look . . . fine. You look just fine, honey." I could tell he didn't mean it, because he looked like he would explode any second from keeping the snorts of laughter in. "You just look so . . . different. Not exactly your sexy self. Are those pleated-front pants?"

Oh, my God. Michael was right. What was I thinking? I was wearing pleated-front pants, combat boots, and a white polyester ascot! Of course I wasn't cute! I could only hope that Michael would forget about this image of his usually (somewhat) cute girlfriend before it had any lasting effects on our sex life. I would never wear my uniform in front of him again. How embarrassing.

I was only grateful that Michael couldn't see me in class the next day, as Chef Jean instructed we accessorize our dorky uniforms with a garbage bag worn as a raincoat. After the morning lecture, Assistant Chef Cyndee handed each of us our empty garbage bag. I almost balked, but the first rule of chef school is to obey all instructions, so on my big black garbage bag went. Attired now in shiny black plastic, we could begin.

As I stood there, sweating even more profusely than usual under my rustling plastic prison, I wondered what our garbage bags had to do with making stocks and sauces, the object of the day's lesson. Apparently making stock was a much more messy, unappetizing project than I had anticipated.

Stocks are the very essence of French cuisine, the foundation on which glorious recipes are built. We had mastered basic knife skills and several techniques for cooking vegetables, and a week into our schooling, we were ready to tackle the preparation of stocks. Bit by bit we were learning the building blocks of basic kitchen technique. A well-prepared stock forms the basis for almost all sauces in the classical culinary repertoire. Stocks also play vital supporting roles in many more complex preparations. This was the focus of our lesson: learning to build the basic stocks, and the nomenclature of the sauces derived from them.

All stocks begin with the same basic ingredients—bones, mirepoix, herbs, water, and time. The mirepoix, a roughly chopped mixture of onions, carrots, and celery—the holy trinity of French cooking—should compose a mere 10 percent of the total weight of the ingredients. All stocks also share the same mixture of herbs, known as a bouquet garni, which is always made up of bay leaves, parsley stems, black peppercorns, and thyme. Salt is never added to a stock; because stocks are a component of a more complex finished dish, the amount of saltiness of the final dish would be too hard to balance if the stock itself was presalted. Also, many stocks are reduced, perhaps several times, before they are used in a sauce. If the stock was salted to taste before reducing, it would be two or three times too salty by the time the stock was actually ready to be used.

Stocks are classified into two categories: brown stocks (*fonds bruns*) and white stocks (*fonds blancs*). Brown stocks such as brown veal stock, beef stock, game stock, and brown chicken stock are darker in color, as the bones and the mirepoix must be browned separately in the oven or on the stove before being combined and simmered in water with tomato paste. Brown stocks are also fortified from deglazing the pans used to brown the bones and mirepoix. The *sucs* (browned proteins fixed to the bottom of pans after searing or roasting) are dissolved in a bit of water or white wine and then added to the stock. The components are then covered with cold water and brought to a simmer. The bouquet garni is then added and the stock cooks slowly, never allowed to boil, for as long as possible, usually eight hours or overnight.

White stocks such as white veal stock, white chicken stock, and fish fumet follow the same basic master recipe, with a few small changes. Instead of browning the bones to be used in the stock, the bones are blanched—that is, they are immersed in cold water, brought to a brisk boil, and immediately drained. The mirepoix, green leek tops, and water are then added to the bones with the bouquet garni. Fish fumet varies from other stocks because carrots are not used as part of the mirepoix (their naturally sweet flavor is considered to be overpowering to the delicate flavor of the fumet). Fumet is also not a long-cooking stock—the flavors should be fully developed in less than an hour, and in the case of small batches, a half hour's simmering time should be sufficient.

All of these directions seemed pretty straightforward to me, but nothing so far explained why the whole class was wearing industrial-size garbage bags. Little did I know.

The class began with the brown veal stock, or *fond brun*, because it is the most important and most utilized of all classic stocks. Two fifty-pound cardboard flats of frozen veal bones were delivered to the classroom. These babies were frozen solid, stuck together with remnants of blood and tissue still clinging to the huge shanks. These veal calves must have been *big*—the bones were easily as big around as my thigh. Chipping them into manageable hunks and then wrestling them into roasting pans sprayed frozen bits of blood all over the room. The bloody ice chips melted in the rising temperature from the blasting convection ovens, and I began to see the wisdom in protecting my freshly laundered chef's jacket from the mist of defrosted blood drops quickly blanketing every exposed surface. The bones and mirepoix were soon browning nicely in their enormous, troughlike roasting pans, and once everything was deeply caramelized, we dumped it all into a huge, fifty-gallon Swiss kettle to begin the long simmering process that would turn these bones and vegetables into liquid gold. We used what looked like a fireman's hose to fill the monstrous kettle with water—Imogene needed all of Angelo's considerable mass and muscle to help her direct the spray into the vastness of the kettle. This was a piece of industrial equipment that could easily have found a new home on some South Sea island as a cannibal's chafing dish. That was it—less than a half hour's worth of work, plus skimming and simmering, and we had the beginnings of the great sauces. Now for the fish fumet.

Fresh from our success with the veal stock, we attacked the fish fumet with a swaggering sense of surety. Stocks are a piece of gé-noise cake—there was nothing to them. Then we opened the bag of fish bones.

Rather, Marita opened the bag and promptly ran screaming from the room. Marita had come to school from her home in Santo Domingo, and while she spoke excellent English in a soft, sweetly accented voice, in her distress she lapsed into a long string of Spanish, and at first we weren't sure what had set her off. No one was particularly anxious to open the bag again, though. Jackie, the darkly lovely but quiet girl who had rocked the seventies look at orientation, helpfully translated part of Marita's remarks. Looking confused, Jackie said she thought she heard Marita say something about . . . monsters. Ridiculous. It was just fish! I prodded Tucker toward the bag, and while I held it, he reached one hand in and brought out what looked like . . . a monster. It was a huge fish head, mouth open in a mute roar, distressingly large tongue evident behind its sharp teeth. I didn't even know fish had tongues. Its bulging, gelid eyes were not yet cloudy. Almost everyone who was crowded around the bag took a long step back, but Tucker was totally unconcerned.

"Look here," he said, his Michigan accent apparent in his vowels. "Everybody just calm down. This is nothing. I've caught bigger fish than this with my dick!" It was not a very politically correct thing to say, but it broke the tension in the class—for the first time, we felt like one team, not twenty-four students. We all laughed at the mental picture: Tucker, White Owl cheroot clamped in his teeth, his checked chef's pants around his ankles, fishing hip deep in Lake Michigan.

There were a few more mean-looking fish heads in the bag, and a great many flaccid fish skeletons. There was also a mop bucket's worth of smelly fish mucus in the bottom of the bag, coating every morsel of fish we touched. Pretty soon the sticky substance was all over everything not already festooned in the fine spray of blood from the veal bones. We dumped everything into the huge sink and rinsed it all off. Then Chef Jean dropped the bombshell. We would have to clean the heads before they were ready for the stockpot. The bright orange gills trailing from the fish heads would have to be yanked off and discarded. The eyes would also have to be removed. Each pair of students would be assigned one head to clean before adding it to the pot. Chef held up one hideously grinning skull and then plopped it on my cutting board.

"Darling, you will do this one. Tucker, he already knows his feeeshes. You should be careful next time you go fishing, you wouldn't want to lose that little bit of bait!" With that, he laughed, and then proceeded to demonstrate how to remove the eyes with a melon baller. It looked so easy when he did it—the whole thing just popped right out like a ripe piece of cantaloupe. I got out my melon baller, situated the sharp edge next to the gleaming orb, and scooped. That's when the eye turned to liquid and shot all over my garbage bag poncho. Ewww. The wisdom of donning the shiny black plastic garbage bags was patently obvious.

Once we finally wrestled the fish into their watery grave in the fish fumet, we were able to continue with our lesson at last. When the stocks finished their long simmer, we would begin to learn the classic sauces derived from them, but until then, we would learn the art of the emulsified sauce. Emulsified sauces can be hot, as in the case of hollandaise sauce, or cold, as in the case of mayonnaise, or room temperature, like salad dressing.

The common element in them all is the emulsifying agent—in most cases, this is an egg yolk, though mustard is also a powerful and useful emulsifier. Emulsifiers work by binding the fat in the sauce with the water-based flavoring, such as lemon juice or vinegar. Try whisking together oil and vinegar for a salad dressing. No matter how hard or long you whisk, and how much air you incorporate, the droplets of fat will eventually precipitate out of the vinegar, and the dressing will separate. Now try adding a tablespoon of mustard and repeating the process. With a few brisk swipes of the whisk, something magical happens: the oil, vinegar, and mustard come together and turn into a thick, almost creamy sauce.

Egg yolks are also great emulsifiers—they bind fats and water-based flavoring together beautifully—and sauces emulsified with egg yolks possess a singular richness. Mayonnaise is one of the only sauces that uses both mustard and egg yolks together, creating a very sturdy sauce thick enough to spread across meats, fish, poultry, shellfish, vegetables, and the lucky sandwich. Usually yolks are used to bind hot sauces such as hollandaise and béarnaise, and occasionally to add heft and richness to soups. In this case, the temperature of each component of the sauce must be perfect in order to keep these rather delicate emulsions from breaking. The clarified butter, which provides the fatty backbone to hollandaise and béarnaise sauces, must be added drop by drop, until it has all been incorporated and the sauce becomes thick, creamy, and glossy. If the fat is added too quickly, the yolks will be unable to absorb the large amount of fat and will not bind the sauce effectively. A good rule of thumb to remember when making a sauce with egg yolks is that one yolk can absorb approximately 200 milliliters (not quite a cup) of oil.

Because these sauces are so delicate and depend for much of their stability on the proper temperature, they usually cannot be held for long periods of time, even kept gently warm in the diffuse heat of a warm-water bath (bain-marie), without breaking (separating) once again into hydrophilic (the water-based flavor and yolks) and hydrophobic (the oil) elements. Even with careful attention to detail, sometimes the sauce will break as it is being prepared. There are several ways to fix a broken sauce. If the sauce becomes too hot, adding a few drops of very cold water and whisking vigorously will usually resurrect it. If the sauce is too cold and has separated, add a few drops of warm water and whisk. Sometimes, even these steps will not save a sauce. If this happens, simply add another egg yolk and whisk vigorously over gently simmering water. This extra yolk will bind any extra oil in the sauce as well as binding with the other yolks. This will almost always work to save a broken emulsified sauce. If even this doesn't work, it is time to scrape the broken sauce onto freshly cooked, piping hot pasta, grate a snowy mound of cheese on top, add a few grinds of freshly cracked pepper and a squirt of lemon juice, and call it the *fantaisie du chef.*

Tucker and I fought over who would prepare the mayonnaise, and in the end we flipped a coin. While Tuck and I were friends and got along well, both of us were supercompetitive and wanted to do everything ourselves. I lost, and ended up holding the bowl steady while Tucker whisked. His mayo was perfect: a rich, creamy sauce with a strong hint of lemon that bore little resemblance to the store-bought version. We ate it straight from the bowl on slices of warm bread from the bread kitchen across the hall. Delicious.

Mayonnaise

1 egg yolk

Juice of 1 lemon

1 tablespoon Dijon mustard

7 ounces (between ¾ and 1 cup) vegetable oil

Fine sea salt and freshly ground white pepper

1. In a small bowl, whisk together the egg yolk and lemon juice until the yolk is pale yellow and airy. Add the mustard, whisking briskly until well combined. While still whisking briskly, add the oil drop by drop, making certain that each addition is well incorporated. The mixture will begin to thicken and will also become much more voluminous. Once the oil starts to be incorporated more readily, it is safe to add a bit more at a time, but remember not to flood it!
2. Once all the oil has been whisked in and is well incorporated, taste for seasoning and add salt and pepper as needed. The mayo is now ready to be spread on sandwiches, used in salads, and slathered on eggs, potatoes, and almost anything else you can imagine. The mayo will keep for a few days in the refrigerator, but is best used when it is fresh.

A variation on the classic mayonnaise is aïoli, the garlicky mayonnaise redolent of olive oil and the Provençal countryside that spawned it. To make aïoli, crush a few garlic cloves well with a mortar and pestle (or in a blender) until a paste forms. Add the egg yolk and the mustard and whisk well. Add the olive oil bit by bit until it is totally incorporated and a thick, glossy, smooth sauce is achieved. But be more gentle with the whisking than when using regular vegetable oil—olive oil is easily bruised, and if treated too roughly, it will taste bitter.

Makes 1 cup

Basic Vinaigrette

The thing to remember when making vinaigrette is that the proportion of vinegar to oil will always be one part vinegar to two parts oil.

Scant ½ cup white wine vinegar

1 clove garlic, crushed

1 medium shallot, roughly chopped

1 heaping tablespoon Dijon mustard

½ cup vegetable oil

½ cup olive oil

Salt and freshly ground pepper

1. Mix together the vinegar, garlic, and shallot in a small bowl and let stand for at least 30 minutes to meld the flavors.
2. Add the mustard and mix. Whisk in the oils in a steady stream until well combined. Add salt and pepper to taste. Whisk again briefly before adding to greens.

NOTE: Strain out the garlic and shallot before serving if preferred. I like to leave them in, but make sure you alert other diners to their presence!

Makes a bit less than 1½ cups

Pâtes Cassées (Broken Pasta)

I went through an inexplicable phase when I could not make mayonnaise successfully to save my life. No matter what I did, I seemed to end up with a runny mess instead of thick, unctuous glory. Instead of tipping these disasters into the garbage, I got in the habit of pouring them over leftover pasta, creating something between hot pasta salad and pasta Alfredo. Michael liked it so much that even now, when I can whip up a proper mayo in a jiff, I will make this dish. It is particularly comforting after a stressful day—it is very cathartic to do something wrong on purpose, and have it turn out so delicious.

While you could use the same proportions of ingredients for regular mayonnaise in this dish, I have tinkered with things slightly to make it even more richly runny, lemony, peppery, and just short of overwhelming. Of course, if you do have a misbehaving mayo on your hands, by all means, use it!

2 egg yolks

Juice of 2 lemons

1 tablespoon Dijon mustard

¾ cup olive oil

Salt and coarsely ground pepper

Small handful (about ¼ cup) roughly chopped fresh herbs (see Notes)

8 ounces pasta, cooked al dente and drained (see Notes)

¼ cup shaved (with a vegetable peeler) or grated Grana Padano or Reggiano Parmigiano

1. Whisk the egg yolks with the lemon juice and mustard. Add the olive oil a drop at a time while still whisking, until the mayonnaise starts to come together a bit. When all the oil is added, you should have something like a thin custard. If it is thicker or thinner, it doesn't really

matter. The joy of this dish is that you can't really go wrong, because it is wrong already.

2. Taste and add salt and pepper to your liking, but be gentle with the salt—do keep in mind that the cheese is quite salty. Fold in your chopped fresh herbs, and pour over your steamy hot pasta. Sprinkle with the cheese.

NOTES: A bit of whatever is lurking in your refrigerator is an excellent finish for this. Fresh thyme, flat-leaf parsley, basil, or a sprig of rosemary would be lovely, and I have even used a soupçon of mint to good effect (but know your audience before trying this). Cilantro, sage, and curly parsley are not happy pairings, though, and if this is all your fridge yields (or if you don't have any fresh herbs at all), a dash of herbes de Provence or a whisper of dried thyme would be fine.

I like to use a short pasta with texture, like cavatappi or campanelle, to trap the yummy sauce, but you could use wide, rustic ribbons of pasta like pappardelle or even fettuccine just as well.

This is delicious hot, lukewarm, or cold from the fridge the next day. Start with some firm slices of *saucisson sec* or salami with cornichons and peppery hot mustard, end with a green salad, a nice fat wedge of sheep's milk Camembert, and some ripe fruit, and you have a wonderfully filling (and fulfilling) meal.

Serves 2 generously or 4 as part of a larger meal

TOAD HALL

As our second sweaty week drew to a close, everyone in class was thinking the same thing: it was definitely time to have some drinks and get to know each other a little better. We had gotten over our first week's jitters, and seemed to be settling into a rhythm as a class—personalities were beginning to emerge, friendships were being struck up, and underneath it all, there was the quiet hum of competition to see who was going to be the top chef.

In the women's locker room after class, Imogene and I had already begun to talk up the idea of a group happy hour, and I was certain that Tucker could rope in all the guys from our class as well. The ovens and burners of our Level 1 classroom blazed away all day long, making the already hot days of June even more unbearable. The temperature in the classroom regularly climbed above 110 degrees. Chef Jean warned us to keep ourselves hydrated, and often took long swallows from his own water bottle. Rumor had it that while we all sucked on ice chips from the freezer, Chef Jean's bottle was filled with chilled rosé wine. I never found out if it was true, but it would explain Chef's increasingly jovial demeanor as the day wore on. I wouldn't have blamed him if it *was* true—there is no better way to beat the heat!

I knew I wasn't alone in fantasizing about a frosty cold drink to put out the proverbial flames when Tucker started rhapsodizing about fishing on Lake Michigan with his dad. The high point of all his stories was not the bigmouth bass he bagged, but cracking open a tall can of Coors afterward. This was not really the beverage choice I had in mind, but even a cold glass of Boone's Farm—a disgusting beverage available at only the very best truck stops and 7-Eleven stores and a favorite from my college years—was starting to sound good by the end of another parching, sweat-soaked day.

Our uniforms—polyester pants, long-sleeve poly-blend jackets, and itchy polyester neckerchiefs—didn't do much to alleviate the situation, either. As I stood over yet another pot of boiling vegetables, I could feel the sweat running in a steady torrent from right underneath the band of my absorbent paper chef's hat, pooling for a moment in the crease of my neck, before descending in a salty flume down my back to soak into the ultrahigh waistband of my checked trousers. Two separate rivers descended down the back of each leg to saturate my socks, already suffocating in my heavy-duty black work boots. My hands became sweaty from the heat and the pressure to churn out perfectly cut turnips, and I began to lose my grip on both my knife and my sanity. Blisters formed from only two weeks of chopping vegetables popped and wept fluid down my hand.

Redemption came at last on our second Friday afternoon. With two more hours to go until class let out, Chef Jean sidled up behind me to monitor my attempts to skim a slick of grease off the top of the veal stock bubbling gently away in the Swiss kettle. I was using a ladle the size of a cantaloupe to corral the scum and fat from the surface of the thirty-five gallons of veal stock simmering below. Steam was drifting up to penetrate my jacket and undershirt before trapping itself in sticky droplets in my bra.

"Ooh la la," Chef exclaimed. "You look *très chaud*. Your face is getting very red. Perhaps . . ." Here he leaned forward slightly, and I thought I caught a faint glimpse of sympathy in the depths of his eyes. It was probably just my own desperation reflected in his eyes. "Perhaps you and the other students would like to join me and the other chefs and students this afternoon for a drink? It is a good idea, *non?*"

I couldn't believe my ears. A drink? A tall glass of chilly alcohol to rest against my fevered brow, to quell the unpleasant, burning sensation in the pit of my stomach and quiet the voice in my head asking me if I had made the right decision giving up my office job to come here.

"Uh, gee, Chef, that sounds great." *Oh, dear God,* I thought to myself, *why do I sound like a high school student accepting a date? Pull yourself together, wipe the slick of sweat off your face, and say something intelligent!*

"Uh, where?" *Great. Great thinking. Impress him with your scintillating conversation.*

"Well, some of the instructors like to go over to Toad Hall on Friday afternoons. Students come, they drink, they hang out, they talk. Sometimes, they like to buy drinks for us."

Oh, wonderful idea! I would herd everyone in class over to the bar after school and make an ass of myself in front of the instructors. No, this is not what I was thinking. Unfortunately, this is what I did. I was actually thinking more along the lines of having everyone in class come, we could buy Chef Jean a couple of rounds of drinks, and I would practice my conversational French on him. If I couldn't manage to be witty in English, I could at least try to be coherent in French. A little lubrication couldn't possibly hurt.

I spread the word—Tucker got the boys interested, and Imogene recruited the girls. The rest of the afternoon dragged by, and finally, it was three o'clock. We packed up our knives and our red toolboxes of equipment and burst from the classroom in one sweaty, excited tidal wave of anticipation. It was like the last day of school before summer vacation, except that we were all looking forward to something a bit more adult than lemonade and Popsicles.

In the locker room, I fought my way over a mess of bodies in various stages of nudity until I made it to the square foot of space I called my own. The locker rooms at chef school were cramped, overcrowded, and always dirty. It was in strange contrast to the polished perfection of the rest of the school. While the kitchens were always immaculate, and the dining room of L'Ecole was a masterpiece of crisply starched, immaculate linen tablecloths, warm ochre-colored walls, and gleaming silverware all precision-placed in neat and orderly rows, the ladies' locker room was a warren of steel-gray lockers, grimy concrete floors, and fluorescent lighting that always seemed to be flickering. There was no room for showers or even benches to sit on. There definitely wasn't room for the ninety-six women (on average) attending the school during the day. Some people were assigned lockers in a bathroom near the pastry kitchens, but this did little to ease the congestion. It wasn't so bad in the mornings, because people from different levels seemed to trickle in at different times (I noticed the more advanced the level, the earlier the people were coming in), but as soon as three o'clock came, classes were over for the day and all the levels plus the pastry students converged in one sweaty, seething mass of humanity, studded with red toolboxes.

In an attempt to bring some level of sanitation to my tiny corner of the locker room, I bought an economy-size tub of baby wipes and handed them out freely to my sweaty neighbors. It didn't exactly take the place of a shower, but at least I managed to remove the pieces of food found stuck in various unexpected places. I haven't the foggiest idea how I managed to get carrot strips lodged in my socks, or how potato peelings found their way even into my underwear. I threw my street clothes on as quickly as possible, forgoing style or even a glance in the one tiny mirror, in favor of speedily escaping the maelstrom of perspiration and grime. Together with the rest of the gals, I bounced out of the service entrance, onto the steamy, scummy SoHo streets. Tucker and the boys came down moments later. Almost everyone lit up a cigarette except Tucker, who smoked one of the stinky, cheap cigars he bought at the deli and insisted on calling cheroots. I didn't smoke, but I was definitely in the minority. Once the instructors emerged, we finally set off, practically running the three blocks to the bar.

Though it was only a few blocks from my apartment, I hadn't

noticed this particular watering hole before, but that wasn't too surprising. It was the very definition of a hole in the wall—a sliver of an
entrance set slightly back from the street, up a few steps. There was a
sign, but it was battered, distressed, and barely legible. This was also
the general theme of the décor once inside the double doors. The
long, low, dimly lit space was populated with a few worn-out tables
and chairs. The aging wooden bar running along one wall had definitely seen a lot of action. The plank wood floors were scarred but
clean, as was the bartender, whom we came to know affectionately
as Bear. In the back were a few more tables, some vinyl benches, and
a pool table. The best part was the air-conditioning. That and the
gleaming polished taps behind the bar. I tried not to be the first one
to order, but I didn't have to worry. It was a stampede: chefs and students, not only from our level, but also the three levels above us, all
descended upon the lone bartender like starving men setting upon a
hapless double cheeseburger.

When I finally fought my way to the bar, I felt a hand on my
shoulder. It belonged to a short, swarthy little man whom I vaguely
recalled from our orientation.

"Hey, you," he said rudely, his heavy French accent turning the
words into a guttural slur. "Don't you know we chefs have seniority?
You wait your turn."

Oh, Lord. It must be a chef-instructor, but who? How did I know
there were still chefs waiting to order? Almost all of them had retired to one table, the conversation among them quieted with the
arrival of a waitress bowed almost double under the weight of the
tray of drinks she carried. What was this chef doing still at the bar? I
could tell he was a chef, all right. He was wearing street clothes, like
the rest of us, but his authoritative belly was plainly visible, as was a
certain Napoleonic look in his eye. The heavy French accent was also
a big tip-off. How could I ease myself out of this situation without
offending this guy, who would probably end up being my instructor
in the next level?

"Would you like a drink, Chef?" I asked. *Brilliant, brilliant move,* I thought. It did seem to placate him, if only slightly.

"*Beh, oui,* why do you think I am standing here?"

A good question, I thought.

"You may buy me a beer," the angry chef ordered. "*Attends, non* . . . make that two. One for me, and one for your own chef."

"Sure thing, Chef," I said. Well, I wouldn't be able to bring Chef Jean a beer myself, but at least this chef would pass it along to him for me.

Actually, I thought I was really killing two birds with one trip to the bar, making friends with my chef and this new chef. Here my happy thoughts were interrupted by the chef still standing at my elbow bellowing, " 'Sure thing, Chef'? Where did you learn to talk? Didn't your chef tell you it is ALWAYS 'Yes, Chef'? Always."

I felt the unexpected sting of the rebuke and spoke before I had time to reconsider—"But we aren't in school, Chef." Big mistake. The chef, who was at least an inch shorter than I, seemed suddenly to tower over me, all ominous slitted eyes and heavily accented syllables. Cowering at the bar, I silently prepared for the outburst.

"Say 'Yes, Chef Robert'!" He pronounced it Roh-bear, *bien sûr.*

I didn't even have to think twice. "Yes, Chef Robert," I said meekly.

Just then, the two beers appeared, and I handed them off to the angry Gaul before me. My hands were shaking very slightly, from prickly embarrassment laced with searing anger, but mostly acidic, stomach-churning shame. I smiled, to show how thrilled I was to be buying him a drink, and realized I was smiling like a moron into empty space. He had turned away with the drinks and scuttled off to join his compatriots.

I couldn't believe how quickly the conversation had gone downhill. I was already beginning to dread the thought of toiling under Chef Robert. I knew who he was now, the infamously vicious chef for all Level 3 students. I could only hope he wouldn't remember me

by the time I made it to his level. *If* I made it to his level. There was
no doubt that nothing I could do in the kitchen under this man's eye
would be good enough. Even if he did succeed in forgetting our first
encounter, I knew I wouldn't be able to.

I bought a hefeweizen beer for myself, a bit of sunshine in a
glass, the creamy light wheat beer given a playful kick with the tang
of lemon wedges, and joined my own little circle of friends.

"What the hell happened, Darling?" asked Tucker, who had
taken to calling me by my last name, like we were both on the var-
sity football team. He had obviously seen the unfortunate incident
at the bar, and his already rather prominent ears were practically out
on stalks in his eagerness to hear what had gone so flagrantly wrong.
The conversation among my fellow classmates sputtered and died
like a faulty pilot light on a Vulcan range, and all eyes turned to me.

I decided to try to downplay the incident. "Uh, nothing. I just
bought a beer for Chef Jean and Chef Robert. That's it. Sort of."

I took a heroic swig of my beer and then another one, fending
off further questions. Pretty soon I was looking at the spent wedge
of lemon at the bottom of my empty glass. Tucker took one look at
my long face, and decided to have pity on his partner. He bought
me, and everyone else, another round of drinks. After quaffing the
second beer, things seemed to be looking up—it couldn't be as bad
as I thought it was, I told myself. Just a slight misunderstanding. I
would win all the chefs over with my kitchen competence and willing demeanor. Hopefully.

Soon, it was my turn to head back to the bar and buy a round.
Ricki came along. Ricki was one half of the team across the aisle
from Tucker and me, and while I admired her ease with her chef's
knife, I didn't know that much else about her. She had many visible piercings, and a few tattoos revealed themselves in the locker
room. It all seemed to portray her as a supertough chick not to be
messed with. But she also had an easy smile, and a southern accent
so glorious and rich it reminded me of lemon meringue pie. I am

a sucker for accents of all types, and would probably have agreed to any suggestion Ricki made in that sweet southern voice. When she suggested that we should buy shots for our classmates, I was all for it. Fifteen kamikaze shots were quickly lined up on the bar and Ricki and I did our best waitress impersonations, sashaying across the length of the room with our loaded trays, under the watchful eyes of the chefs.

I was trying to forget my earlier humiliation and focused all my attention on perfecting the right amount of dip and sway in my cocktail waitress strut without dumping shots down my shirt. Thirty seconds later, things were looking even better as fifteen shots were simultaneously drained and fifteen shot glasses were banged down on the table. I had never had a kamikaze shot before and thought they were a revelation. I asked Ricki where she had gotten the wonderful idea for these delicious shots. She flung down her shot glass and wiped her mouth with the back of her hand before answering, and I realized that her glass had joined a flock of other shot glasses gathering in formation in front of her.

"They're all I drink," she slurred, stifling a hiccup.

Fortified with the fiery alcohol, I felt like now would be the ideal time to begin my campaign to win over Chef Jean. I could just make him out in the gloom of the dark bar, still sitting with the other chefs. As I was screwing up my courage to wander over and throw myself into the lion's den, he suddenly got up and made his way to the bar, empty glass in hand. Marvelous! I shot out of my seat, knocking it over in my hurry, and scurried over to intercept him before he could place his order.

"*Bonjour,*" I shouted, perhaps a bit too loudly. "Make it two," I added, turning to the bartender, who was just setting a small Stella Artois in front of my astonished professor, "and put it on my tab."

That sounded awfully good, I thought. Now it was time to get out my rusty high school French, dust it off, and get to know Chef a little better. For fifteen minutes, I babbled on in broken French, interspersed liberally with sweeping hand gestures, gulps of Stella, and long pauses when my increasingly fuzzy brain searched in vain for a long-forgotten verb form.

Chef looked at first startled, then confused (my vocabulary was not what it used to be), and finally his face broke into a grin, and he began rapidly firing French at me. I think I got most of it, though I got lost in the middle of his anecdote about jam-filled omelets—at least, I think that is what he was talking about. Another round of Stellas appeared before us, and I plastered on a grin and thanked Chef for his generosity, and looked around for a potted plant or anywhere to dump the suds as quickly and quietly as possible. This is when the wheels began to come off. I was in the middle of a long story about some seared veal kidneys I had eaten in a little bistro in Nice when I felt someone grab my elbow. I turned, a bit wobbly on the stool, to see Tucker mouthing frantically at me.

"What are you doing?" Tucker hissed, but before I could think of a way to say good-bye to Chef *en français,* Tucker physically dragged me to my feet and led me back toward the bleary ring of faces at our classmates' table.

I was filled with triumph: I had done it! Made friends with Chef, and worked on my French. Multitasking was definitely my middle name. Wait a minute, no, it wasn't. What was my middle name? Tucker interrupted this fuzzy train of thought to say, "You looked like a total freak over there. What were you doing?"

I didn't care what Tucker thought. I was happy that I had worked up the courage to try out my French on Chef. I was taking a big chance in quitting my job to go to chef school. What was a little embarrassment at my pitiful French grammar?

As I looked around the table at the faces of my new friends, I realized someone was missing from our merry little band. I peered around, trying to match up the red faces around me with the class roster, when a large pyramid of spent shot glasses that took up almost half our table caught my eye. Ricki.

"What happened to Ricki?" I asked Tucker. He sighed deeply, and pointed. Stretched out on the vinyl bench, hidden from the gimlet eyes of the chefs by a protective screen of red toolboxes and knife bags, was a deeply slumbering Ricki, drunk as a skunk and completely dead to the world.

Well, we couldn't just leave her there, I thought. We would have to resuscitate her and somehow transport her back to the Upper East Side, where she was subletting a tiny studio apartment. But how? Usually, this was not a logistical problem that would have stumped me, but my mind did not seem to be working with its usual speed. It didn't seem to be working at all, in fact. As I stared contemplatively at the supine form of my classmate, Tucker swung into action. Jared, by far the biggest member of our class at almost six and a half feet tall, was enlisted to prop up Ricki's limp form and propel it through the bar with speed and stealth. Tucker scurried outside to Broome Street to hail a cab. It was my job to wake up Sleeping Beauty and get her sufficiently upright and ambulatory so that she would not have to be carried out of the bar. I started by gently calling her name, and then nudging her softly on the shoulder. The snoring noises became markedly louder, but she didn't stir. I shook her shoulder harder and practically shouted her name, but still nothing. I looked around, hoping that inspiration would strike before the cabbie waiting outside lost patience, when someone plunked a large glass of ice water down next to me. It was the bartender, Bear. He took one look at the situation, snorted, and returned to his lair behind the bar. I drank the water, and then dumped the ice down the back of Ricki's shirt. Bingo! She shot up, right into Jared's grasp. I festooned her swaying form with her toolbox and knife kit and sent her out to the waiting cab.

I decided maybe it was a good time for me to depart as well. Tucker and I settled up the surprisingly expensive tab we had run up, and slowly made our way home, pausing every block or so to rest. Even though the sun was still high in the sky, it seemed like it had been a very long day. When we finally made it to my apartment, all I could think about was collapsing gratefully onto my bed. I mumbled good-bye to Tucker and staggered up the three flights of stairs. Finally I managed to get my door open, drag myself inside, and face-plant at long last on the cool cotton sheets of the bed. I was exhausted from waking up early, my feet hurt from standing all day, my hands were covered in blisters, and my head was already pounding from that kamikaze shot. I would just lie here for a minute . . .

Michael found me several hours later, facedown, arms and legs splayed out like a starfish at low tide, with my shoes still on. Regaling him with the story of the afternoon, he seemed somewhat doubtful that I had been quite the social success with Chef Jean that I had originally thought, or that Ricki, or anyone else, could have possibly been in worse condition than yours truly. Remembering some of the things I had said, I thought he might be right. Michael was also surprised to find me in bed at six o'clock in the evening. It was not like me at all—I was always going: making dinner, doing yoga poses, working on a knitting project, talking on the phone, all at the same time. His pet name for me was the Energizer Bunny.

Michael did not seem pleased that the Energizer Bunny was now on the loose with a bunch of hard-partying chefs. Despite my assurances that nothing could be less sexy than a long day spent sweating over tiny vegetable dice, and the fact that he had seen how very unappealing my uniform was, it seemed that all the time I was spending with my new pals was making him jealous. I loved Michael for all the ways he wasn't like my friends: he worked in an office as a successful real estate investor, he had normal hobbies (playing basketball and poker), read long biographies, and he could spank me soundly in our marathon games of backgammon. I didn't care that his fridge contained only bottled water, a bottle of Rao's vodka sauce, and a magnum of Dom Perignon when I met him, or that he used his oven to store the rugs he brought back from Turkey. The fact that he couldn't boil water was endearing to me, but

Michael seemed to feel that suddenly we had nothing in common, and I might run off with someone whose *sauce gribiche* swept me off my feet. While Michael sulked and played an online poker tournament, I lay in bed, too tired to even look for the take-out menus, and I wondered: Had I bitten off more than I could chew? Was school too much for me and for us?

Kamikaze

While my first experience with this deadly little drink was not the spectacular evening I was hoping for, I don't blame it on the kamikaze. Use the very best liquor you've got and freshly squeezed lime juice (or, even better, Key lime juice) and drink in moderation. I have tinkered with the classic recipe for the shot to make it a bit more sophisticated. My version is below.

1 ounce best-quality vodka (I like to use Grey Goose L'Orange or Ketel One Citroen)

1 ounce Grand Marnier or other top-shelf orange liqueur

1 ounce freshly squeezed lime juice

Grated zest of 1 lime

¼ cup superfine sugar

2 lime wedges

1. Fill a cocktail shaker with ice. Add the vodka, orange liqueur, and lime juice and shake well.
2. Prepare an old-fashioned glass: Mix together the lime zest and sugar and place in a shallow bowl or on a plate. Run a wedge of lime around the rim of the glass, and then dip the glass into the sugar mixture, making sure that a liberal amount of sugar and zest adheres to the rim of the glass. Fill the glass with ice.
3. Strain the drink mixture into the waiting glass and garnish with another lime wedge. Sip slowly!

Makes 1 drink

EGGSTRAVAGANZA

*O*f stocks are the foundation of French cuisine, eggs are the mortar that binds (sometimes quite literally) the bricks together. It is said that a chef earns his toque when he is able to prepare eggs in a hundred different ways—one recipe for each pleat in the tall hat.

Even though I ended up with egg on my face after the fiasco at Toad Hall, I still love eggs, from deviled to poached to fried. I was really looking forward to today's lesson on eggs, but I wasn't sure how I was going to feel after sampling a dozen different egg recipes. But other than a possible egg overdose, I wasn't really worried about doing well—who couldn't make an omelet already? Me, apparently.

After the morning lecture, we dispersed to our workstations, each team burdened with a flat of thirty eggs. With hundreds of the fragile things rolling around the classroom, something messy was bound to happen. Sure enough, as Penny, the middle-aged biddy who had dominated Dean Jacques Pépin's attention at orientation, ambled back to her workstation at the back of the class, clutching her flat of eggs to her chest, her enormous bosom caused several innocent eggs to jostle out and splat against the tiled floor. A half dozen had gone before she noticed the slimy trail of yolk and shells she left in her wake.

While this muddle of Penny's making was funny, it was also a slippery mess, and Penny was unable to wrangle the mop and clean it up without help. Suddenly twenty students were busily weighing out ingredients and rereading recipes, eyes averted. Tucker and I threw ourselves into the breach. We wiped and mopped while Penny stood by, babbling unhappily. We had barely started classes and already Penny was becoming a problem for us all—the egg incident was only the latest in a growing series of mishaps. Penny was always last to finish her dishes, and she had already set her workstation on fire—before our third week of class. Penny was constantly holding up the class one way or another, by asking hundreds of questions during lecture, or telling interminable stories about her hometown in Indiana that drove us all up the wall.

I made excuses for Penny, thinking how difficult it must have been for her to come to New York from a small town, how hard it was to adjust to the grueling schedule of chef school after being a homemaker for twenty years, how different everything was from her expectations. It must have been hard to be the only fluffy, middle-aged housewife in the midst of rambunctious teens and twenty-somethings. Still, Penny was a catastrophe.

When we finally finished helping Penny mop up her latest messy disaster, Tucker and I were free to begin with the program of recipes slated for the morning. I was glad that I hadn't eaten any breakfast; our first recipe was for coddled eggs, a dish my father had made for me when I was small and home from school with the flu. Coddling an egg is an extremely gentle procedure. The egg is cracked into a buttered ramekin, bathed with a bit of heavy cream, and popped into a warm oven. The egg cooks slowly, almost poaching in the cream, yielding a soft, rich dish that verges on custard. I ate all of my coddled egg, and finished off the rest of Tucker's, too.

With a bite of this simply prepared dish, I was suddenly whisked back to my childhood. I remembered the tiny surge of excitement at being allowed to stay home sick from school, of a fever soothed with ginger ale, crackers, and love in the form of a sunny yellow yolk breaking open in a cloud of warm cream, spiked with freshly ground pepper and grains of crunchy sea salt that melted on my tongue.

Chef Jean applauded our clean dishes and winked at us. "I see you are hungry," he said. "Well, you will need to be to make it through class today." That sounded slightly ominous. Part of our education here at school was not only to learn to prepare the classic French dishes, but also to learn to taste food properly. All chefs must taste absolutely everything that comes out of the kitchen, several times over, from the first addition of herbs to the last-minute adjustment of seasoning before the finished dish heads out the kitchen door to the diner. This is the most basic of safeguards: no one will ever receive a dish that is less than perfect (in the chef's opinion) if the chef has personally made certain that all the elements meet approval from his or her rigorous and well-developed palate. Of course, in order to develop this palate, one must begin at the very beginning and taste everything. So in class we were responsible for tasting not only our own creations, all the way through the cooking process, but also for tasting the final products of our neighbors. Comparing and contrasting twelve different versions of the same dish, three or four times over, would educate our infantile sense of taste more quickly than a single meal in a five-star restaurant. Even so, I wasn't planning on wolfing down too many more egg dishes. I am no Cool Hand Luke. A taste here, a taste there, and I would fulfill my duties to my palate and my classmates as restaurant reviewer, without popping out of my increasingly snug chef's pants.

Our next project was the perfectly poached egg. There are few more versatile methods for preparing this most versatile of ingredients. A poached egg could be served warm, doused in the lemony bite of hollandaise sauce, or chilled and trapped within the gelid confines of a salty aspic. It could be served at room temperature, perched atop peppery bitter frisée, ready to bathe the greens in warm, but not yet set, yolk. Poached eggs are also very easy to prepare in large quantities, and may be held for several hours or even a day in the refrigerator, before being rewarmed with a quick dip in simmering water.

The whole class managed to poach their eggs properly and plate them up with a minimum of fuss and bother. We were all obliged to try everyone else's eggs—after a few bites, though, a plain poached egg can lose some of its appeal. By the time I took a bite of Jared's egg at the back of the classroom, farthest away from my station, it was stone cold on the plate, its once runny yolk congealed into something resembling wallpaper paste. I was already experiencing egg overdose, and we hadn't even made it to lunch yet. Luckily, there was only one more recipe to go before we were free at last to lunch on something other than eggs. All that remained to be prepared was an omelet.

As quintessentially French as a baguette, the omelet, that staple of the brunch menu all over the country, was the last—and most difficult—technique we would be attempting before lunchtime. Piece of cake, I thought. I had been making omelets since I was little and had to stand on a kitchen chair to reach the stove. Chef Jean called us over for a demonstration before setting us loose with our own nonstick pans. Feeling confident in my ability to prepare an omelet, I scarcely paid attention to what Chef was saying as he heated the small pan, well greased with a knob of butter, and beat two eggs together in a bowl. I nodded somewhat impatiently as he talked about not overwhipping the eggs, so that they would not become tough, and grimaced only slightly when he tasted the raw eggs for the correct balance of seasoning before pouring them into the sizzling hot skillet. But then everything I thought I knew about making an omelet went out the window. Instead of letting the eggs set in the pan without moving them, Chef began to scramble them rapidly as soon as they hit the hot surface. What was going on? Chef caught my astounded look from a corner of those all-seeing eyes, and began to laugh.

"Not what you expected, eh?" he asked me.

The eggs were now practically finished cooking, an opaque pale yellow instead of runnily transparent. Chef stopped scrambling them just when they were cooked but before they began to bunch up in curds on the bottom of the pan. Suddenly, he pulled the pan off the heat, held it high in the air for a moment, and then brought it down with a resounding bang on the grates over the flame. We all jumped in shock, and Chef chuckled at the looks of astonishment on our faces. The lumpy surface of the omelet had become smooth as silk. Chef tipped the pan up, slid the finished omelet onto a plate, brushed it with melted butter, and added a small rounded scoop of the tomato, onion, and green pepper filling known as *pipérade*.

"Voilà," he said. Chef had prepared a flat omelet perfectly in a little over forty-five seconds. He wiped out the nonstick pan and began the whole process again, demonstrating the rolled omelet. Once again he brushed the pan lightly with melted butter and in went the gently beaten eggs, Chef's hand becoming a blur as he used his wooden fork to scramble quickly, gently. Then, just as the eggs turned opaque, up went the pan in the air, down it came with a crash, and the eggs smoothed out to a calm, pale yellow sea.

Now Chef tipped the skillet up to a 75-degree angle, with the handle grasped firmly in his left hand tilted high in the air, and the eggs slid easily to the edge of the pan, making a small crease in the middle of the omelet, half the egg ready to slip out of the pan and half still clinging to the bottom. Into this he popped a scoop of the filling and then—one-two—with a deft flick of the wrist so quick I almost missed it completely, Chef used the handle to flip the pan all the way over, the velocity folding the rest of the omelet neatly together before depositing it, a perfectly plump, football shape, squarely in the middle of the waiting plate. Chef covered the omelet with a fresh linen napkin and gently pressed it more firmly into shape. A quick brush with melted butter to make it shine, and there was the most gorgeous pale golden omelet, positively glowing under the hot kitchen lights.

If it sounds confusing, that's because it is. There is a lot of whipping, shaking, banging, and flipping, all in the time it takes to pour a glass of water. We stared, mesmerized, at the two omelets looking so lovely and creamy on their plates.

Angelo nudged me. "Did you see him smack those eggs? That was hot! Smack that!" he said, whipping me in the rear with his side towel. I had the feeling he wasn't talking about the eggs.

"And that melted butter just dripping everywhere? Ohhh, yeah. This is my kind of recipe." Nope, definitely not talking about the omelets. I smacked him right back with my own side towel. This was not the time for the sexual double entendres endemic in kitchens. Suddenly omelets seemed downright scary, and I had a bad feeling I had underestimated this lesson.

Assistant Chef Cyndee handed out twenty-four nonstick pans, and off we went. Nonstick pans were a precious commodity in the school kitchen, and were kept locked up in the storeroom downstairs when not in use. Before we were allowed to actually touch them, Chef made us all promise never ever to use anything but wooden utensils on them. If there was a scratch on one of the pans when we were done with the lesson, Chef assured us with the utmost Gallic sincerity that he would personally beat the guilty student to death with the pan himself. With that warning ringing in our ears, we began. As soon as we had each produced a perfect omelet, we were free to break for lunch. I took a deep breath, put my pan over the flames, and prayed.

"Go!" shouted Chef Jean. "Now: whip, season, taste, pour, scramble, bang, and onto the plate. No, ONTO THE PLATE! THE PLATE!"

I banged my pan down again, more in frustration than anything else, as Tucker slipped his omelet seamlessly onto the waiting plate. My omelet wasn't going anywhere. Worse, it was starting to brown around the edges. Real French omelets have no marbled brown bits of color, only pale perfection and are still even slightly runny—*baveuse*, a word for which there is no real English equivalent. I pulled my pan off the burner and got out my spatula. It was cheating, but I was desperate to get the sucker out of my pan and try it again. Gently I eased the tip of the spatula under the obstinate egg. Ever so carefully I levered the spatula underneath, tipped the pan forward over the plate, and shoved. The omelet came out, at last. In three pieces. Crap. Quickly, I stuffed the pieces in my mouth and chewed. Definitely too done. It tasted more like an old tire than an egg. Yuck. I swallowed with difficulty and turned around to find Chef Jean staring at me, his eyes twinkling as he took in the traces of egg in the pan, on the plate, and on my chin.

"Try more butter," he said, before moving away to help the next failed omelet maker, as wails of "Chef! Help!" went up like air-raid sirens throughout the classroom.

I put a great whack of butter in my pan and off we went again, this time to try the rolled omelet.

"Go!" shouted Chef Jean.

And again: Crack the eggs, beat, season, taste, pour, scramble, bang, and now grab the handle, tip the pan, add the filling, fold over, and—this time things were going well for me, it was all coming together, literally. All I had to do now was get it out of the pan and onto the plate—position plate and flip. This is when my omelet fell on the floor, smearing filling all over the burner, the cutting board, and my shoes. How could I have missed the plate entirely? I stared down at the mess in disbelief. I scooped everything back up and buried the failure in the garbage. Perhaps there was a bit more Penny in me than I would ever care to admit.

I returned to my workstation, where Chef Jean was once again hovering, with a smile at the corners of his mouth.

"Try it again, but maybe not so hard this time, eh? Be gentle. It isn't going to leap out of the pan and bite you. *Bon, allez!*" Easy for him to say.

Tucker had once again produced a gorgeous specimen, and was out of the classroom, his apron streaming behind him. Traitor, I thought. Partners are supposed to help each other. Again, I prepped my pan, beat the eggs, and churned out another omelet. Somehow this one got cut in half as I was flipping it onto the plate. I crammed half into my mouth and forced Ben, Junior's partner and the fourth member of our little kitchen island, to wolf down the other half, before Chef could see the carnage. The third rolled omelet came out of the pan and made it to the plate before oozing filling out of the bottom. I ate this one, too. The fourth omelet was too brown. I made Junior, who was still laboring over his own omelet attempts, eat this one. The fifth omelet stuck to the pan again. By now I was the only one left in the classroom, and had no one to pawn off the wrecked omelet on. I closed my eyes and ate this one, too. The sixth omelet, I forgot to put filling in. The seventh omelet looked more like a flattened basketball than a plump oval. The eighth omelet was not perfect by any stretch of the imagination, but it was definitely an omelet, not an egg-themed train wreck. I stood, the total chaos and destruction of my efforts piled around me like snow drifts: my shoes, pants, and apron were splattered with bright red tomato and pepper filling; eggshells littered my cutting board and the stove, and some were even hidden in my pants pockets. Chef Jean had returned from lunch, looked at my last effort, and smiled.

"Good," he said. "Now go home this evening and do it again."

That evening, Michael and the cat had omelets for dinner. I had had my fill of eggs for quite a while.

Oeufs Brouillés (Gently Scrambled Eggs)

These succulent eggs bear as much resemblance to the leathery American breakfast staple as the NFL does to the sport of le football. These eggs take time and patience and are better served as part of a special dinner that encourages lingering and savoring every mouthful, rather than as part of a quick and dirty eat-and-run sort of meal.

8 fresh large eggs

4 tablespoons heavy cream

Generous pinch of salt

Several grinds of fresh pepper

4 tablespoons (½ stick) unsalted butter, softened

1. In a large bowl, whisk the eggs gently with 2 tablespoons of the cream and the salt and pepper.
2. Place a large, heavy sauté pan over very, very low heat. Gently pour in the egg mixture and add the butter. Whisk slowly but thoroughly, never stopping for a moment. Eventually, the eggs will begin to coagulate into small, fluffy curds. This should take 10 to 15 minutes.
3. When the eggs are set but still quite soft and a bit runny, remove the pan from the heat and stir in the remaining 2 tablespoons cream. The eggs will continue to cook a bit even off the heat, so remove them a little before you think they are quite ready. Adjust the seasoning as needed and serve on warmed plates.

Serves 2 for dinner or 4 for brunch. Can be doubled easily.

NOTES: I like to use a well-seasoned cast-iron pan of my grandmother's. Add a generous scattering of Parmesan or even shavings of fresh truffle for that very special person.

Perfect Poached Eggs

Poached eggs do not require any special equipment, contrary to what the kitchen gadget stores would have you believe. The only equipment needed is a large pot of salted water, an ice bath at the ready, a slotted spoon, and a thermometer. Bring the water to a steady, gentle simmer. Crack the egg gently, and with a steady but patient hand, pour the egg into the water. That's it. No swirling and dropping the egg into the vortex left by the spoon, no special egg holder, nothing. The egg will hit the bottom of the pot and spread out just a bit. There will be a few loose "strings" of white that trail away from the central mass, but these are easily trimmed when the egg has finished cooking and been plunged into its ice water bath.

The quality of the egg being poached is very important in this method: the fresher the egg, the more tightly it will hold its shape in the simmering water. An old egg will be looser and less cohesive, due to the breakdown of the proteins. A very old egg should not be poached at all; better to use it in a recipe calling for hard-cooked eggs or for baking—the older the egg, the easier it is to separate the white from the yolk.

Once the egg has been gently slipped into the water, be sure to keep an eye on the temperature. While it is easy to poach a half dozen or even a dozen eggs at once (if your pot is sufficiently large), the addition of so many cold things to the simmering water will drop the temperature dramatically, and it will take quite some time to return the water to its proper temperature. Conversely, it is also easy to let the temperature get too high. This will cause the egg to cook too quickly or, if the water begins to boil, may even break down the delicate texture of the egg, leaving you with something akin to egg drop soup. Once the egg is perfectly cooked, simply scoop it from the hot water with a slotted spoon and slide it gently into the waiting ice bath. If you aren't sure how done your egg is, scoop it up gently in the spoon and prod the yolk very lightly with the tip of your finger. It should provide a bit of resistance—no resistance means a raw yolk, and a firm lump means an overcooked yolk; you want something in between. The dip in ice water will stop the cooking immediately.

Once the egg is cool, remove it from the ice water and hold it in the palm of one hand. Using kitchen shears, trim any strings or asymmetrical bits so that the egg presents an even appearance. Place the egg on a sheet tray covered with slightly damp paper towels, cover tightly with plastic wrap, and set in the refrigerator until ready to use.

POUR SOME SUGAR ON ME

*E*very few weeks, the school sponsored after-school programs for the students to expand our culinary horizons. There was a lecture on making sausage, hosted by Chef Septimus; a demonstration on smoked salmon, complete with samples and fresh bialys, from the owners of Acme Smoked Fish in Brooklyn; and a jam-packed tour of the open food markets of Chinatown, a stone's throw from the back entrance of the school. This last was an incredible discouragement because as we walked by stalls filled to bursting with exotic dried meats, fish, mushrooms, and spices; huge bins of produce, giant melons, and coconuts; and fishmongers whose wares were still flipping their fins, waggling their antennae, or scuttling around their plastic prisons, nothing seemed to be fresher. But our guide explained that most of the fish came from New York Harbor or the East River and were so contaminated they were not safe to eat. She pointed out the baby turtles for sale by the scoopful, telling us they weren't pets but meant for the dinner table, and that we shouldn't even think about buying them, let alone eating them, because they were filled with salmonella. Ewww. Under her practiced eye, we started to see the bounties of Chinatown differently. Instead of the briny fresh smell of a fresh catch, I could smell the fetid, oily smell of an old dock at low tide. The fish scales stuck to the steaming hot pavement and to the soles of our shoes lost their rainbow luster and instead became a symbol of the severe cultural differences between Eastern and Western ideals of sanitation. The dark, mysterious little stores selling dried mushrooms, glass jars of powders and potions, bins of rice, foil-wrapped candies, boxes of fantastically gnarled roots, and huge tins of smoky black tea became not outposts of an impossibly ancient culture in a thoroughly modern city, but black-market racketeers selling dried monkey's paws, teeth from endangered snow leopards, powdered horn from the last unicorn in existence. Chinatown still holds lots of glamour and the spicy scent of mystery, but I don't think I will be buying turtles there anytime soon.

The best after-school programs were the ones featuring the world-famous chefs who were also deans at The Institute. The school was lucky enough to have an incredibly illustrious roster of deans on the letterhead, and while Jacques Pépin, Alain Sailhac, and Bobby Flay weren't exactly lurking in the classrooms teaching us how to peel veggies, or swinging by the coffeepot to shoot the breeze, they were regular visitors to the kitchens, and even more often to the restaurant. Jean-Georges Vongerichten, fresh from opening his Chinese venture 66 in TriBeCa and coauthoring a wonderful cookbook with Mark Bittman, gave an afternoon demonstration of his Chinese-French fusion technique, complete with samples for the audience. Needless to say, the school's auditorium was packed to the walls with students, chef-instructors, and even members of the support staff.

As we slowly made our way from cooking vegetables and making simple stocks and sauces to learning to poach eggs, the chef demonstrations became more and more interesting. Having some inkling of the effort involved in making those perfect cubes of vegetables and tomato-skin flowers made these demonstrations more personal, and we were able to see so much more that went on before the chef used his sleight of hand to transform *mise en place* trays of prepared ingredients into the stuff of the *New York Times* dining section. It was also a wonderful excuse to snag a cushy seat in the auditorium and rest after a long, hot day in the kitchen classrooms, and soak in the air-conditioning.

The pastry arts students tended to have their own chef demonstrations, complete with celebrity wedding cake makers like Ron Ben-Israel, whose atelier was a few blocks away from school. There were truffle-making demonstrations and long lectures about the logistics of turning edible ingredients into architecture (it helps to keep the room cold!). There generally wasn't a lot of crossover between the two disciplines, though there were plenty of pastry students at Vongerichten's demo, and Imogene and I had crashed the truffle-making demonstration to eat as much of the super-high-quality chocolate as we could. Dean Jacques Torres was coming to demonstrate how to spin and pull sugar, and a bunch of us Level 1 students were going to go, not only for the massive amount of air-conditioning we could expect to bask in, but also to bask in a bit of the reflected glory of celebrity.

At last we ended our own long, hot day spent churning out stuffed vegetables, everything from mushrooms, zucchini, and eggplant, which were at the very height of season, to butternut and acorn squash that were so unripe, they fought us every step of the way. Ben, Tucker, Junior, and I trooped to the blissfully chilly auditorium and grabbed seats near other members of our class. Sitting next to Ricki was Mimi, the vaguely unpleasant woman who had used her vintage Kelly bag to assault me at orientation. (Well, at least it was couture, I told myself, when I saw the bruise in the mirror.) Mimi had not warmed up to me in the slightest, for some reason. She continued to snub both Tucker and me, and Ben and Junior by association. While I was envious of her fabulous wardrobe, it turned out Mimi was no great shakes in the kitchen. *Ha,* I thought to myself, *I may not have an "It" bag, but at least I can wield eight inches of honed steel!* Even to me, it was only cold comfort.

Angelo and Jackie were also here, which made sense. Jackie's ambition to be a food stylist was naturally piqued by the prospect of the exotic and no doubt gorgeous creations that Dean Torres would be conjuring up, and I kept forgetting that despite his tough-guy image, Angelo was a trained artist whose keen eye and sensitive touch had distinguished him from the rest of us ham-handed fry cooks several times already. Sitting with them was Keri, which *was* a surprise. Keri was a very nice girl, just out of junior college and on her first trip east from Utah. With her blond hair and blue eyes,

Keri was the ultimate image of the All-American Girl, something that seemed to drive certain male members of our class to distraction. Unfortunately for them, Keri was a devout Mormon, here at chef school just to learn to cook. She was at the demonstration this afternoon for the simplest of reasons: "I love candy!"

As my fellow students and I took our seats, the president of the school stepped up to the podium and introduced Jacques Torres, and I immediately forgot about everybody else. Though Dean Torres was a soft-spoken man with a Gallic accent, his actions spoke more loudly than words, certainly much more loudly than the raised voices of many of the chef-instructors. With a large copper pot of boiling sugar-water, a candy thermometer, and some gel food dye, Dean Torres began to pull the sugar into shapes. After spreading the molten sugar onto a cool marble slab and folding it over and over until it became glossy and opaque, Dean Torres pulled on a pair of gloves and began to stretch and pull the sugar into panes of translucent sugar glass, as delicate and beautiful as crystal. Using an inverted bowl, he quickly made a series of caramel cages, arches of crispy caramel used to decorate crème brûlée, poached pears, and apple tarts. With a long steel rod, Dean Torres wrapped long strands of hot sugar around and around, making them twirl through the air as effortlessly as if he were playing with a yo-yo. The sugar twined around the cool bar and then slipped off to create spiral towers. With the food coloring, Dean Torres tinted some of the sugar paste and then began pulling it into fantastic shapes, heating it under a lamp when it cooled and became brittle, until he had made delicate sugar sculptures of flowers, fruits, even a tiny cat. Smiling at us as we sat transfixed by the gorgeous creations that he seemed to pull out of thin air, Dean Torres casually snapped off the stem of a rose he had fashioned with a skill that I imagined God himself was envious of. He casually crunched the candy between his teeth. *"Merci beaucoup,"* he said before leaving the stage, trailing talent and a bit of stardust behind him like a glittering path of sanding sugar.

THE UPPER CRUST

I have found that many people, when the subject of a favorite food comes up, revert back to a certain memory. Almost all of these memories take place in childhood, when a heaping plate of Thanksgiving bounty or a homemade caramel apple from Halloween made an indelible impression in the mind and on youthful taste buds.

I have an incurable sweet tooth and, as I am from the South, my favorite food of all time is pie. The forbidden pleasure of cold apple pie for breakfast, the heavenly lightness of a slice of lemon meringue, an illicit nibble of crispy crust from a chocolate pie right out of the oven—these all make my mouth water in a way that filet mignon never could. My family traditionally has five pies for Thanksgiving: apple, pumpkin, pecan, chocolate, and buttermilk. Everyone has a different favorite, and fights break out when it is suggested that this year we do without one of the selections. Making pecan pie with my grandmother is one of my very first memories—rolling out chilled dough with a child-size rolling pin; helping to tip the pecans and their sticky-sweet trapping of warm Karo syrup and spice into the waiting crust; slipping the pie into the hot oven to bake; and waiting (an interminable hour!) for the payoff: golden brown and bubbly perfection.

My mother taught me to make piecrust in that modern marvel of kitchen wizardry, the food processor. The stainless steel blades cut in chilled butter lumps in seconds, and a crust can be made in this machine in far less time than it takes to measure out the ingredients. So important is pie to my life, and the food processor to making piecrust, that I shipped mine to England when I spent a year abroad in college, studying at Oxford. The thought of life in that rainy, chilly climate without the benefit of flaky layers of pastry trapping warm apple slices was too much to bear and I gladly paid the outrageous shipping charges.

Child of the late twentieth century that I am, I had never made pastry crust by hand, or even with a pastry cutter. As much as I loved pie, and doing things in the authentic way, I never mustered up the courage to attempt the daring feat of producing a perfect short crust using nothing but a bench scraper and my own hands.

Chef Jean was very excited to begin our instruction on the proper way to make pastry dough and an apple tart—the French way, not the vulgar American version so beloved by all of us. I was soon learning that the proper way to do things was inevitably and always *The French Way*. Any other method or variation of ingredients or procedure was nothing but a bastardized imitation, a pale impersonation of the original, and personally offensive to Chef's delicate sensibilities. For instance, the *tarte aux pommes* is a much more elegant, refined version of dessert than the typically American overblown double-crusted mile-high apple pie (Chef Jean shuddered at the mere mention of it). In the true, understated French version, there is only a single bottom crust, spread with a chunky puree of apples sweetened with just a hint of sugar, a perfectly symmetrical layer of wafer-thin apple slices fanned across the top. No cinnamon, no nutmeg, no excess sweetness, merely fruit and buttery, flaky crust. A pure incarnation. The crust must be without fault—golden brown, even thickness, and texture just balanced between crisp and tender. Chef informed us we would be making such a crust with our bare hands. It came out sounding more like a threat than a promise that he would teach us the proper way of achieving this. I never thought the prospect of golden, flaky pastry would fill me with terror, but chef school was turning out to be full of frightening food encounters.

As always, Chef Jean demonstrated the procedure first for all of us. He measured out flour and dumped it into a pile right on the marble-topped table. Using a measuring cup, he shaped the mountain of flour into an even ring, with a small circle of countertop visible in its center. It looked like a snowcapped ridge circling the mouth of a sleeping volcano. Into this he dumped very cold butter that had been broken into small pieces. Using his bench scraper, Chef began to flick the flour over the mound of butter until it was completely buried. Now the bench scraper became a blur of motion as he began to cut the butter and flour together, chopping up and down and up and down over the mound of flour until the butter had been completely incorporated and the mixture looked like pale yellow cornmeal. He quickly ran his hands through the mixture, rubbing them together to ensure that the butter was fully incorporated. It really looked like the sand on the shores of the Côte d'Azur, and I wasn't surprised when Chef mentioned that this process was actually called *sablé*, which means sandy.

Once again, using the scraper, Chef mounded the mixture up into a small hill on the marble, and then made a well in the middle. This time, into the well went a few splashes of ice water. It seemed as if the water had no sooner hit the marble than Chef was once again flicking the flour mixture back into the center and chopping and scraping the ingredients together. It seemed like a miracle that he could combine everything together so quickly that the water didn't even have time to leak out of the churning flour surrounding it. So far, he had barely touched the pastry at all, merely attacked it with his razor-sharp scraper. But now that the water was totally incorporated, Chef quickly gathered the dough together with his hands into a loose pile. Taking a healthy pinch of dough between thumb and forefinger, he smeared it against the marble. His other hand deftly used the bench scraper to sweep up the dough and deposit it onto a second pile. Both hands were working simultaneously, doing totally different things to the dough, while Chef kept up a running commentary on the procedure. The smearing of the dough against the work surface is called *frottage* and ensures that the butter, flour, and water are all evenly incorporated into the dough and there are no lurking pockets of butter. In less than thirty seconds Chef had completely frottaged the dough and gathered it back together into a compact heap. He swiftly shaped this into a flat circle, wrapped it in plastic wrap, and popped it into the freezer. He checked his watch—precisely one minute and seventeen seconds had elapsed since he began the recipe. Wow. Chef had made *pâte brisée* by hand as quickly as I could make it in the food processor. This was definitely going to take some practice.

Before we students could begin our assault on pastry, however, the temperature in the room would have to be brought down a bit. Even though we hadn't turned on the ovens yet, the sticky July heat outside melted into the heat of the classroom and the mercury was quickly climbing to above 100 degrees. There were no air conditioners in chef school—real restaurant kitchens were rarely air-conditioned, and we were not being coddled. Only the pastry kitchens for the pastry students were kept cool to prevent their fragile confections from melting—and we regular culinary arts kids were jealous. The thermometers we kept tucked in the pockets of our chef's jackets showed just how quickly the temperature climbed from the relative cool of the locker rooms to the sweltering triple digits of the classroom.

In such hot weather, it would be very difficult to keep all the ingredients as cold as they must be in order to make a crust that would not collapse into a greasy mess once it was heated in the oven. Also, while the teacher's demonstration station was equipped with a marble top, which is an ideal surface on which to make pastry of all sorts, the class would have to make our pâtes on the stainless steel counters of our workstations.

Stainless steel conducts heat extremely well, and our workstations were already blood warm to the touch in the stuffy air of the classroom. We began by washing down all the countertops thoroughly. Every evening, after the night classes went home, the cleaning crew would polish every surface of all the kitchen class-rooms with stainless steel polish, which left everything sparkling but also left a faint chemical film behind. After cleaning the counter-tops, we measured out all of our ingredients, from flour to butter to salt to ice water, and put everything—even the flour—in the lowboy refrigerators. While the ingredients chilled, we filled sheet trays with ice and placed them on all the countertops, to try to bring down the temperature of the steel work surfaces and the classroom in general.

While we waited for the temperature to drop, Chef Jean told us stories about working in restaurant kitchens. In this city, most restaurant kitchens were (and still are) located in the basements, and sometimes the sub-basements, of buildings. I think he was trying to make us feel better about our current conditions in our cushy class-room, but the thought of being trapped on the line in a restaurant kitchen ten feet below street level filled me with a sense of panic and cold dread. What if there was a fire? Is this really how I saw myself, sweating and churning out below-average piecrusts in some lesser circle of hell for the next five years?

I didn't have long to wonder about my possible future, though. While I was still envisioning building-collapse scenarios, ending up trapped next to the deep-fat fryer, Chef called us back to the pres-ent, to our hot little classroom, which somehow didn't seem quite as hot as it had before, and ordered us to begin to produce pastry.

"Make it quick, *vite*," he said. "You don't have all day. Imagine you are Junior here, and you are going to get lucky for the first time." We tried to stifle our giggles.

Chef smiled slyly. "Well, maybe not quite that quick, eh? Do it right, at least!" With that, we all erupted in loud guffaws, while poor Junior turned red as a raspberry. We all knew that despite Junior's boasts, he was fresh out of high school in his tiny hometown in rural Maine, and still a virgin, to his everlasting embarrassment. Sweet little Keri was the only one to miss the joke, but Angelo hotfooted it over to whisper an explanation in her ear. She, too, turned brick red. I had the distinct impression that Keri was getting a completely different sort of education than her strict Mormon parents were paying for. To say that Keri was as pure as the driven snow wouldn't be true—she was much more pure than the snow that blanketed Manhattan every winter. Keri came to New York City from a small town in Utah, near Salt Lake. At nineteen, Keri was the youngest of eight siblings—and one of the youngest members of our class—and she seemed to be astoundingly naïve about some things. Her wide-eyed innocence was charming, and complemented her blond hair, blue eyes, and baby face. Chef school seemed like an odd choice for Keri—it was so visceral, full of the booze, sex, and general depravity her Mormon background had shielded her from.

But the fun and games were over, and we removed the pans of ice from our workstations and attempted to mimic Chef's swift and self-assured style. While it took us all quite a bit longer to complete the task that Chef Jean had made look so simple, everyone eventually turned in a lump of roughly doughlike texture and approximately circular proportions at the end of ten minutes. While we labeled the pale lumps with our names and returned them to the lowboy refrigerators to chill once again, Chef explained the concept of the *tarte aux pommes* to us.

This regal dessert resembles an apple pie only in that both desserts have apples as a main ingredient. Much as a croissant found in a patisserie in Paris bears only a faint resemblance to the monstrous croissants found everywhere in America, the *tarte aux pommes* only scantily recalls its distant cousin on this side of the Atlantic. The two desserts highlight the basic differences between French and American cuisine, and perhaps even French and American people themselves.

I am the first to admit that before chef school, I thought that bigger was always better, especially in terms of dessert. I have always been a fan of an extra scoop of ice cream, extra sprinkles, heck, an extra cookie after that brownie. I didn't really care how delicious something was: if it was sweet, I wanted two. It wasn't so much that I was willfully ignoring my taste buds; it was more that I was unaware of the panoply of tastes possible. My taste buds were sleeping. I realized that perhaps I was missing something as I watched Chef Jean wax rhapsodic over the simplicity of the French apple tart. His eyes shone with a fervor approaching fanaticism. His hands, never still when discussing food, became positively spastic as he attempted to kiss the tips of his fingers, pat an imaginary crust into a tart pan, and demonstrate the delicate thinness necessary for the apple slices garnishing the top, all at the same time. His voice even seemed to rise higher and higher as his praise for the simple majesty of the *tarte* grew. This, apparently, is what all apples aspire to. I began to feel sorry for those poor *pommes* that were merely candied, or covered in caramel, or, worse still, became part of the puree served atop pancakes with a mountainous dose of whipped cream at the IHOP.

As I watched Chef Jean, I began to wonder what it was about this dessert, which was really only dough, apples, and a bit of sugar, that would make this jaded, eaten-everything-under-the-sun chef so fulsome in his praise. What else could possibly be in this simple confection to make it so good? While I pondered this question, I had my epiphany. It wasn't what was in the *tarte*; it was what *wasn't* in it that made it so transcendent. It had no bells and whistles, no secret spice, no unexpected jets of cinnamon foam garnish to surprise and titillate the palate. It was the very best of a simple thing, and only a palate that could recognize and appreciate the best tastes could really appreciate this stark perfection. Like a Zen koan, the *tarte aux pommes* presents a challenge to the neophyte, a seemingly unanswerable puzzle that can be solved only with proper preparation and insight, but one that would surely lead to nirvana for those worthy few who could provide the right answer.

I was so electrified, thinking that perhaps a slice of this simple dessert could unlock all the great mysteries of the kitchen—and that I had, in fact, found the culinary Holy Grail (in Level 1!)—that I missed part of the next instructional demo. Chef was forced to actually wave a side towel in front of my face to break my trance.

"Hello, Darling? Am I boring you?" Chef Jean asked, only partly joking.

I couldn't bring myself to tell Chef that I was hoping for a religious experience by eating apple pie, so I ducked my head and tried to mimic his deft actions once again. We peeled bowls of apples, both Golden Delicious and Granny Smiths to add a layer of complexity to the filling, and after coring and roughly cutting them into large chunks, set them to simmer in small pots with water and just a quick dash of sugar to bring out the sweetness of the fruit.

After twenty minutes or so, the apples had softened and the water had evaporated, leaving us with a pot of something resembling rustic applesauce. We stirred constantly until the apples were cooked through and beginning to break down, careful not to beat all the chunks out.

"Leave it a bit interesting, eh? Not like baby food," Chef directed.

While the apple compote chilled in an ice bath, we returned to our lumps of dough. Armed with heavy wooden rolling pins, we pulled our chilled dough circles from the lowboys and began to roll them out. Once the dough had been rolled out into a thin, even circle, it was ready to press into the waiting tart pan. The air was soon full of flour as overzealous students added handful after handful to their dough in order to ensure that it would not stick to the work surface. Chef Jean took a shot of flour right to the face as he was prowling the aisles of the classroom, and exploded, a French Krakatoa.

"What the hell are you doing? What is all this flour? If you did it right, you need no big handfuls of flour! Just a dusting! A sprinkle! *Un petit petit peu!* Morons!" Chef shouted, blowing little puffs of flour off his face with each furious syllable.

In a paroxysm of rage, he grabbed the nearest dough lump and tore it into two pieces. We were shocked, thinking that he had destroyed someone's effort in a fit of pique. But no. Angry though he might have been, Chef was never vindictive. He held the two flaccid pieces of dough up and showed us the insides. It was plain to see that there were large gobs of butter that had not been properly incorporated into the whole. We gasped and gawked at the poor performance of our classmate, like motorists passing a particularly gruesome traffic accident. No one got out to help, however. I felt like kissing the feet of the patron saint of bakers that Chef hadn't chosen my pitiful dough for an object lesson. Chef took a deep breath and began to rework the dough he had destroyed, slapping small pieces of it against the work surface in *frottage* to thoroughly incorporate the rogue lumps of butter. Soon the dough was once again a homogeneous whole, and Chef rolled it out in a few brusque movements of the rolling pin. Carefully he folded the dough in half, and then in half again. Scooping the little package up, he placed it over the buttered and chilled tart ring and unfolded it, its halves of dough fluttering open like a paperback caught in a high wind. He tucked the dough in with deft pats and then pinched a decorative edge around the sides with his meaty thumb and first two fingers, spinning the tart ring around like a child's top.

His good humor once again restored, Chef explained that a further spell in the lowboy to chill the dough and let it rest after being rolled out would ensure that the dough would not shrink up in the oven, leaving too much filling and not enough crust. Rolling out the dough must be done very quickly, like mixing the dough once water has been added, for the same reasons: the more dough is worked and played with, the more structure is created. Structure in this instance means the formation of strong strands of gluten, which give bread its marvelous chewiness but wreak havoc with the texture of pastry dough. Letting the dough rest after working with it allows the molecules of gluten to loosen the bonds they form with each other, enabling the dough to "relax" and perform properly. This was another revelatory moment for me. For years I had been making piecrust, rolling it out, and sticking it straight into the oven without any additional rest, despite my grandmother's insistence that a "nap" would produce better crusts. I thought it was just an inefficient step I could cut out of the procedure with impunity, but I was wrong. I cast my eyes up to heaven and said a little prayer to Nan, thanking her for all the insights she gave me and letting her know that I was using them at last.

Once all the dough had been rolled out and placed, more or less successfully, into the tart rings, and after another long stint in the lowboy refrigerators, we were ready to assemble the tarts and bake them. First, in went the simple, rustic apple filling we made, now cool to the touch. Next came the thin apple slices on top for garniture.

For Americans, cleanliness may be next to godliness, but for the French, garniture *is* God. We carefully peeled, halved, and cored two more apples each, and then set each half on the cutting board, on its side. Using our chef's knives, and all of our remaining patience, we made paper-thin apple slices, hundreds of them. Very few of them were actually any good, but by the time I had worked through my second apple, they were looking a bit more even. The apple slices were then fanned out over the filling in two concentric rings, the first, larger ring running clockwise, and the next, smaller ring running counterclockwise. Because there is some small, deeply ingrained part of me that seems dyslexic, I made my rings counter-clockwise first, and then clockwise. A small mistake, but one immediately obvious to Chef, who made me pick all the apple slices off and start over again, going in the correct direction.

"See? *Much* more beautiful," he said, when I had replaced the slices, now all marching in neat circles, the right way. I couldn't see the difference, but reminded myself that the French have a mania for both the intricacies of bureaucracy and rigidly formal gardening in addition to a stranglehold on the world's best desserts. Perhaps it all went hand in hand. After arranging the two overlapping rings of apple slices, there was still a bit of the filling showing in the middle of the tart. The remaining apple slices were arranged in a tight, overlapping concentric circle, cored sides touching the apple filling, winding ever tighter until the remaining surface of the filling was covered with a rose made of apple slices. A few tiny circles of apple were stamped out of a stray apple slice to provide the proper degree of botanical verisimilitude to the rose, everything was washed gently with clarified butter, dusted lightly with a bit more sugar, and slipped into the waiting oven. Since the apple filling is already cooked, the tart is finished when the dough is fully cooked through and golden, and the apple slices have caramelized and are glowing brown, like a sunbather in a secluded cove of St. Tropez (Chef's words, not mine).

I spent the forty-some minutes waiting for my tart to come out of the oven kvetching with Angelo, whose dough had been the unlucky recipient of Chef Jean's object lesson. Nominally, we were making another pâte crust for the afternoon's recipe, quiche Lorraine, but while Chef was in conference with Cyndee about the progress we were making as a class, Angelo slouched over to Tucker and me to vent his feelings. Angelo's station was on the other side of the classroom from us, but we had quickly become friends—he was very talented and driven, but he also liked to have a good time, slurping down beers and shots with us a few afternoons a week at Toad before catching his PATH train back to Jersey.

"Asshole!" Angelo huffed, his Jersey boy muscles bulging with emotion. "Why pick on me?"

"Your pretty face," I replied. It was so much fun to tease Angelo, to see his blue eyes widen in laughter before he delivered an always witty, and usually dirty, rejoinder.

"Seriously, Angelo, today was just your day. We all have them," Tucker added.

And it was true, we all did. While Chef was never deliberately malicious or mean-spirited in his critiques of us, there usually was one person who felt the sting from the sharp side of Chef's tongue a bit more than everyone else. I had been the unlucky student once, and while I was grateful for the lessons I had learned, I was not eager for a repeat performance.

At last, Chef deemed our tarts well baked, and out of the huge ovens they came. But they were not quite finished. A thin glaze of apricot preserve would need to be applied to the top so that the tart had a shiny, "come hither" look.

"Like a stripper putting on lip gloss," Tucker whispered to me.

I was too besotted with the gorgeousness of my own creation to pay any attention to Tucker's redneck observations. I reverently painted on the apricot glaze with my pastry brush (a tool that looks exactly like a small paintbrush from the hardware store, but costs about five times as much) and waited impatiently for my masterpiece to cool. This was it, the very essence of French cooking—a dessert that made much of its very simple ingredients, prepared in a regimented, time-hallowed manner, and decorated with dizzying attention to detail. Now I was to taste this apple tart from the tree of knowledge, and know food with all the glory of God—as a true chef, in other words.

Like the sound of one hand clapping, my first attempt at a *tarte aux pommes* lacked the resonance I was hoping for. It was good, even delicious in its own way, but it was not the religious experience I had anticipated. There was no jolt to my taste buds, no heavenly choir, no path to nirvana magically appearing before me. There was just a glimpse: a tiny twinge, somewhere in my hippocampus, of some-thing greater. It wasn't enlightenment in a blinding flash of bril-liance. More a quiet awakening, the gentle warmth radiating from a tiny crumb of knowledge. I was learning. Slowly.

Pâte Brisée (Short Crust)

Food Processor Method

This is it: the basic short pastry crust that all other short crusts are based on. It can be used for everything from an apple tart to a rustic tomato and herb pizza (my favorite meal in the summertime). With a few modifications (egg yolks instead of ice water, some confectioners' sugar, a sifting of cocoa powder with the flour), this recipe can be used in hundreds of ways.

1 cup plus 1 tablespoon all-purpose flour, plus extra for rolling

1 teaspoon fine sea salt

8 tablespoons (1 stick) unsalted butter, well chilled and cut into small lumps

1 to 2 tablespoons ice-cold water

1. Dump the flour and salt in the bowl of a food processor and blend briefly to combine. Add the butter all at once and blend in short on-off bursts until the mixture resembles very coarse cornmeal. Add 1 tablespoon of the water and blend briefly. The dough should begin to come together. If not, with the motor still running, carefully add a few drops of water at a time until the dough just begins to clump. Continue to blend only until large clumps of dough form.

2. Remove the dough from the bowl of the processor onto a large square of plastic wrap. Using the plastic wrap to guide the dough (especially helpful when the dough is a bit too sticky from overzealous watering), gently pat it into a rough disk shape. Wrap securely in the plastic wrap and stow in the refrigerator for at least 15 minutes, until the dough has fully chilled and is firm to the touch.

3. The longer the dough is chilled, the better off it will be, I think. Should the dough be very firm when removed from the fridge, don't attempt to manhandle it with the rolling pin—it will only cause cracks

to form in the dough and frustration to boil over in the chef. Leave it alone on the counter for a few minutes. The warmth from the other things you no doubt have going on in the kitchen should be sufficient to warm the dough enough to roll without letting it get sweaty. On the other hand, beating the dough with hearty thwacks from your rolling pin will soften the dough without the chance of it overheating.

4. When rolling out the dough, be sparing with additional flour. It is tempting to create a snowstorm on the work surface, to ensure that the dough will not stick during the rolling process and will make it from the work surface to the tart or pie pan without tearing. Resist this impulse! A scant flick of flour on the rolling pin, work surface, and each side of the dough should be more than sufficient to prevent sticking. Watch the dough as you roll it out: it should move with the pin a bit. If it doesn't, there is a sticky spot underneath somewhere; use a scraper to gently unstick things and add a whisper of flour.

5. Once the dough has been rolled out to ⅛ inch thickness and a roughly 12-inch circle, fold the circle in half, then half again. Place this in one quadrant of the pan and unfold. Press the dough into every little nook and cranny. Be generous with the dough (there should be very little to no dough left over). Keep tucking until there is only enough dough left for a small decorative edge.

6. Do your dessert a favor at this point and stick the crust back in the fridge to chill one more time before baking. It will make a more delicious, beautiful dessert, and will also give you time to finish the filling.

Makes one 8- or 9-inch pie or tart crust

Buttermilk Pie

This is, hands down, my favorite way to use pâte brisée. *My fanatical love of this pie, and the driving desire to have it as much as possible, is probably what spurred my culinary ambitions from early childhood. It is also very southern and reminds me of the long line of excellent cooks I come from. It is a wonderful antidote to those days when taxi drivers snarl at you, the laundry loses your shirts, and you get caught in the rain without an umbrella. A great ending for a barbecue supper—pulled pork, coleslaw, sautéed string beans fresh from the garden, a long summer evening, and this pie. Heaven.*

3 tablespoons all-purpose flour

Pinch of salt

Generous pinch of freshly grated nutmeg

4 tablespoons (½ stick) butter, softened

¾ cup sugar

4 egg yolks

1 cup fresh buttermilk (see Note)

Juice of 1 lemon

1 tablespoon grated lemon zest

1 generous teaspoon pure vanilla extract

1 recipe Pâte Brisée (page 81), rolled out into a 9-inch pie pan and chilled

Fresh berries, for serving

1. Preheat the oven to 350°F.
2. Sift the flour, salt, and nutmeg into a small bowl and set aside.
3. In a medium bowl, cream the butter and sugar until pale and fluffy. Add the egg yolks one at a time and whisk until well combined.

Add the buttermilk, lemon juice, zest, and vanilla, stirring after each addition. Sift in the flour mixture slowly and whisk until thoroughly incorporated. Pour into the prepared crust.

4. Bake in the middle of the oven until puffed and set, 35 to 40 minutes. Let cool to room temperature before serving.
5. Serve with a bowl of fresh berries.

NOTE: Fresh buttermilk can be found at farmers' markets and some upscale groceries, and makes a delicious difference to the taste and texture of this pie, but supermarket buttermilk works just dandy, too.

Makes one 9-inch pie

ONE POTATO, TWO POTATO . . .

While each day at chef school seemed like one long, tiring, sweaty stint at the stove, the weeks of Level 1 were flying by. We were more than halfway through our first level and I was struggling, no doubt about it. While my attempt at an apple tart was passable, and I was able to cook carrots to the basic degree of acceptability, and I hadn't burned anything (at least not recently), I couldn't help but feel less than thrilled with my progress so far. My phone calls to my mother had become a soap opera chronicling day-to-day life at chef school, full of dramatic twists and turns, each recipe I prepared a cliff-hanger. Every call ended the same way: me, full of despair, whining about the latest disaster, my mother's soft voice radiating calm and assurance. She had been through all this, and I believed her when she told me that I could do it.

Still, it was difficult. While Chef Jean would never actually compliment any of our efforts, it seemed somehow that whenever he orbited by my station on his rounds, I was doing something wrong. Inevitably, Chef would waggle one long, scarred forefinger in the general direction of my chest and make that noise peculiar to the French, a sort of tooth-sucking, tut-tutting noise. It embodied frustration on my part and disappointment on his. But I was determined to get better, to avoid hearing that brisk "tut tut tut" one more time. I studied, prepared, and practiced. I went through a metric ton of vegetables refining my knife skills. I chopped, peeled, shredded—and started over again from scratch. Blisters became calluses. I was hoping that I would be able to show Chef Jean that I had what it takes to be a chef with our lesson on potatoes. Potatoes I could manage, I was sure of it.

The humble potato's dirt-crusted exterior and pockmarked skin do little to endear it to the highly refined aesthetics of a classically trained gourmet. Despite garnering millions of corpulent admirers with its deep-fried, fast-food perfection, the potato's glorious incarnation as the "French" fry is a bit of a misnomer. The French did not eat potatoes until relatively recently in their nation's long history of gourmandizing. The starchy tuber was considered fit only to feed hungry livestock until the mid-eighteenth century. In an effort to find a more abundant, inexpensive source of food for the peasant class during an especially wet year that caused the wheat crops across the country to fail, the eighteenth-century agronomist and economist Antoine-Auguste Parmentier proposed that the potato play a new role: as a starchy staff of life necessary to the survival of the French peasant. But to take something seemingly fit only for the pigs to eat and expect a French housewife to serve it at her dinner table was out of the question—*quelle horreur!*

The French peasant did not welcome change, and so a vigorous image makeover of the potato was begun. Many classic potato recipes now go by lofty-sounding names—from the decadent *pommes de terre à la duchesse* to *pommes de terre Anna* (said to be named after one of the Russian czar's children) to *pommes de terre dauphine, pommes de terre marquise,* and even *potage Parmentier,* the rich and creamy potato-leek soup named after the potato's first French champion. Other potato recipes are a reference to places—from the rather (suitably) boring boiled potatoes of *pommes de terre à l'anglaise* to the more decadent creations known as *pommes de terre à la Lyonnaise, pommes de terre à la Parisienne, pommes de terre à la Savoyarde,* even *pommes de terre Pont-Neuf,* named for the oldest bridge in Paris. Naming some potato recipes after glamorous places and members of a royal family may seem like second nature to our advertisement-laden society—*pommes de terre Paris Hilton,* anyone?—but it was a revolutionary bit of marketing in those days. And it worked.

Another reason for the success of the potato in France is its extreme versatility: what was once fit only for the family cow could also be dressed up with the addition of a little cream, a bit of butter, perhaps a truffle or two, to be served as part of Christmas dinner. There are hundreds and hundreds of recipes for potatoes—mashing, baking, boiling, and frying are only the beginning. Potatoes are also easily maleable. Their strong starch molecules are a marvelous building material, and not only for the moats, castles, and volcanoes often sculpted on dinner plates. By the nineteenth century, chefs like Marie-Antoine Carême were sculpting elaborate fantasies of edible potato starch architecture to grace the finest banqueting halls in the world. The French, with their intense flair for decoration, came to embrace the potato with open arms.

We, too, were ready to embrace the potato. Who wouldn't welcome the chance to make and eat the scads of French fries we would be churning out? Unfortunately, my extremely high–waisted chef's pants, complete with pleated waistband, had already grown a bit tight, and I wasn't sure how the carbohydrate-rich lunch was going to square with my more recent efforts to restrain myself in the kitchen. With the student loan weighing down my already sluggish bank account, I could barely afford to buy a Diet Coke, and a new, roomier wardrobe was out of the question. I would have to try to resist the temptations that continually presented themselves in front of me. After the French fries, of course.

After our morning lecture, we broke into our teams to begin peeling potatoes. Mountains and mountains and mountains of them. I suddenly understood why institutions, from colleges to jails to the army, had switched to powdered potatoes—no one, not even prisoners, should have to peel such large amounts of this vegetable. My vicious French peeler seemed to be working against me. I was afraid of its sharp twin blades—I knew they were waiting for my attention to wander, just for a fraction of a second, to gouge a deep trench into my hand. I was clutching the peeler so hard that I began to get a nasty blister on my index finger. Still, there didn't seem to be an end in sight—every potato I peeled and then plunked into a bucket of cold water only seemed to send another tumbling down the pile to my waiting hands. Tucker, who never complained about the interminable prep work involved in all of the recipes, began to move more and more slowly. At last, we finished our pile. Chef Jean noticed, and immediately volunteered us to help schlep in the *other* fifty-pound sack of potatoes that needed to be peeled. Even Tucker was aghast, and actually committed the first cardinal sin of chef school: Never *ever* question a direct order.

"Oh, come on, Chef. We aren't going to use that many potatoes today, are we?" As soon as the words left his mouth, a collective hush fell over the classroom. I tried to make myself as small and unobtrusive as possible. *Be the potato,* I mentally chanted, hoping to escape the incipient wrath of a Frenchman whose judgment had been questioned. *Just be the potato.* I willed myself to become one of the pile of dirty lumpish tubers. I knew I should stand by my partner, share the onslaught of abuse, but I could feel my loyalties shriveling under the heat of Chef's blazing stare. *Here it comes,* I thought. Invective like a bolt of lightning would come down from on high and strike Tucker stone dead. I held my breath.

But there was no explosion, no blinding white light that swallowed Tucker whole. Chef Jean merely pinned Tucker to the spot with his piercing stare, testing the sharpness of a paring knife against the callus on his thumb. One long moment passed, and then Chef said, very matter-of-factly, "No. It is true; we are not going to be using all of these potatoes in class. But the Level 2 students in charge of family meal today are short-handed, and so we are going to help them out. That is what good chefs do. When one falls behind, is in the weeds the whole shift, you help them out. You do what you can to make their life easier, because one day, it will be you."

With that, Chef dumped the sack of potatoes out on the front counter. He didn't say another word, but one by one, we filed up to the front and took a bowlful of potatoes back to our workstations. We peeled the extra potatoes, not because Chef had asked us to, because, really, he hadn't. We peeled the potatoes to help out someone else, because soon we might find ourselves in their chef's clogs. I was amazed at what a virtuoso of guilt Chef Jean was.

Once we had peeled enough large brown Idaho potatoes to fill all four industrial-size garbage bins in the room with potato peelings, we were ready to master the vegetable. We would start with the art of the French fry. Or, because it would be too egomaniacal even for the French to call it that, the *pommes frites*. Fried potatoes are divided into categories depending on how many times they are immersed in bubbling hot oil before they are fully cooked. There are the fries fried once, including the *pommes cheveux, pommes pailles, pommes gaufrettes,* and *pommes liard.* Twice-fried potatoes include the *pommes allumettes, pommes mignonettes,* and *pommes Pont-Neuf.* There is only one type of potato that is fried three times, the show-stopping *pommes soufflées.* In total, there are almost a dozen ways to enjoy fried potatoes, each one specifically designed to accompany a different meat or fish.

The type of fried potato most Americans are familiar with, as a supersized side to their hamburger meal, is made by a two-step process. The potatoes are cooked in oil ranging from 300° to 320°F until the insides are cooked and fluffy but the outsides remain pale, with no hint of color. Then, right before being served, the potatoes are dipped once again in oil, this time a bit hotter, from 350° to 375°F, to cook the outsides to a perfect golden brown. In fast-food restaurants, the potatoes are cooked through the first step, then flash-frozen, shipped, and browned when you decide whether you would like fries with that. Almost all other fried potatoes are fried only once, in peanut oil heated to 350° to 375°F. The oil is hot enough to prevent soaking into the potatoes, but not so hot that it would cause the potatoes to brown before the insides are cooked. The difference between these different sorts is merely one of shape.

But before a potato can be fried, it must be peeled and cut to the appropriate size and shape. To this end we had all been equipped with a French mandoline, widely regarded as the most vicious of the various bloodthirsty tools we budding chefs would be working with. A French mandoline is a beautiful, intimidating piece of equipment, all gleaming stainless steel and wickedly sharp blades. And heavy as sin. I actually had one of my own, tucked away in a kitchen drawer at home. I was too frightened of it to confront it directly, and every time I opened the drawer to retrieve the lemon zester or a stray piping tip, it seemed to stare balefully at me, its various limbs folded under it as if preparing itself to spring right at my throat. I tried not to think about the monster while I contemplated its more work-worn cousin, lying here on my cutting board, doubtless just aching to chop off one of my fingers. Chef Jean explained how to coax its hinged legs out from underneath its heavy, rectangular body before maneuvering it into proper working position: nose to the ground, working bits—a sliding plane and fan of razor-sharp teeth—erect and in their proper places. Armed with a naked potato in one hand, we steadied the mandoline with the other and began to slice.

Mastery of the mandoline is dependent on a forceful hand and a large reserve of patience. I thought I was finally making friends with my mandoline, but it was uphill going. The blade seemed so dull, I really had to push *hard* to get any slices out at all, and they certainly weren't very beautiful or even. I was valiantly struggling, whispering words of encouragement to the little stainless steel beast, when I heard a snort of derision from behind me. It was Assistant Chef Cyndee, who was rapidly becoming known as a mean-spirited witch. She never missed a chance to belittle one of us, to openly mock our best attempts at the curriculum recipes, to move at least one in our class to tears with her parodies of our efforts. When I heard that lewd giggle behind me, I knew my enemy was not the piece of machinery in front of me, frustrating my efforts, but the snake behind me, her fangs already out, dripping with poisonous sarcasm. I braced for the assault, willing myself not to turn around but to continue to work, however unsuccessfully, at my task. I knew she wouldn't be able to restrain herself for long.

She didn't. Suddenly she whipped the mutilated potato from my hand and spun me around. "What, exactly, do you think you're doing?"

There was no answer for the question that wouldn't reek of insubordination, so I just stood and waited.

"I don't think I have ever seen this before. Chef, come over here and look at this. This is priceless." Here she paused for breath before moving in for the kill.

"This idiot . . ." she started. Oh, how the word stung. Assistant Chef Cyndee could barely walk and chew gum at the same time, and yet she had every right, in the trenches of kitchen warfare, as my superior, to call me an idiot—"this idiot has been using the mandoline backward. Everyone, come here and have a look at how NOT to use kitchen equipment."

Here she surrendered herself to loud, piercing laughter that shook her plump frame and caused her significant backside to sway like a cow having an epileptic seizure. The truly horrifying thing was that she was right. I *was* using the mandoline backward. Somehow I had reversed the instructions Chef had given us on setting the blasted things up. It seemed that I was, in fact, a total idiot, and quite possibly a moron. Why hadn't I realized my mistake? I could feel my face burning with shame, and I was sure that everybody else was secretly snickering along with the horrible Cyndee. This was not something I would be able to live down anytime soon. To my surprise, when I caught the eye of Ben, the tall, very quiet, and hardworking student who made a fourth at our kitchen island, he wasn't laughing at my misfortune at all—he shot me a deeply sympathetic look. Even Chef Jean seemed to pity me as I stood there, red-faced. He flipped the mandoline into the right direction, ran a fresh potato over it a few times, and handed it to me. "Voilà. Now try it." I did. Much better. Perfectly shaped potato matchsticks cascaded effortlessly from the mandoline. I quickly shredded another three potatoes and soaked the shards in water, rushing to catch up with the rest of the class.

At last we were ready to begin churning out fries like a bunch of line cooks at McDonald's. Once we had enough potatoes cut and soaked, we dried them thoroughly—water must never come into contact with hot oil. Not only do they not mix, but water actually causes the hot oil to "jump" out of the fryer, and all over the kitchen, and sometimes all over an unsuspecting chef. The potatoes must be bone dry before they hit the hot grease, not only for the taste of the finished dish, but also because it might save one's skin.

The best oil for frying potatoes, or indeed any food, is one that has both a high smoke point and a very mild to no flavor. Vegetable oils are a good choice and peanut oil is particularly good. The oil should always be hot before the food to be fried is added—if the oil is not hot enough, the fat will be absorbed by the food, which will become soggy, sopping with grease, rather than ethereally light, with that crunchy texture that makes fried foods so delicious.

The peanut oil filled our heavy cast-iron kettles halfway (any further and the oil would bubble over when the food was added) and was heating on the stove. As Tucker and I wrung out water-logged potato sticks, we kept a wary eye on the temperature gauge, checking it every fifteen seconds or so to make sure our oil was not too hot. Chef Jean had begun the lecture on frying potatoes by instructing us what to do in case a grease fire broke out in the kitchen. His tone was grave, and the spark customarily in his eyes, even when he was berating one of us, was absent. Nothing is more dangerous in the kitchen than a grease fire, as it quickly spreads throughout the hot, confined space of the kitchen, propelled by the wind from the giant exhaust fans. In case a grease fire did actually break out, we should immediately alert Chef, and get as far away from the flames as possible without stampeding like frightened cattle. We were not to try to put out the fire with water, as nothing exacerbates a grease fire more quickly than some jackass throwing water on it (Chef's words). We were not, under any circumstances, to be one of those morons. It would look bad for Chef if one of his Level 1 students was the one to burn the school down. In case of a dire emergency (I wondered at what point a roaring fire in the kitchen went from a regular emergency to a dire one), we could attempt to quell the flames with a snowstorm of flour. While flour can catch fire, it is considered to be flame retardant, and would, in mass quantities, work to smother the flames. I tried not to picture the mess that would result from such an incident, especially after the chemical fire extinguishers were triggered and drowned us all in foam.

With Chef's warning still ringing in our ears, we watched the heavy-duty temperature gauges immersed in the oil like nervous hawks. At last, we had some very dry potatoes, and our pot of peanut oil was just the right temperature. We dumped in a batch, and watched with something close to panic as the oil bubbled up, almost over the blackened sides of the pot, before at last subsiding. I stood with the strainer known as a spider clutched in my hands (which smarted very slightly from a few grease spatterings—the potato sticks hadn't been quite as dry as we had thought), while Tucker stood with a sheet pan lined with paper towels and kosher salt at the ready.

As we watched the matchsticks go from waxy paleness to golden perfection in their second dip in hot oil, our stomachs began to rumble. I hadn't eaten fast food in years, but suddenly there wasn't anything I craved more than one of those little crispy spears. We scooped them from the hot fat and shook them out onto the tray, making great haystacks of fried potatoes, crystals of salt settling gently on their surfaces like snowflakes.

Without even waiting for Chef's inspection of our efforts, we began to shovel them into our mouths. They were burning hot, but absolutely divine. Soon our salty fingers were scraping empty plates, and we eagerly began to work the mandolines to create more. We weren't the only ones, either. All around us our classmates wore greasy grins. The lure of fried food suddenly dawned on me—this heavenly lightness, earthy crunch, and satisfying starchiness spoke to some long-buried instinct, the hunter-gatherer gone to the food court. But these potatoes were so much better than the ones traditionally served in little paper sacks or cardboard containers, often only lukewarm and limp. Nothing beats the taste straight out of the deep fryer!

After gorging on what seemed like basketfuls of *pommes frites,* we were ready to undertake the *pommes soufflées.* There is no American cousin to the French souffléed potato, perhaps because there is no way to take a shortcut in its long preparation. *Pommes soufflées* are the only potatoes that require a three-step frying process. The potatoes are sliced thin, less than an eighth of an inch, and then cut into decorative shapes. Unlike other types of fried potatoes, these slices should not be washed and drained before being fried. The extra starch left clinging to the potatoes is partly responsible for their eventual, dramatically puffed appearance.

The potato shapes are fried gently in 280°F oil for approximately five minutes, until the interior has softened. They are then transferred to oil that is slightly hotter, 350°F. The little potato slices will puff up like tiny starchy balloons but should still be very pale, with no color. Next, they are drained, where they will deflate. Just before serving, the potatoes are immersed once again in the hot oil where they will reinflate and turn golden brown. *Pommes soufflées* must be served right away, as they will lose their delightful puff when cool. These potatoes are really the essence of frivolity, meant to amuse the eye and delight the palate, but only for a fleeting moment. From peeling to final immersion in oil, they entail hours of work when prepared in large batches, but are meant for a mere second's enjoyment. This, too, is a very French *truc,* or trick, that serves to constantly amuse and baffle the Francophile gourmand. Because of the detailed nature of the recipe, Chef Jean demonstrated to us how to perfect the *pommes soufflées* without setting all twenty-four of us at it. We were not yet ready to be trusted, it seemed, with this particularly tricky feat of culinary legerdemain.

It did seem like magic when, from the bubbling fat, Chef produced the perfect little souffléed potatoes, so different from anything we had ever seen, and so different from the potato's humble brown and lumpy beginnings.

The Most Decadent Potato Puree

This recipe calls for a potato ricer, which really does make the final puree much lighter. If you haven't got one, use a masher or a whisk. Do not use a food processor! You will end up with a gummy, sticky mess.

4 large Idaho potatoes, washed and peeled (about 2½ pounds)

Kosher salt

1 cup heavy cream

8 tablespoons (1 stick) unsalted butter, plus more if needed

½ cup cream cheese (½ of an 8-ounce package)

White pepper

1. Dice the potatoes into 1-inch cubes and place them in a large pot with enough very cold water to cover. Add salt—the water should taste briny, like the ocean—and bring to a boil. In the meantime, preheat the oven to its lowest setting.
2. Once the potatoes are easily pierced with a knife, they are ready. Drain the potatoes thoroughly and spread them out on a sheet pan covered with paper towels. Place in the oven to dry out the potato chunks well.
3. Meanwhile, bring the cream to a boil in a saucepan and simmer until it has been reduced by half. Add the butter and cream cheese and blend until smooth.
4. Put the potatoes through a ricer and then spread them out once again on the paper-lined sheet pan; place in the low oven to dry briefly. The potatoes should not cook or brown even slightly; they should merely give up any lingering moisture.
5. Place the potatoes in a bowl and whisk in gently the butter-cream mixture, incorporating lots of air. The potatoes should not feel dry or mealy, but moist and rich. If they are not quite moist enough,

continue to add butter, 1 tablespoon at a time. Adjust the seasoning with salt, and add a generous grind or two of pepper. If not serving immediately, keep warm in a bain-marie in gently simmering water until needed.

Serves 6

PLUCK U.

hough it was as hot as ever, as June slid into July we passed the halfway point of our first level and began to really pick up steam, moving from endless days of dicing vegetables and whisking eggs into omelets to more substantial fare. At last, we were to learn about meat and fish, beginning with poultry.

All birds, whether tiny quail or gigantic turkeys, are built the same way. Legs, wings, thighs, breasts, wishbones. Learn to dismantle and prepare one, and you could handle them all. We were starting out class one morning with a giant, economy-size box of chicken carcasses—chickens are by far the cheapest poultry, not to mention the most plentiful. The stray feather or two stuck to the box was a sign of freshness, surely. But these little pluckers weren't the sort of chicken I was familiar with. Forget the plump, pale yellow skins of the Oven Stuffer Roaster, or the superhealthy pedigree of the organic chickens bought from the Greenmarket in Union Square. These were industrial chickens, and once we had separated them into individual specimens—they came out of the waxed cardboard carton in a solid three-foot-square block—we noticed that some had unique physical characteristics. Ricki picked up a carcass that was missing its left leg—not just the last leg joint and claw, which are always removed at the processing plant here in the States—but the whole leg, up to the thigh joint. Jared pulled out a chicken with an abnormally short wing. But despite the few with mutant defects, most of the chickens were whole, and we plopped them on our cutting boards, waiting for instruction, like first-year medical students ready to open up our first cadavers.

Unless you are killing your own chicken, the specimens available for sale today all have some basic level of preparation already done to them. By the time they reach the store, they have already been trimmed of their head and neck, and as mentioned, the last leg joint and claw have been removed. This is a step that isn't done in other countries, and I remember my initial confusion when looking for dinner at an open-air market in a small village in France. All the chickens looked *different* to me, somehow, and it took me a moment to realize they all seemed to have *very long legs*. Also, traditionally, American chickens' body cavities have been cleaned out and dressed. The internal organs have been removed and the cavity rinsed of any remaining blood and viscera. Depending on the chicken, some of the internal organs, including the heart, gizzard, and liver, are returned to the now-empty cavity. Lastly, the feathers have been plucked, leaving the pale skin intact.

Even with this prepreparation, there are a few additional steps that should be taken to ensure that the poultry will cook evenly and have a beautiful outward appearance. The wings should be trimmed at either the first or the second joint (depending on how the chicken will be cooked). The wishbone is also usually removed, making carving easier if the bird is to be roasted whole, or just to make further dismantling of the carcass less of a hassle.

Now, everything comes down to whether you will be using the poultry whole or in pieces. Whole birds are used mainly for roasting, and whether it is a turkey or a Cornish game hen, all birds cooked whole should be trussed. Trussing ensures that the bird will maintain a compact shape and retain its neatly symmetrical appearance for service. It also ensures that the bird will brown and cook more evenly than if it was left to loll in the roasting pan like a fat man asleep on a beach chair.

There are two ways to truss a poultry carcass: using kitchen twine and a trussing needle, or using kitchen twine on its own. We were to learn how to truss birds with a needle. Chef Jean was adamant that we were not to learn the shortcuts in preparing anything, including chickens for roasting.

"Even if you have to prepare a hundred chickens, I want you to use your trussing needle on all of them. Practice, and get quick with that needle. You should be able to truss a bird in thirty seconds!" Chef obviously had high hopes for us working in a chicken joint.

I imagined being faced with a whole carton of chickens to prep, truss, and roast every morning, and vowed that wherever I went to work, they would not be serving rotisserie chicken.

A trussing needle is a very handy piece of kitchen weaponry, and can be used not only to prepare poultry for roasting, but also for many other finicky tasks. It is a good eight inches long, with an elongated eye at one end and a flattened point at the other. The tip is flat so that while the sharp point easily pierces through flesh and sinew, it leaves a minimal tear in the skin. And boy, is this needle sharp. I was bent over my chicken, trying to wrestle the wishbone out of the breast without breaking it in two and cutting myself with the razor-sharp bits of bone, thereby introducing salmonella directly into my bloodstream, when I was stabbed in the ass with what felt like a white-hot poker. I am ashamed to admit I shrieked "like a total girl," as Tucker informed me.

I whirled around and confronted my attacker. To my shock, it wasn't one of the usual suspects—Angelo practicing his version of flirting, or Tucker, out to jokingly sabotage my progress, or even clumsy Junior. Standing before me, brandishing his poultry needle with an incredibly wicked grin on his face, was quiet, unassuming Ben. Ben, who had said less than twenty words in class all semester. Ben, who shared the kitchen island with Tucker and me. I didn't know he had it in him. Angelo or Tucker? Sure. Ben? No way! But the miscreant stood before me, still brandishing his razor-sharp weapon.

"Ben?" I couldn't believe it.

"I gotcha!" he chortled. "You should have seen the look on your face!"

I could only imagine, as my face went redder at the thought of the noise I had let out, like a squealing piglet. And then I suddenly felt a breeze, a breeze that seemed to be blowing right across my bare cheeks. No, not the ones currently stained scarlet with embarrassment, the other ones. I was trying to get a glimpse of the damage done to my chef's pants when Chef Jean finally intervened. He didn't even have to utter his customary "What zee hell are you doing?" He just grabbed the sleeve of my jacket as I spun around in circles, trying to get a good look at my ventilated ass, and marched me out of the classroom.

"Find a new pair of pants," he hissed before slamming the door behind me.

I slunk off to the women's locker room, where I used the full-length mirror to survey the damage. Not only was I bleeding from a puncture wound on my right cheek, the speedy exit of the trussing needle had ripped a large hole in the seat. Apparently, the chef's pants that cost sixty dollars—more than a decent pair of Levi's—were made to withstand little more than grease splatters. Every move I made caused the rip to get wider and wider, leaving a nice peek-a-boo view of punctured posterior. I quickly opened my locker, searching through the drifts of dirty socks and sweaty tank tops for my spare pair of pants. Then I remembered. Like an idiot, I had taken them to the cleaners, after a particularly messy class—only a professional would be able to get all that caked-on egg splatter off. Which is where they still were, no doubt clean, pristine, and of no use to me whatsoever.

I didn't have the technical abilities or the inclination to jimmy anyone else's locker open, and searching through lockers full to bursting with sweaty underwear, old issues of *Gourmet* magazine, and extra measuring cups wasn't very appealing. But I could feel the moments ticking by, and I knew that if I wasn't back at my station soon, not only would I miss out on learning how to properly truss my poultry, but I would be in for a public tongue lashing from Chef. I would have to think of something, quick.

Thank God that at one point in my career I had worked at a totally dead-end office job. While my typing skills never really got a lot of use, and my understanding of the ink-stained inner workings of the copy machine was hazy at best, I had managed to pick up some useful skills. I could use a FedEx packing slip to remove all the cat hair from my cashmere sweater. I could also, with the aid of my trusty Swingline stapler, mend falling hems. This was definitely a fashion emergency of the first order. I fled the locker room in hot pursuit of office supplies.

Clutching my rapidly unraveling pants tightly to my rear end, I sped down the halls and barreled through the double doors that segregated our classrooms from the civilized world of the support staff. We were not allowed much interaction with this segment of the school population, and every office seemed to be occupied by an unfamiliar, unsmiling, and definitely unsympathetic face. Then, around a corner, I finally found a familiar face: Rose, the very pleasant lady who had shepherded us through orientation what seemed like years ago. I hoped she remembered me; I was about to throw myself on her mercy.

"Rose! Hi!" I plastered a big grin on my face, so that she wouldn't think I was totally out of my mind. "You don't happen to have a stapler, do you?"

Rose looked up from her computer screen and, after a moment, connected the name embroidered on my chef's jacket with our previous encounter. "Oh, Katherine . . . hello. Er, ah, yes, I do have a stapler. Do you need it? For, er, *class?*"

I snatched the implement from her desk without waiting for her to ask any potentially embarrassing questions. "I'll bring it right back!" I shouted over my shoulder, as I sped away to the bathroom to do a quick repair.

I returned to class triumphantly, just in time to truss. No time to mete out vengeance to Ben, but I kept up a running volley of dirty looks over to his side of the cooking island, just so he knew he wouldn't be getting away with this, not by a long shot. First, though, we were busy roping flaccid chicken carcasses. All of us were waving our deadly trussing needles, though they were now being used for their proper purpose. Threaded through the eye was almost a yard of kitchen twine—actually unbleached no-nonsense cotton string— and we were ready to begin the operation.

The only problem was, none of us seemed to have the firmest grasp of chicken anatomy. As Chef shouted from his position at the front of the room "STAB! Through the right wing, neck skin, back fat, back fat, neck skin again, and OUT through the other wing! Pull hard!" we stared down at the suddenly uncharted chicken terri- tory before us. I knew damn well which wing was the right one, and neck skin I also had down, but back fat? Which part? How could I see back fat when I was busy petting the thigh of my chicken absently, as if to reassure my patient that this wasn't going to hurt a bit? Thankfully, I wasn't forced to ask the latest in a long series of stupid questions—some other moron out there in the class beat me to it. I was secretly reassured to see that my partner, Tucker, had no real idea of what he was doing either, and though he had taken the plunge (literally) and stabbed the right arm of his chosen target, the bird seemed to be suffering from a mere flesh wound.

Chef seemed to finally notice the sea of perplexed faces staring back at him because he stopped playing cat's cradle with *his* chicken, quickly untied her, and started over, much more slowly, so that the rest of us could catch up.

Once we finally got our chickens neatly pinioned, all that was left was the actual roasting. Led on once again by Chef, soon we were all searing and salting and then slipping our little chickens in the ovens. In about an hour, we each had a perfectly roasted chicken ready for lunch.

As I followed Chef's instructions for carving my chicken, I was struck with the perfect plan for revenge on Ben. We were using a boning knife, a big curved monster of a blade, and a carving fork—what my grandfather called a "pig sticker," a stainless steel fork with six-inch tines of wicked sharpness. Even sharper than a trussing needle. As the prongs gleamed under the bright kitchen lights, I thought to myself that vengeance was mine. Dutifully I cleaved the thighs and drumsticks from the body, and gently sliced down each side of the breastbone to separate the breast meat from the carcass. Then, I sliced each breast in half, one half with the wing bone, one half without. Every chicken was inspected by Chef, to make sure that the chickens were properly cooked, our slices were even, and there were no bits of bone lingering in the meat. Then, it was all ours to eat for lunch.

While everyone was eating, enjoying the fruits of hard labor, I struck. Feigning innocence (not easy for me), I casually ambled over to Ben and Junior's side of the kitchen, the carving fork concealed in the folds of my apron. When Ben turned toward his plate, which sat on his carving board, I struck, jabbing the pig sticker squarely into the seat of Ben's pants. His squeal was music to my ears. While Ben danced around the classroom clutching his rear end, the whole class exploded in laughter.

Finally Ben calmed down and came over. I was bracing for the worst, and eyeing the various knives spread around the room with some trepidation—had I started a war I couldn't win? But Ben was smiling, and held out his hand (the one that wasn't gingerly rubbing his bottom).

"Truce?" he asked.

"Truce," I answered, shaking his hand.

"Beer?" Ben asked, a twinkle in his eye.

"I'll buy," I replied.

The least I could do was buy a round—after all, Ben was the one eating crow.

Perfect Roast Chicken

This is the secret to those golden brown, crispy-skinned chickens that seem beyond the grasp of the average home cook: The chicken does not go into a hot oven pale and uncooked. It first must be browned in vegetable oil in a hot, hot pan. Even better, if you have the time to let your chicken sit overnight in the fridge without its wrapping, the skin will dry out and be even crispier when roasted.

1 chicken, preferably organic and free-range (about 3 pounds)

Kosher salt

1 small onion, roughly chopped

1 stalk celery, roughly chopped

1 medium carrot, peeled and roughly chopped

Freshly cracked pepper

Vegetable oil

1. Preheat the oven to 450°F.
2. Pat the skin of the chicken dry. Gently tip a generous handful of salt into the cavity of the chicken (only inside the cavity!), being careful to get no salt whatsoever on the skin. (This is a cardinal sin in the kitchen—salt causes moisture to be released from the meat and coagulate on the surface. Moisture on the surface of anything means that no matter how hot the pan is, the meat will not form that lovely crust of caramelization that tastes so good and keeps the interior so moist. Poultry has a nice built-in pocket for any and all seasonings. Salt the cavity liberally, and as you season, remember to be generous! What are you saving that salt for?) Once the chicken is seasoned, pack the cavity with the mirepoix (the onion, celery, and carrot) and pepper to taste. Get ready to brown.

3. Place a large ovenproof sauté pan (not nonstick) over high heat. Turn that flame up as high as it will go and heat the pan until it is very hot. Pour a bit of oil in the pan; it should immediately begin to shimmer but not smoke. Quickly slide the chicken gently into the hot pan. There will be some spitting, so stand back a bit. Brown the chicken on all sides over high heat—back, breast, and sides. This should take about 3 to 4 minutes per side.

4. Remove the chicken from the pan—gently, to avoid puncturing or tearing the skin. (This is hard to do faultlessly. I have found that inserting my tongs into the body cavity will sometimes work well. If you get truly stuck, sliding a flexible spatula underneath the chicken and resting another spatula gently on top of the chicken for balance will usually do the trick to get the bird out of the pan. A further piece of advice: Take the pan off the heat if you think you need some more time to remove the chicken successfully from the pan. There is no need to rush or to let the poor thing burn.)

5. Drain most of the fat from the pan. Return the chicken to the pan breast side up, and pop it into the oven. After 15 minutes, turn the oven down to 400°F.

6. With a spoon, gently scoop up some of the fat from the bottom of the pan and baste the chicken with it. All that time spent browning the skin of the chicken means that it is already gloriously crisp and (hopefully) perfectly browned. Baste using only the clear fat in the pan—using some of the opaque "juice" from the chicken will only make this crackly skin soggy. Fat will just crisp it a bit more. Depending on the size of the chicken, at 400°F, most chickens will be done after another 30 to 40 minutes. Continue to baste with the hot fat accumulated in the pan every 15 minutes or so.

7. Use an instant-read thermometer to test for doneness. Insert the point into the thigh of the chicken, being careful to avoid the thighbone, and when the internal temperature registers 155° to 160°F, the bird is done. (I know, I know, if you read the care labels on poultry, they advise that you cook until the temperature reaches

180°F, or until the bird spontaneously combusts, whichever comes first. That bird, too, will be done, but so dry I don't really advise eating it. Do keep in mind that after the bird comes out of the oven, the internal temperature will continue to rise by as much as 10° to 15°F, and this can mean a perfectly cooked chicken becomes overdone. It can always go back in the oven for a moment or two, but nothing can save it when it has been in too long.)

8. Remove the pan from the oven, and as before, gently remove the chicken from the pan. Put it neck-first into a stainless steel bowl, breast up. (Putting the roasted bird in a bowl neck down and breast up is supposed to enable the juices to flow gently back into the breast meat. It sounds weird, but Chef Jean swore it worked, and he was right.) Tent the chicken *very* loosely with foil. (If the foil is too close, it will trap steam—this means that the skin will quickly go from crunchy to soggy.) Let the bird rest for 10 to 15 minutes. Check the temperature in the thigh again if there is still some question about the degree of doneness.

That is a perfectly roasted chicken.

BIKE ACCIDENT

It had been an awful day at school. Everything had gone wrong, from spilling my coffee on my uniform in the morning to struggling over a cheese soufflé that failed to rise in the afternoon. I blamed Tucker for overcooking the béchamel sauce that is the base of every soufflé, and Tucker blamed me for underwhipping the egg whites—a ridiculous charge. I whipped the eggs until they were so stiff they could have arm-wrestled with Angelo, but the whites were left to sit, waiting for Tucker to cook and cool his béchamel, and so they deflated. We ended up bickering throughout the afternoon, and even Chef Jean couldn't get us to quit our sniping at each other. When class finally let out for the day, I was in such a bad mood that I stomped out of the classroom without even telling Tucker good-bye.

At least the schools were finally out for the summer, and I would not have to hurry uptown to tutor my flock of spoiled, lazy students. Most of them were good kids, and they certainly had a lot on their plates, from advanced placement classes to piano lessons to ballet and baseball and soccer and charity work. But there were a few students who were simply too lazy to do their own work. I was paid fifty bucks an hour to read *Pride and Prejudice* aloud to one freshman from Dalton, a spoiled scion of a sporting goods empire, because it was "too boring" for her to read herself. Her mother offered me five hundred dollars to write her final English paper for her, and while I needed the money badly, I couldn't say yes. It was too much like selling my soul. Not to mention that her English teacher would not have believed for a moment that "little Andrea" had managed to write anything other than a text message.

With no plans for my afternoon, I decided to go for a run in Hudson River Park, along the West Side Highway. Even on a hot afternoon in July, there would be a cool breeze coming off the river, and it would be a good way for me to relax and forget about my quarrel with Tucker, my less-than-stellar performance so far in chef school, and even keep my rear end in pre–chef school shape in the event that I was ambushed by Ben again.

I hurried through the crowded streets of SoHo to my little apartment, threw on my running shoes, and hit Spring Street, following it west against traffic to the river. I jogged along, watching the landmarks of the West Village slowly come into view on my right as I ran uptown. There was the small clutch of strip clubs and peep shows, a last holdout against the wealthy gentrification slowly changing the face of the West Side and of the city as a whole. *Well, if I flunk out of chef school,* I thought gloomily to myself, *I could always get a job at the Carousel Club. And then again, maybe not,* I thought, as I glanced down at my less-than-curvaceous frame.

I thought about the progress I was making so far. Or not, as I sometimes felt. I had learned to use my knives properly, and could turn vegetables into perfectly even matchsticks or fine dice. I could roast a chicken pretty well, and had turned out some beautiful omelets at last, but there were still so many things I couldn't do, or couldn't do well enough. While Tucker and I had gotten the hang of making French fries pretty easily, I couldn't exactly go home and polish my skills in my tiny galley kitchen, which was the size of a dishwasher. More recently, we both had failed at making soufflés, and as much as I wanted to blame Tuck, I knew that it was my fault, too. I had tried to make a *tarte aux pommes* as a special treat for Michael, but my homemade *pâte brisée* crust was gummy. I felt like I was going backward instead of forward with my skills; gone were the days when I could mindlessly whip up some new recipe for dinner—cutting out time-consuming steps, chopping any old way, using whatever pan I had handy. Now I repeated lessons learned in class over and over, trying to get every single part absolutely perfect. Even making something a dozen times was no guarantee I would have every step memorized and perfectly executed. And even if I did finally make a perfect béarnaise sauce, or my *oeufs en gelée* were breathtakingly gorgeous, Chef Jean would never see them. He only saw my fumbling efforts in class. I longed to imitate his polished maneuvers, the offhand confidence instilled in his gestures. His every movement, from rolling out dough to adding a pinch of salt to the whisking egg whites was swift and certain. I knew that it took Chef Jean a lifetime of kitchen work to perfect this, but this knowledge didn't stop me from wanting to be that good, right now!

As I thought about how long it would take me to be a chef like my teacher, the glass-and-steel Richard Meier high-rises on Perry Street loomed up on my right. Once I drew even with them, I knew it was time to turn around and sprint for home—a round-trip of about three miles. I slowed from a run to a trot, checked the traffic around me on the bike path, and crossed on the crosswalk. As I was halfway across, head down, still thinking about Tucker and how school was going, someone shouted "LOOKOUT!"

WHAM! The next thing I knew, I was sitting on the tarmac of the path, ten feet from the crosswalk. Blood was running into my eyes and down my white T-shirt and making a puddle on the ground around me. One of my tennis shoes had come off and was lying on the ground, looking lonely. I was confused. What had happened? Someone was retrieving my shoe, and someone else was holding me down, telling me not to move until the ambulance got there. Ambulance? A few feet away, I saw a bicyclist pulled over, the front wheel of his bike bent and one of his handles twisted in the wrong direction. *Oh. I must have collided with the cyclist. But where did he come from?* I had looked both ways before crossing on the crosswalk. The only person around had been a woman doing yoga on the grassy median. She was still here, holding a T-shirt to my head to stop the bleeding and talking to the EMT workers who had parked their ambulance right on the path, lights flashing and siren wailing.

"That man flattened this poor girl!" the woman said, and I was grateful that someone was here to stick up for me. The medics loaded me into the back of the ambulance, and a police officer was talking to the cyclist as we pulled away. We shot through the rush-hour traffic to St. Vincent's, the overcrowded, overworked, under-funded hospital that serves most of lower Manhattan. On the way, one of the medics took down my information, checked my blood pressure, disinfected the many cuts and scrapes that covered most of my body—I had several square feet of road rash on both thighs and calves, and most of the skin on my right arm had been scraped away—and entertained me with stories of how they were often called to another culinary school uptown to treat the many deep cuts and burns the students received. I started to feel better about my own career at school—at least I hadn't chopped a finger off yet!

The medic (named Jim) looked at the cut on my scalp, which was still bleeding profusely. "Oh-oh. Looks like stitches for sure. Mmmm, it's a bad one. You might need a dozen of them. That's an ugly cut. We'll definitely have to shave off some of that blond hair of yours." With that, he began quizzing me to see how my response time was. It was slow, and I was still a little fuzzy. I couldn't remember anything about the accident, or anything leading up to it, just the failed soufflé, which I told Jim about in detail. Jim let me talk, and even use his cell phone to call Michael. It took me a long time to remember what his cell phone number was. When I finally did get through, I told Michael to meet me at the hospital.

When we arrived at St. Vincent's, Jim helped me out of the am-bulance (I was still feeling a little wobbly) and into the hallway of the ER. He handed my file to a nurse, covered me in a blanket—the afternoon was still very warm, but I had started to shiver with cold. Shock and leftover nerves, Jim told me, nothing to worry about. Then he was gone and I sat alone in the hallway for what seemed like hours. Finally, a frazzled nurse swept by and, without even glancing at me, said, "The doctor will see you in room 3. Please have your insurance card out so that we can make a copy for our files."

Oh. My. God. I had just realized I didn't have health insurance. When I quit my job, I thought about signing up for the supplemental COBRA insurance, but at $150 a month, I just couldn't afford it. And I definitely couldn't afford this. The ambulance ride alone was enough to bankrupt me. In a panic, I fled the ER, tearing past the security guard and right into Michael's arms. He recoiled. I was still wearing my bloody shirt, and dried blood flaked off my face. Michael can't stand the sight of blood, and while I could tell he was concerned, he was also trying very hard not to look at the blood, the scrapes, or the bruises rapidly forming. So he was looking everywhere but at me.

Early evening was falling, and Michael hailed a cab. He was trying so hard to comfort me, without actually coming into contact with any of the nasty-looking scrapes or cuts still oozing blood, or touching any of the bruises that seemed to be sprouting like dark purple fruit everywhere. (I could feel the one on my bum with every pothole the cab hit. It was sure to be the size of a stockpot.) He settled for squeezing my hand—I didn't have the heart to tell him he was only grinding stray bits of grit more deeply into the road rash on my palm. He was even paler than I, and it was easy to see that he was really upset. When we finally arrived at the apartment, Michael let me in (my key chain had been broken and the keys lost in the accident) and then dithered in the doorway. A quick check in the mirror showed just how bad it was. I looked terrible, more like steak tartare with a side of overripe eggplant than a person. I showered off the blood, trying to avoid getting anywhere near the head wound (which was still trickling blood) and put myself to bed. Instead of joining me, Michael hemmed and hawed and finally came out with it.

"I thought I would play poker with the boys this evening, but you don't look so good." Michael had begun playing poker in an underground club on West Fourteenth Street a few evenings a week. I usually didn't mind, since I was busy working in the evening anyway, but lately I had begun to come home late at night to an empty apartment, and the dinners I cooked got cold on the stove before Michael came home from playing poker, sometimes as late as one or two o'clock in the morning. I was getting tired of spending my evenings with Spankie—her green eyes were no match for Michael's big brown ones, and, frankly, she always had tuna breath.

I sat in bed, my head pounding, every bone and muscle in my body sore. I felt even worse than I looked. I stared at Michael, who was hovering like an anxious student waiting for a pot of water to boil. I didn't think I was up for Michael's version of tender loving care, which veered toward microwaved Hot Pockets, chicken soup straight from the can, and celebreality TV on VH1. I definitely couldn't face that. "No, go ahead. I think I'm just going to crash. I mean, get some sleep." Michael looked so relieved, his "Thanks sweetheart! Feel better! I love you!" came floating up the stairwell as he hightailed it to the club.

Hmmmph. He didn't have to agree quite so easily, I thought to myself as I threw back some Tylenol and carefully eased my bruised butt into bed. I didn't even feel like having dinner—for the first time ever. This was not the way I had imagined my relationship going. I wondered if Michael and I had come to the end of things, after almost two years together. Were we just going through a phase, or was this the end of us?

TASTES LIKE CHICKEN

When I finally saw my doctor after my run-in with the cyclist, it turned out that I had a major concussion, a black eye, and three cracked ribs. Nothing could be done about any of these injuries, but Dr. Tay gave me a break on my bill, thank God. Michael was horrified that I was in such bad shape. He brought me a gigantic bouquet of peonies, my favorite flower. Their intoxicating scent filled our apartment and put a huge smile on my (slightly battered) face. He was being a real sweetie—leaving me little love notes by my coffee cup in the morning, making plans for a vacation getaway after school was over. He *was* being a bit secretive, having whispered phone calls to his friends, and suddenly declaring his sock drawer off-limits, but I was busy recovering from my accident and thought nothing of it. I had enough on my plate.

The concussion was making me nauseous, and I left class several times over the next few days to throw up. Taking a sick day was out of the question; since school was only six months long, the students were not allowed any absences, and missing even one day would put one too far behind in the curriculum. So I was not in the best shape for one of our last classes in Level 1: Organ Meat Day.

Even for someone who has no food prejudices, the words *Organ Meat Day* are a little disconcerting. Coming at the end of our first level, it seemed like the tough final of a Biology 101 class, designed to weed out the weak of heart and stomach. Students in the more advanced levels could be relied on to taunt us by telling stories of the truly unique smell and disturbing feel of the various organs we would be preparing, and partaking of, in this segment of the curriculum. I am not afraid of organs. When I lived in England, I read

Nose to Tail Eating, the seminal organ meat cookbook by Fergus Henderson, with a sense of slavering anticipation. I love to make chicken liver crostini—the creamy richness of the liver plays up the dense, chewy texture of a good hunk of ciabatta. I had eaten tender, barely seared veal kidneys garnished with shaved black truffles in a brasserie in Nice. For a time in college, I had even been premed, and had fearlessly dissected my fetal pig, Sweetpea, before tucking into a BLT.

I was born in Virginia, a land where pickled pigs feet in gallon jars are available on the counter of many a gas station, right next to the cash register. I had also spent my very first years living on a farm, and had even eaten the occasional rabbit that lost a fight with the tractor. I think that experience of living closer to the land and to my dinner has made me more pragmatic than many of my peers. Chicken breasts come from chickens, not from Styrofoam trays in the grocery store. Even that gorgeous slab of perfectly marbled New York strip steak once came from a living, breathing animal, one with big brown eyes and impossibly long lashes.

I don't think it's wrong to eat meat, though I did go through a vegetarian phase (don't all high school girls?), but I have found myself becoming increasingly disgruntled with the American desire to divorce the act of eating meat from the animal it came from. I have been very lucky to be one of the few who were raised with an appreciation of the balance between people and animals. If we are going to raise animals and then eat them, then we should consume as much of the animal as possible—including the heart, the liver, and the kidneys. We should relish every aspect of the animal that has become our dinner. It is comforting that the French are a nation of eaters who preserve this tradition, of taking a delight in what the overhygienized Americans have deemed offal. They seem to be on a more intimate footing with their food—they love the living animal, love the filet mignon, love the *pieds et paquets* (lamb foot and intestine stew), love the *tête de veau* (calf's head). But despite my attempts to practice this overarching view of my role in the food chain, I still remember the shock I felt the day that I asked my mother where our bull calf Bosco had gone, and she had responded, quite matter-of-factly, "The freezer."

Fortified with the courage of these convictions, I refused to be swayed. I would relish every bite of every organ. Or so I thought. The Day of Organ Meat dawned, a fiercely hot, sticky morning in July, when the chewing gum on the sidewalks of SoHo was already hot enough to liquefy and cling to my shoes like sticky barnacles. SoHo in the summer becomes the province of movie crews and tourists, both of whose antics are enough to drive the hapless resident to the brink of insanity—if your block hasn't been shut down for filming and stepping foot outdoors doesn't bring shrieks of "You idiot! You walked through our shot!" from some production assistant, then you are unable to walk at all due to the herds of slow-moving roving tourists.

In class, it was my turn to help Assistant Chef Cyndee wheel the provisions for the day to the classroom. There, resting on the cart, was a calf's liver that was as big as a pickup truck's engine block. The size of this baby was enough to make me wonder what sort of mutant factory-farm animal this had come out of. It was enormous. As the cart bumped its way down the hall, the dark red, shiny surface rippled slightly. And of course the visceral realities of the day's preparation didn't end there. There were also pale globes of thymus gland, laid out in their stainless steel tray as if fresh from some surgeon's operating room, and going by the ridiculous alias of "sweetbreads"—these, at least, were quiescent on our trip to the classroom. A bag of veal kidneys slumped dejectedly, like a drunk on a crosstown bus, at the bottom of the heap.

Organ meats are divided into two classes: the red and the white. Liver, tongue, and kidneys are red in hue, and so make up the *abats rouges*, the red organs. Brains, head, sweetbreads, feet, and marrow make up the *abats blancs*, the white organs. Organ meat comes primarily from cows, usually calves; lambs; and, to a lesser extent, pigs. While the rising concern about BSE (bovine spongiform encephalopathy) or "mad cow disease," has not reached the fever pitch in the States that it has in Europe, the recent discovery that two cows did test positive for the disease has been enough to dissuade me from eating calf brains—so far. BSE is transmitted primarily through the brains and nervous systems of animals by proteins called prions. Until recently, animal feed was routinely made from the unwanted portions of slaughtered animals (everything from tails to eyeballs, including large portions of the central nervous system), a sort of Soylent Green technique that might cause widespread infection if one infected animal were to enter the food chain. While the FDA has ended this practice, I can still think of no better reason to eat grass-fed beef. Thankfully, our syllabus for Organ Meat Day spared us from the prospect of brains and a possible lawsuit for contracting Creutzfeldt-Jakob disease, the unpleasant—and fatal—form "mad cow" takes in people. Indeed, our only experience with the *abats blancs* would be the sweetbreads. Most of our time in the kitchen would be spent preparing liver and kidneys, certainly enough gore for the faint of stomach.

Almost all organ meats must undergo elaborate preparation before they can be cooked. While practically every portion of meat must be trimmed to remove fat and connective tissue, to make them more aesthetically pleasing to the diner, most organ meats must first be peeled (like a banana). Organs are encased in a translucent, slightly shiny membrane that, I suppose, helps keep them together and functioning in the crowded morass of the abdomen. Thankfully, Chef Jean took on the task of peeling the huge hunk of liver, standing at the head of the classroom and gently peeling back the membrane before portioning the meat into pieces for each of us. Of all the chef-instructors, Chef Jean had the most deft and delicate touch with the knife, quickly and easily breaking down a carcass while he kept up a running commentary about what to do and what not to do. I could easily imagine him as a surgeon, calmly cracking open a chest cavity while first-year residents gathered around to catch a glimpse of the gore within. But perhaps not all the students were so eager to catch a glimpse of Chef's busy and bloody knife at work.

Marita, one of my fellow classmates, suddenly staggered back from her usual place right in front of Chef Jean. She looked decidedly green, a bizarre contrast to her deeply tanned complexion and thick braid of dark hair. With a mumbled excuse in her delectable Dominican accent, she fled from the room. When she returned, still a bit green around the gills, she explained that she was a very strict vegetarian, and while she was more than happy to prepare meat, the sight of all the flaccid organs lying before her had been a bit too much to take. I remembered my days of vegetarianism and thought Marita, a lifelong veggie, was very brave to take on the challenge of getting a culinary degree in the face of so much red meat.

Chef Jean, as usual, was unsympathetic. I am not even sure there is a word for vegetarian in French, so perhaps Marita's discomfort was lost in translation.

Each of us was given four slices of deep red liver with which to make . . . liver and onions. Of course, we used extra-rich demi-glace and slowly caramelized onions, and garnished it with fresh parsley, but ultimately, after almost an hour's effort, and with the classroom redolent of the metallic smell of iron-rich tissue being sautéed, I was struck with the realization that I had produced the exact same meal my mother had made, and I had refused to eat, hundreds of times in my young life. I was becoming my mother, as I passed the plate on to the students in the bread classroom across the hall, wheedling them to "just take a little bite. It's delicious!"

While twenty-four of us churned out twenty-four plates of liver that wouldn't be eaten, the sweetbreads were lurking. Many of the white organs have to be *dégorgés* (disgorged) before they can be used. Disgorging is the technique of soaking meat in cold water to flush out any lingering blood and juices. Usually organs must be disgorged for anywhere from an hour to overnight. Sweetbreads must be disgorged, blanched, and then pressed under something heavy, so that excess water will be removed and the thymus gland becomes a more regular shape. Each team of two students was given one gland. My partner in crime, Tucker, and I began to work with ours, but as I was trimming the line of connective tissue that almost bisects the gland, the slimy thing suddenly shot off my cutting board and scored a direct hit on Tucker's clean chef's jacket, leaving a disturbingly damp imprint. Luckily, my sloppiness went unnoticed by Chef, and the other students seemed to be having problems of their own. Still, we bravely continued. We browned it, and then braised it slowly in Madeira, white wine, and demi-glace. A final garnish of peas, turnips, pearl onions, and carrots added color to the brown sauce and off-white meat. In humans, the thymus gland is responsible for building the body's immune system. As I chewed a bite of the surprisingly soft flesh, whose flavor was a more delicate, nuanced riff on liver's single blaring note, I couldn't escape the thought that this was something that was meant to be "good for you," a prophylaxis eaten in the hope of staving off some disease for which there was no cure.

So far, I had not been the fearless eater I had hoped to be on Organ Meat Day. I had envisioned myself gobbling down delicacies, urging my fellow students to overcome their finicky prejudices toward these overlooked treasures. It wasn't shaping up as I had imagined. In fact, it really wasn't going so well at all. It turns out I just don't like liver. One bite was enough for me to confirm this, and even the gentle nudging from Chef couldn't make me finish my braised sweetbreads. I was chagrined at the thought of being so provincial, of having a palate that was raised on roasts and steaks and yet was unable to appreciate the full-flavored, nuanced taste and texture of organs. This was a horrible revelation—how could I be a foodie if I couldn't appreciate these things? Even worse, as a chef, I certainly couldn't publicly extol the virtues of the fried gizzards on my menu if I privately shuddered at the thought of actually eating them. I did have hope, though. We were scheduled to spend the afternoon working with kidneys, and kidneys I could definitely do. I like kidneys. No, I love kidneys—I had eaten kidney pie in England and seared kidneys in Nice. I had enjoyed kidneys in other countries—I couldn't be provincial! I was a kidney aficionada. I could still save face and be the offal-phile I so badly wanted to be.

Kidneys fall in the class of red organs and must be prepped before cooking. Veal kidneys are considered the crème de la crème of all types of kidney, and so that was what we were working with. Because their flavor is so delicate, and presumably because they come from animals that are so young they haven't really had time to *use* the organ all that much, veal kidneys require no disgorgement before use. They must merely be peeled and the fatty tissue removed before being sautéed, fried, or seared. But veal kidney isn't the smooth, red, bean-shaped organ that it is in humans. It looks more like a postmodern space station—small globular spheres held together by thick yellow ropes of fat. But I was not going to be deterred from my quest to prove my foodie chops and educate my palate. I carved off several spheres and trimmed them, splitting each one in half. Now they were more reassuringly like those morsels I had once slurped up with such self-assurance.

Sauteuses were placed over high flames and oil began to shimmer in pans, ready to sear the kidneys to a crisp and seal in the juices. I was ready. My mouth was even watering slightly. Twenty-four budding chefs added kidneys to hot pans, and suddenly, horribly, the ammoniac reek of urine filled the air. Twenty-four noses wrinkled in unison, and with one voice, we shrieked "Gross!" The smell was vile. It was invasive, pervasive, and I could feel it bonding on a molecular level to my skin and hair. Chef Jean threw himself into the situation, which was quickly reaching the level of open mutiny.

"Babies!" he taunted us. "You don't like that smell? Wait until you try some!"

The thought of eating something that smelled like, well, animal pee was almost beyond even my gag reflex. Almost. Still, I kept going, deglazing the pan with Cognac and adding heavy cream and Dijon mustard to the well-browned lumps still sizzling away. The sauce thickened up and looked almost innocuous, a velvety light beige that smelled more like shallots and mustard than anything else. I ladled my kidneys out onto the plate and napped them cautiously with the sauce. A dash of fresh parsley for presentation, and it was suddenly the moment of truth. I maneuvered a forkful into my mouth, preparing to choke down the most vile organ encounter yet.

It was shocking.

Delicious.

The kidneys were crisp, then soft, and the sauce was vibrant with the tang of mustard and the decadent rich smoothness of cream.

I ate the whole thing. Even Chef was impressed.

Chicken Liver Pâté

This is a nice, simple way to ease yourself into the organ meat milieu. We have been making it for years and serving it as an afternoon snack on Thanksgiving and Christmas to tide over hungry guests before the big meal is ready. The richness of the shallots and Cognac elevate the humble chicken liver without overwhelming the delicate flavor.

3 medium shallots, finely chopped

1 large clove garlic, finely chopped

16 tablespoons (2 sticks) unsalted butter

1 pound chicken livers, trimmed

Salt and freshly ground pepper

¼ cup Cognac (the best you can bear to part with)

¼ teaspoon freshly grated nutmeg

Pinch of ground allspice

Ciabatta bread or crackers, for serving

Sour gherkins (cornichons), for serving

1. In a large, heavy skillet over moderate heat, cook the shallots and garlic in half of the butter, stirring, until softened, about 15 minutes.
2. Pat dry the chicken livers and season with salt and pepper. Add the livers to the shallot mixture and sear until just pink inside, about 5 minutes.
3. Melt the remaining butter in a small saucepan and set aside.
4. Add the Cognac to the livers and carefully tilt the pan until the liquid almost touches the edge. Ignite the Cognac with a long match and stand back! Shake the pan until the flames subside.
5. Transfer the hot mixture to a food processor or blender. Add the

nutmeg, allspice, and salt and pepper to taste. Puree the mixture until very smooth.

6. Pack the pâté into a 2-cup crock or several small ramekins. Film the top of the pâté with the melted butter—this prevents the pâté from oxidizing and changing color. Refrigerate until ready to use.

7. Bring to room temperature before serving. Serve with chewy ciabatta bread or crackers and tiny gherkins.

Makes about 1½ cups

FIDO, THE FIGHTING LOBSTER

Juuly became August and our time in the Level 1 kitchen was almost over. My black eye had faded from the color of candied violets to the pale yellow of sautéed onions. In a few more days we would be leaving the relatively sheltered confines of our sweaty but safe kitchen-haven and begin working in the cavernous Level 2 kitchen, learning more classic French dishes and putting together the family meal to feed the students, faculty, and support staff every day. While we had already begun our mastery of vegetable dishes, poultry, soups, tarts and pastries, and even organ meats, we hadn't yet begun to study the mysteries of the deep. We had all heard that the lesson on shellfish was the very best day of Level 1, better even than the lesson on ice cream and frozen desserts, because on Shellfish Day, everyone in class got to have a lobster of their very own for lunch.

I had only ever had lobster once before in my life, on a spectacularly bad Valentine's Day date in college. While I had no intention of ordering something that, to me, looked like an overgrown sea cockroach, my overbearing date had other ideas. "Get the surf and turf," he grunted, his hockey player's muscles dwarfing the spindly chair on which he sat, the table he was resting his ham-hock hands on, indeed, everything in the room. "I'll eat what you don't want," he graciously offered. Which, it turned out, meant that after my first bite, everything on my plate was his. Nevertheless, five years later, armed with a decidedly more adventurous palate and the ability to successfully dismember the sucker, I was excited for another crack at *homard*.

First, though, at nine o'clock precisely, we began the day with oysters. Raw oysters. Nestled in wooden crates packed with seaweed, their wrinkled, craggy shells poking through the ice like bits of some shaggy reef, they weren't really a good pairing with my morning coffee. Champagne would have been a much better choice. But they were delightfully cool to the touch, and after several false starts with a curved oyster knife, I had jimmied the hinges apart on one particularly large, lusty-looking fellow, and without any palate-numbing additives—not lemon, mignonette, or the bright ketchup obscenity of cocktail sauce—I swallowed it down whole. An immediate briny tidal wave of flavor caught me up in its big, mighty ocean arms and propelled me off toward an absolute, intoxicating love of seafood.

There was an entire box of oysters to be consumed, literally dozens and dozens to be wrenched open and sucked dry before moving on to mussels, clams, and scallops, those lesser bivalves, whose role in our morning would be as an appetizer along the lines of a shellfish soup. After quaffing almost a dozen oysters all by myself, I wasn't terribly eager to begin the rather arduous process of cleaning and debearding the mussels, or scrubbing the shells of clams, but the lure of a sunny Provençal-style stew, suffused with the happy summer flavors of saffron, tomatoes, and garlic, cheered me through the long process.

Once we had cleaned and prepared the clams, mussels, and scallops, we were ready to begin making our shellfish soup. After the tedious preparation of the bivalves, the rest was a walk in the park. A few shallots, nicely *ciseléd*, some diced tomato, quantities of garlic paste, and a liberal guzzle of extra virgin olive oil, and that was all. Into the pot went the oil, shallots, and garlic to turn golden and fragrant before we added the pulpy, sweet tomatoes. While this simmered nicely over a low flame, Chef told us a story of how, as a boy, he gathered mussels with his grandfather for market near the small seaside town where he grew up, on the border between France and Spain.

"Actually," Chef said, "I am not really *français*. I am a Basque."

This surprised me, as I had ignorantly assumed that all Basques were "freedom fighters." But here was Chef, his quintessentially Gallic features relaxed in a serene smile as he recounted scenes from an idyllic childhood, one filled with farm-fresh eggs, lazy milk cows, and pike just caught in mountain streams. The recipe we were making was not really Provençal, it was Basque, and a bit of Chef's own past he was sharing with us. I was suddenly anxious to prove I could reproduce something from such a rich food heritage, something delicious that would remind Chef of his homeland. I was also inexplicably homesick myself for the rolling green hills of Virginia, the cows and chickens that had populated my own childhood, the taste of my mother's cooking.

The ingredients in front of me were a far cry from the shrimp with grits of my childhood, however. Once the garlic and shallots had softened and become fragrant, and the bright red tomato concassé had cooked down into a rich savory compote, we added a cup of dry white wine and a few precious strands of saffron. Saffron stems are actually the tiny stamens harvested from a variety of crocus that grows on the hills of Spain. Saffron turns everything it touches a brilliant yellow, and adds an exotic, pungent sweetness with a whisper of metallic tang. As soon as the strands hit the pot, the air was filled by the gasps of some of my fellow students who had never seen the little flower's brilliant powers of transformation. Once the saffron had added its distinct voice to the rising chorus of flavors in the pot, we began to add the mussels, clams, and scallops.

Clams are almost always the first to go into the pot, as it takes a little time for the heat to penetrate their thick shells and persuade them to open. The mussels go next, as soon as the clams have just begun to look like they might at any moment begin to open. The scallops go in last, as they have, by far, the most delicate flesh. The scallops should, in fact, merely poach in the juices released by the mussels and clams. Once all the shellfish begin to open like delicious blossoms from an undersea garden, the stew is ready.

We all carefully arranged three scallops, five clams, and seven mussels in each bowl, the odd numbers remaining an all-important, mystical element to French cuisine. The red tomatoes, yellow saffron, even the shiny black of the mussel shells seemed to take on a fierce intensity against the sturdy white china bowls. A sprinkling of finely minced parsley on top added even more color and vibrancy to the dish, and as always, after a careful visual inspection of each plate, counting to ensure we had indeed arranged the proper number of bivalves in the proper proportions, Chef dipped his large tasting spoon into each bowl, to check authenticity and correctness of the seasoning. His somewhat froglike, protuberant eyes fluttered closed after each mouthful as he rolled the flavors around in his mouth. Finally he admonished us—"Eat! Eat! It will not stay warm forever! Tell me what you think."

I heaped my spoon with a bite of stew, the bright yellow sauce studded with small nuggets of jewel-bright tomato and pale purple, fragrant shallot. The taste of sunshine and lazy seaside afternoons filled my mouth in one vibrantly buoyant wash of perfectly harmonized flavors. I didn't need to hear Chef's stories of his boyhood to suddenly appreciate and understand the magic of place; it was all there in the bowl before me. The class was silent as we took in the perfection of the simple dish, so accurately and effectively evoking a lost moment and a culture none of us had ever experienced. The reverence and appreciation were palpable.

"This is what cooking really is," said Chef, his bright eyes smiling at us all. We were beginning to understand.

As marvelous as it was, however, it was *not* the lobster that we had been promised, tantalized by, and teased with since the beginning of classes in June. There also didn't seem to be any more plywood boxes stuffed with the fruits of the ocean, either. Where were the lobsters?

We were beginning to get restive, having cleaned the kitchen up for the morning and replaced the various implements from our shared *batterie de cuisine* in the large stainless steel armoire, and had begun to sharpen our knives—a task Chef set us to whenever there was a free moment in the kitchen. Whenever he saw two or more students congregate and begin to talk, he would run over, flapping his arms as if he were driving a flock of poultry before him, shouting "*Va, va.* Go, go find something to do. A chef's hands must never be idle. Sharpen your knives." My paring knife was beginning to take on a decidedly snub-nose look to it from too much time spent grinding against the whetstone when the door to the kitchen swung open with a bang and we all stood to attention.

This was beginning to be a habit, as we had already been the subjects of several surprise inspections by visiting deans in our short stay in the Level 1 kitchen. These inspections, in which the dean would stalk up and down the rows of nervous students, barking comments like "Stand up straight" and "Shave that facial hair before you come to this kitchen again," reminded me of some five-star general inspecting a fresh shipment of raw recruits, and once the door had slammed shut behind the departing figure, there was an audible sigh of relief, from both students and chef.

But this was not a surprise inspection; it was David, the majordomo of the storeroom. David could provide anyone with anything, from nonstick pans to any type of vegetable you could imagine to lobes of fresh foie gras to canned black truffles, these last pricey delicacies kept in a specially locked cabinet to which he had the only key. Rumor had it that the special cabinet also housed a veritable cornucopia of illegal pharmaceuticals as well. David was *the* connection. This time, though, he came heavily burdened, like a short Cuban Santa Claus, with a huge plywood box slung over his stevedore's shoulders, a box stenciled with the words CAUTION! LIVE LOBSTERS! CAUTION! Lunch had finally arrived.

We circled like a school of sharks. I don't think anyone actually bit David in their eagerness, but there were a lot of big, white teeth showing. Swearing good-naturedly at us in Spanish, David dumped the box at Chef's feet and fled—there was definitely blood in the water. Chef cuffed the hands already tearing at the plywood and called for silence. We were to return to our stations, and Assistant Chef Cyndee would dole out to each student one lobster. There would be no trading, no returns, no refunds. Tucker and I exchanged chagrined looks. This was not a good thing. Cyndee's antipathy for us all was obvious, but she seemed to have a special loathing for my partner and me. I blamed it on Tucker's super-nerd habit of asking Cyndee endless questions about the food, the recipes, the curriculum, and kitchen lore in general, none of which she knew the answers to, and Tucker blamed me for being blond and for smiling too much. I think we were both right.

Sure enough, Tucker and I predictably ended up being the last ones to receive our bounty. Tucker's lunch was so small it looked more like a crayfish than a lobster. Mine was slightly bigger, but it was missing one of its claws. It was also very, very angry. Cyndee tossed the disgruntled crustacean onto my cutting board, making it even more furious. It scuttled for cover behind a large stainless steel bowl. I didn't know lobsters could move that fast. Using my large strainer as an improvised lacrosse stick, I eventually scooped up the errant lobster and deposited him in a large stainless steel container called a squareboy, where Tucker's tiny lobster was already cowering in a corner. My lobster immediately began to advance, antennae bristling ferociously. He was definitely a fighter. I named him Fido on the spot, and left him to menace Tucker's lunch while we gathered to watch Chef's lobster demonstration.

Chef was holding Amanda's lobster up in one hand and explaining how to tell the boys from the girls. Apparently it has something to do with the excessive number of legs hiding under the thorax. However, there were so many of them, and they were all waving wildly as Chef poked the underbelly gently with a paring knife, that I lost track of whether boys or girls were supposed to have more and just tried not to think about my lunch having sex.

Just then, Amanda's lobster began flapping its tail and struggling mightily to free itself from Chef's iron grip. Gently, using the butt of a large knife, Chef began to stroke the lobster on the back of its head, behind the bulging eyestalks and flopping antennae. Right away, the lobster stopped struggling. Chef placed it on the cutting board and explained that this petting would calm the lobster, and it would eventually even go to sleep. He continued petting the little guy, now actually singing "Frère Jacques" while we smiled at each other.

Suddenly, just as Chef began the third chorus of *"dormez-vous, dormez-vous,"* he brought the knife down with a *thwack!* and sliced the lobster's head in half. "Dead," pronounced Chef, with satisfaction. "He didn't feel a thing." I wasn't so sure, as I watched the legs twitching wildly and the eyes still moving about on their stalks. Amanda seemed to be in shock. "It is kinder than letting him boil, my dear," Chef said, as if to comfort her. He dropped the carcass into a large pot of cold water, added a handful of salt and dark green seaweed, which had come as packing material in the crate, and put the lid on. Turning the flame up to high, he instructed her to bring everything to a boil, and then turn it off. The lobster would poach for a few minutes (depending on its size) and be tender and succulent without overcooking.

We returned to our stations, and I checked on Fido. He was sitting on Tucker's lobster, and waved his remaining claw up at me. I couldn't tell if it was a wave of greeting or a challenge, like a boxer brandishing one gloved hand, but I did know one thing: I didn't really feel like having him for lunch anymore. I picked him up and began to stroke the back of his head, even scratching behind his ears, if he had any ears, that is. Around me, everyone was either busily braining their lobsters or placing them into the pot live, preferring not to stare death directly in the face. Tucker executed a perfect three-point shot, tossing his lobster into the waiting pot from two feet away, and turned to wait for my guy to join his.

I looked down at Fido, whom I was now cradling gently against my chef's jacket. His big black eyes looked back, and one of his antennae gently tickled my chin.

"I can't," I said. "I just can't. Look at him. He's so cute!" Tucker rolled his eyes and called Chef over. Chef plucked Fido from my grasp. "No! Don't kill him!" I shouted, fearing the fate Chef had just administered to Amanda's lobster. Chef sighed deeply, put Fido down on the cutting board, and reached for my just-sharpened paring knife. Instead of killing him, though, Chef merely sliced the rubber band off Fido's remaining claw. I swooped down and picked Fido up again, ready to bring him home and install him in the bathtub of my tiny apartment. Now that his claw was free, though, Fido had other plans. He clamped down on my thumb with all his might. I tried to drop him, but he was hanging on, literally, for dear life. I tried to shake him off to no avail. Blood was beginning to well, and rained down on my workstation from my now-mangled digit. Calmly, Chef grabbed Fido and yanked. Fido let go of my thumb at last, and without further bloodshed, Chef flipped him directly into the waiting pot, slammed the lid on, and turned up the gas. Fifteen minutes later, my thumb now cocooned in bandages, I was eating lobster tail with drawn butter. I discovered I love lobster.

It was a good thing, too. That weekend, Michael took me on a surprise trip to Nantucket. As we sat on a picnic bench, munching on huge, deliciously sloppy lobster rolls from a tiny roadside shack, Michael suddenly dropped to one knee, whipped out the beautiful ring he had been hiding in his sock drawer, and, with a drip of mayo still clinging adorably to his chin, asked me to marry him. I said *yes!* and kissed him mightily, mayonnaise and all.

Preparing Shellfish

There really is no upside to cleaning bivalves—it is a long, wet, chilly process. Even if you are eating them raw, as with oysters and some varieties of clam, there is a great deal of prep work involved. The bivalves are given a thorough going-over—the shell should be tightly closed, or if it is a bit open, it should snap closed when you tap it gently with a knuckle. There should be no sign of foreign visitors, from small crabs to a vicious variety of sea worm that burrows right through the calciferous mantles and feasts on the plump flesh. Once you have established that all the bivalves are alive, give each a brief bath in very cold water and quick scrub with a wire brush if it has any undesirable bits clinging to it. These undesirable bits can be clumps of mud or stray pieces of shell, even the contributions from passing seagulls, so you want to make certain the shells are thoroughly cleaned.

Oysters and clams to be eaten raw are now ready to be opened. Remember to open just before serving—even on ice, the creatures do not last long once they have been wrenched apart and exposed to the air. Using a towel or an oyster glove (a delightfully medieval kitchen gadget made from fine-gauge chain mail, to be worn on the hand holding the bivalve), hold the oyster securely. The towel (or oyster glove) provides purchase on the slippery surface of the shell, and also protects one's hand from the inevitable nicks and cuts accrued from exerting a great deal of force on a knife against a small, slippery object that does not wish to be opened. Make certain the flatter of the two shells is facing up—the bulk of the oyster is nestled against the curved shell. I find it easiest to situate the oyster so that the hinge is facing me. I then insert the tip of the oyster knife slightly to the right of the hinge. Then I wiggle and pry a bit, edging the knife in deeper, before sliding the knife up to the hinge and twisting to pry it open. Some oysters give up more easily than others. Once the hinge is opened, slide the knife gently through the oyster, as close to the top of the shell as possible, to detach any bits of muscle clinging to the flat shell. Remove the top shell, being careful not to spill any of the precious liquor. Use the slightly curved shape of the oyster knife to slide underneath the oyster, detaching the strong muscle from the bottom shell, but leaving the flesh intact and in place. Gently snuggle it into a bed of crushed ice, and it is ready to enjoy. Clams are treated in precisely the same manner, except that the knife should be inserted directly into the hinge and pried open that way.

Mussels, scallops, and clams that are not going to be eaten raw need some preparation. Mussels, in particular, are a pain in the ass. Not only do scads of them seem to die in between checking them for life the first time and giving them a bath, but they all must be debearded with a sharp paring knife to remove the furry, greenish brown ropes of fiber emerging from the shells. Don't pry too hard, or you will kill the things, but try to get as much of it off as possible. Once mussels have been cleaned and debearded, they are ready to go. In classic French cooking, unless one is making bistro fare, mussels are used only to make stock. They are sautéed in a deep covered pot with some shallots, chopped parsley, and a bit of white wine. Once they have opened their shells, they are strained out, and the cooking liquid is used as stock in other recipes. The mussels themselves are then usually used to feed the kitchen staff—a tasty, easy meal. While the mussels are still warm, add another healthy jigger of white wine and a generous dollop of crème fraîche. Toss lightly, and serve over big rustic pasta ribbons.

Clams do not have to be debearded, but they are often quite sandy and gritty. For this reason, they require a longer soak, and sometimes a bit of further coercion to ensure they give up their mouthfuls of sand before they are cooked. My mother has always sworn that sprinkling the clams with some cornmeal and then letting them soak for a half hour will cause them to release their sand and become plump and happy on the cornmeal. A last meal, as it were.

With clams you suspect of being particularly gritty, several baths may be in order—clams seem to wax and wane with grittiness, being less so in the winter and more so in the summer.

Scallops, by comparison, are a total joy to clean. Yes, they must be rinsed and brushed and checked for signs of life, but that is pretty much it. The shells themselves were a revelation for me—a tiny replica of the shell in which Botticelli's Venus chose to rise from the sea, its perfect, arching fan shape pleasing both to the eye and to the hand. The shells remind me of an Old Master's deft brushwork, shading from fawn to caramel to tawny chestnut before repeating in endless waves. It is too bad that they make me sick to my stomach.

Oyster Stew

We always serve this stew on Christmas Eve in my family, and it is perfect for a festive winter meal.

1 medium shallot, finely diced

6 tablespoons (¾ stick) unsalted butter

2 pints shucked select oysters, with their liquor

1 cup heavy cream

1 cup whole milk

Salt and freshly ground white pepper

Pinch of cayenne pepper

Dash of Worcestershire sauce

4 tablespoons crème fraîche

1 scallion, thinly sliced on the bias

Red and green hot sauce, for serving

1. In a pot, gently sauté the shallot in the butter over low heat until the shallot is soft, about 5 minutes. Add the oysters and their liquor and cook just until the edges start to shrivel. Add the cream and milk and season with salt, pepper, cayenne, and the Worcestershire. Cook just until heated through.
2. Divide the crème fraîche among four soup bowls. Fill with the oyster stew. Garnish with the scallion and a few dashes of hot sauce.

Serves 4

AN END AND A BEGINNING

This was it, our very last day in Level 1. We would be making ice cream, sorbets, frozen soufflés, floating islands, and delicate tuiles—vanilla cookies rolled into tiny cigar shapes. In other words, dessert, dessert, and more dessert. In the late afternoon we would have a lecture from our new, Level 2 chef, Chef Pierre. Then we would say good-bye to Chef Jean. Monday morning we would report to the Level 2 kitchen downstairs.

This was also the last day of our one-on-one work with our partners. Tucker and I had become such a good team, working together so seamlessly, I was really worried about who I would end up with in Level 2. During this new, intermediate level, the class would be broken into actual brigades, like the military unit, with five students in each. In these brigades, every two days we would rotate through the four different stations in the kitchen—garde-manger, *poissonnier, saucier, patissier,* and finally the dreaded family meal station. The work would be more challenging and the pressures more intense than ever. I just hoped I would survive.

There was a palpable current of nervousness running through our ranks that morning, and we twitched and whispered back and forth during Chef's last lecture on the miracle of ice cream, and how, contrary to history books, ice cream was not invented in Turkey or other hot, dry places in the Middle East, or by the Italians transporting ice from the hills and flavoring it with fruit, but by the French (surprise, surprise). As a properly brought up Virginia native, I did know that Thomas Jefferson was famous for serving the confection at Monticello, his gorgeous homestead near Charlottesville, in Virginia's Albemarle County. No doubt Jefferson brought back this enticingly cool, delicious novelty from his time spent as minister to France after the Revolutionary War. Whether or not the French truly did invent the concept of ice cream, they certainly refined it to glorious new heights. The French are credited with adding egg yolks to the cream base, creating a stable, superrich product with superior freezing capabilities and a more luxurious texture and excellent mouthfeel—commercial production food-speak for that sinfully rich, slippery feel really good ice cream makes in the mouth. Cooking this egg-milk-cream mixture yields a creamy, very thick sauce, which is actually crème anglaise. The mixture could be made into *pots de crème* or crème brûlée, or used as a sweet soufflé base. Or it could be churned into ice cream, the perfect antidote to this sultry, sad August day.

Even as we listened to Chef's last morning lecture, the whispers and note passing and general anxiety reached such a pitch that Chef paused, midsentence, to reprimand us one last time.

"*Bonjour, classe! Bonjour!* Focus on your Chef. I am still your teacher, for another few hours, at least. You will have plenty to talk about later, after Chef Pierre speaks to you."

This sounded ominous, a threat akin to the "I'll give you something to cry about!" threats I dimly remembered from childhood. I loved Chef Jean. His occasional outbursts and sarcastic comments were well worth the twinkle in his eye and broad smile when he praised the results of three hours of hot, sweaty work at the stove. I felt like I had finally learned something in the past months, despite having to start from absolute scratch and relearn the very basics, from knife techniques to making stocks to pastry, all over again, the proper way. I could also understand some of Chef's frustrations with us. At times, it seemed as if he had a classroom full of hyperactive schoolchildren, all armed with a plethora of very sharp metal objects. Was Chef Pierre going to put up with our antics? Or was he going to crack down, disciplining us harshly for every little mishap?

Despite Chef's attempts to quell us, the unrest continued unabated. Alliances were quickly being cemented between partners, and many of us were cautiously putting out feelers to other partnerships—trying to decide if we could work well with someone else, and if so, what were the odds that we would actually end up together? I was hoping and praying that I would at least get to stay with Tucker, and maybe even Imogene and her partner, Amanda, would be a good fit. Ben and his partner, Junior, who shared our kitchen island, and whose friendship we had sealed the day I stabbed Ben in the ass with my carving fork, would be ideal, but the odds were heavily stacked against us. The four of us were all obviously very close, and I had heard that the chefs tried to break up friendships when creating brigades, hoping to curtail the amount of goofing off.

Throwing up his hands in despair at our flagrantly bad behavior, Chef Jean decided that we would work as a class today, with no individual projects. I wasn't sure whether this was because we were so unfocused we couldn't be trusted with a flame or because there was only one ice cream machine, and it would have taken all day for each person to make his or her very own batch. In any case, we would be making two flavors of ice cream: plain vanilla and chocolate with caramelized almonds. I hoped I would get picked for Team Vanilla—I love the pure, rich flavor of cream, intensified with a subtle sweetness and heady hit of rich vanilla paste, peppered with tiny flecks of the bean. I had long been suspicious of ice cream with added flavors and textures. I remembered one long-ago Fourth of July when my mother made blueberry ice cream—the blueberries froze into petrified projectiles, hard enough to chip one of my baby teeth. Nothing for me would do but plain old, straitlaced, straight-up vanilla. So of course I ended up on Team Chocolate.

"Ewww, chocolate," I whined to Angelo, as all of us chocolate people clumped together at one end of the room like dregs at the bottom of a cold cup of coffee. Angelo stared at me.

"You are the only girl I know who would complain about

chocolate. It's perverted." Since *perverted* was Angelo's favorite adjective, and he used it indiscriminately to describe everything from génoise cakes to carrots to classic kitchen techniques, I wasn't sure if he was insulting me or not.

He went on, "Vanilla is so blah. So boring. It's the color of my grandmother's cotton underpants. Chocolate is dark, mysterious, a little naughty. Vanilla is for good girls. Chocolate is for bad girls. Devil's food cake is chocolate. Hell, there's a naked lady on all the boxes of Godiva's chocolates. Hello? Naked hot chick equals chocolate. So then, chocolate equals naked hot chick. Duh."

His logic was definitely perverted, but at the same time I found myself secretly wishing I was not at the moment wearing cotton underpants, and that I was that hot chick on the box of chocolates. I didn't dislike all things chocolate, just chocolate ice cream, really. It just seemed so, so . . . brown. In general, brown is not a good food color—for instance, brown bananas: not good. While we all tried to cook everything to the elusive "golden brown" shade Chef always talked about, that was really more of a wildflower honey hue. Chocolate ice cream was just plain dirt brown, and it stained everything, from fingers and faces to shirts and dresses. Maybe I didn't like it because it was unforgiving and messy. Maybe I *was* a little too straitlaced—who else in the world was worrying about whether the stain would come out in the wash when all thoughts should be occupied with the dark pleasures of chocolate?

As if reading my thoughts, Angelo looked deeply into my eyes and said, "You need to loosen up, Darling. Live more. Get that nice white chef's jacket a little dirty once in a while." Maybe he was right. Nice-girl vanilla is all well and good, but how could I appreciate it without dipping my toes in the chocolate fountain?

I quickly shelved these thoughts for closer inspection later, preferably over a glass of wine. The thought that I was as interesting as someone's grandmother's underwear was definitely too sobering to be considered while in a sober state. Chocolate was Michael's favorite flavor—maybe it was time I tried a hit of chocolate myself to spice things up. I squeezed my engagement ring, hanging from a chain around my neck to keep it safe. I still couldn't believe it—me, getting married! I couldn't spend time thinking about my relationship now, though. If I was going to have to take a walk on the dark (chocolate) side, then I would have to pay attention and learn how to do it properly.

Making chocolate ice cream is much like making regular vanilla ice cream, except for the addition of semisweet chocolate chips in the base. While the cream and milk are being heated, the chocolate is tipped in to melt. As this mixture is brought up to about 175°F, the egg yolks are whisked together with the sugar and vanilla, and beaten until the yolks are very pale in color and the mixture has almost doubled in volume. This process is known as *blanchir* (to whiten), for the yolks and sugar are properly mixed when the bright orangey color of good egg yolks has paled to a pastel yellow. Once the milk and cream have begun to steam on the stove, almost but not quite boiling, the yolk mixture is gently tempered with the hot milk. Tempering requires a steady hand and a quick whisk—the purpose is to bring the temperature of the yolks up to the temperature of the milk so that they can be mixed together and cooked further without causing the yolks to cook and curdle. A dribble of the hot milk is added to the yolks and whisked in thoroughly. Then another dribble of milk is added and the process is repeated until the yolk mixture is almost as hot as the steaming hot milk. Once this happens, the yolks may be dumped in the pot with the rest of the milk and cooked until the mixture thickens and coats the back of a spoon.

Once the mixture has hit 180°F and coats the back of a spoon nicely, it is quickly taken off the flame and strained through a fine-mesh sieve, which will catch any lurking protein clumps that may have escaped even the most assiduous stirring. Ideally, it should be strained directly into a container waiting in an ice bath. The ice bath is crucial for this because the ice cream base must be perfectly chilled before being spun in the ice cream machine, and even in an industrial freezer, it would take forever for this to happen without some help. While our chocolate base chilled in its ice bath, we began to make the caramelized almonds.

Making caramel is another process that seemed like alchemy to me before chef school. Like making ice cream, I didn't understand how necessary some steps are to ensuring the delicious taste and texture of the final product. While I had been making ice cream on my own for years, rarely would I go to the trouble of properly tempering my yolks before adding them to my milk. I also skipped chilling the base down thoroughly before churning, the result being that my ice cream was grainy—filled with tiny ice crystals that crunched against the teeth and left a strangely empty taste on the tongue. Now I understood that some steps shouldn't be skipped, and some things in the kitchen couldn't be made to rush. Making caramel is very simple, but like making ice cream, attention must be paid, and all the steps must be followed. Chef school was teaching me these steps, but more important, it was teaching me patience. My old habit of rushing through recipes, taking shortcuts whenever possible, began to melt away as I understood that there was a reason for every single step, and that the final product would taste infinitely better if I spent the time to do everything properly, with care. My cooking in Level 1 had improved tremendously in spite of all my fears and uncertainties, and I even mastered caramel. Eventually.

According to Chef, making caramel was easy: Put sugar in a pot. Add enough water to make the sugar like damp sand. Heat. Use a pastry brush to swab down the sides of the pan occasionally with fresh water. Cook until golden brown. To stop the cooking, dip the bottom of the pan into an ice bath. Simple. As I stared down at my small simmering cauldron of sugar water, I felt the familiar urge to rush things bubbling up inside me. Nothing seemed to be happening. I was terrified to turn the flame up higher, but I was sure I was doing something wrong. Where was the golden color? Why wasn't it working?

"Chef!" I called, unable to hold myself back a moment longer. "Chef, something's wrong with my caramel!" Chef Jean dashed over, the thought of burnt caramel, the same temperature and smell of boiling road tar, uppermost in his mind. We regarded my pot of merrily boiling sugar water in silence for a moment.

"Why isn't it working?" I said, trying to keep the sharp edge of frustration, keener than a knife's blade, from my voice.

Chef Jean checked the flame, swabbed down the sides of the pan with cool water, and finally turned to me. His glasses flashed as he shook his head slowly from side to side. I started to squirm, wishing I hadn't called attention to myself, that this last day with Chef Jean would be full of praise, not remonstrations.

"You want everything to go well, to be perfect. Life isn't like that, you know. Fixing your mistakes is an important skill to learn. So is patience. There is nothing wrong with your caramel. Watch, and wait for it. Some things just can't be rushed. See?" Chef showed me the light brown color suddenly fanning out through the boiling sugar.

I rushed to grab the pot off the heat, but Chef slapped my hand away. *"Attends,"* he said. "Just wait."

The sugar became browner and browner, and I was beginning to panic. It was going to burn! I was never going to learn to do this properly! Then, just when I was beginning to vibrate with impatience, Chef said, "Smell."

I took a big whiff, and could smell the sugar just going from lily-sweet to being tinged ever so slightly with the pleasantly acrid scent of burning leaves. "Now!" shouted Chef, and I plunged the pot of caramel into the ice water bath, stopping the cooking instantly. The caramel was a gorgeous, mahogany brown, like a perfectly broken-in, vintage leather handbag. I added a big handful of slivered almonds, and poured it all out onto a greased sheet pan to cool.

We each added a bit of our almond toffee to the chilled chocolate base, and got ready to spin the whole thing in the big, industrial-grade ice cream machine. This was nothing like the hand-crank model I remembered churning as a child. Instead of making ice cream in an hour, this stainless steel beauty would make it in less than ten minutes. There were no sore arm muscles from all that cranking, but there was no ice cream–coated dasher to lick at the end of the process, either. Some part of me scorned the modern convenience of it, and my Catholic-tinged soul whispered, "It won't taste nearly as good if you didn't suffer for it."

We would just see about that. In it went, and seven minutes later, out came beautifully smooth, dark chocolate ice cream. It would need to go in the freezer for a few minutes to firm up a bit, and then we would have ice cream—chocolate and vanilla—for lunch.

While we waited, Chef announced our new teams for Level 2. Against all odds, Tucker and I were still together. We were also with Ben and Junior. We were also the only team short a person—the other four brigades all had a full complement of five students. This meant that we would have to do a bit of a scramble to keep up with each day's tasks, but I felt a sense of pride and accomplishment—Chef Jean thought we could handle it. We wouldn't let him down! We were all busily discussing our new alliances, the noise of conversation threatening to sweep us away in one giant wave of excitement and anticipation, when the door to the classroom flew open. There he was, silhouetted for a moment against the gleam of stainless steel pots and pans before marching to the head of the class, an impressive paunch (the sure sign of a true seasoned chef) leading the way. Chef Pierre was here to give us our lecture on the next level. Conversation immediately dried up like a kitchen sponge in the broiler. We fled to one end of the classroom—there was a bit of a skirmish as we all tried to stand as far away from the head of the class as possible. Chef Jean made the introductions and then retired to the back of the room with a spoon to check on the ice cream.

Our first encounter with Chef Pierre began with a bang—he

clapped his massive, much scarred hands together and grinned down
on us. I noticed he seemed to be missing some important teeth.
Maybe his bark would be worse than his bite. Maybe not. He
seemed to have only one volume—full blast. As he shouted at us,
telling us that we were in for a very challenging few months, I could
see my fellow classmates staring at him, completely mystified. Chef
Pierre's French accent was so thick, no one could understand a word
of what he was saying. I thanked my lucky stars I had taken all those
years of French classes—I was able to decipher every third or fourth
word. Perhaps he was just trying to put the fear of God into us, I
thought, as Chef Pierre graphically detailed exactly what he would
do to us if we misbehaved. It involved lots of knives and disembow-
elment, I think. At least, that was what his sweeping hand gestures
seemed to indicate. Who needs teeth when you're that good with a
knife? He finished threatening us and stood back, his hands folded
over his stomach, which was straining at the buttons on his chef's
jacket, seemingly satisfied with the reaction his indiscernible and
somewhat spittle-flecked tirade had induced. He looked like a fire
hydrant in checked pants, and seemed as tough as pig iron. I was
terrified. I think we all were.

Chef Jean thanked Chef Pierre and as our new professor swept
magisterially out of the classroom, we returned to our lesson on ice
cream. Everyone was dealt a scoop of each flavor. I tasted the vanilla.
It was delicious—smooth and creamy. But a little, well, blah. I tasted
the chocolate caramel almond. A rush of dark chocolate flavor was
punctuated with the bittersweet crunch of caramel, smoothed with
the almost floral flavor of the almond slivers. It was definitely complex, almost too much for my virginal palate to handle. But what
was that elusive flavor undercutting the heavenly chocolate? A definite tang, a slightly bitter bite lurking somewhere in the toffee clus-
ters. Then I realized: it was fear. Fear of the trials and tribulations
waiting for us in the new level, fear that I was still just beginning to
learn the proper way of doing things. Fear that I was secretly a very

boring person who was clinging to habits (and vanilla ice cream) instead of trying new things. I felt unprepared for the next chapter in chef school, and for the next chapter in my own life. What would happen? I thought about what Chef had told me about making caramel—have patience, let things happen. It was good advice, and as I licked the last bit of ice cream from my spoon, I decided to follow it.

Vanilla Ice Cream

This is a basic ice cream base that makes delicious plain vanilla ice cream. It can also easily be altered to make a myriad of variations, from strawberry to chocolate, with the addition of a cup or so of the desired flavoring.

8 egg yolks

2 cups sugar

2 cups whole milk

2 cups heavy cream

1½ teaspoons pure vanilla extract

1½ teaspoons vanilla paste

1. In a bowl, whisk together the egg yolks and sugar until the mixture is a very pale yellow and the sugar is well dissolved. The mixture will come close to doubling in volume.
2. Heat the milk and cream in a large pot over low heat. Add the vanilla extract and paste and stir gently, to ensure the mixture does not burn on the bottom. Once the mixture begins to steam, remove it from the heat.
3. Working quickly, add a scant ladle of the hot milk mixture to the egg yolks, whisking briskly. Once this has been incorporated, add another ladleful, again whisking briskly. The yolk mixture should get gradually warmer without cooking the yolks. Keep adding ladlefuls of the hot milk to the eggs, whisking all the while, until the yolk mixture is hot.
4. Add the yolk mixture back to the milk mixture and heat gently, stirring with a wooden spoon, until the temperature reaches 180°F, just a breath away from a boil. Immediately remove the mixture from the heat and strain it through a fine-mesh sieve into a stainless steel bowl placed in an ice water bath. Chill.

5. Follow the directions for your ice cream machine. Once the mixture has been spun, remove it from the machine, pack into a covered container, and freeze to firm and ripen for a few hours.

For chocolate ice cream:

I prefer a one-two punch of chocolate flavor—if you're going to have chocolate, make it CHOCOLATE! I sift 1 cup of unsweetened cocoa powder into the 2 cups of sugar, and add 8 ounces of chopped semisweet chocolate to the milk and cream to melt. This makes a deep, dark chocolate ice cream that should satisfy even the most fervent chocoholic.

LEVEL 2

STABBED IN THE BACK

At this point in my chef training, I understood the importance of the tools we used in class every day. The strainers, the Robot Coupe, the pots and sauté pans were all integral to our preparations, but most important to our work was our battery of chef's knives. Intimidating in their wicked sharpness and seemingly monstrous size on that very first day of class, our personal arsenal of weaponry had quickly become a constant companion. We had all received identical knife kits at the start of our studies, complete with chef's knife, carving knife, fillet knife, vegetable peeler, paring knife, and an extremely vicious blade almost fifteen inches long called "The Slicer," like the title of a low-budget horror film, in which it could easily star. Months of daily use and regular sharpening had given each knife a unique appearance, one immediately identifiable to its owner. I could tell the difference between my paring knife and Tucker's from across the kitchen. While Chef Jean had cautioned us to clearly mark our knives, by engraving them or marking the handles with distinctive electrical tape, it hardly seemed necessary, though we all chose different colors and wrapped the handles of our blades accordingly. Who would confuse my already battered chef's knife with its distinctive burr halfway down the blade with their own? In a school where everyone was identically equipped, who would want to steal my knives?

Of course, I was wrong.

Before we could begin our servitude in Level 2 under the watchful eye of Chef Pierre, the current Level 2 students would have to take their midterm exam in the kitchens. So, on our first day of Level 2, we were not faced with the scowling visage of Chef Pierre at all. Some of us were to hear a lecture on food costing and some of us were to help out with the preparation and support for the Level 2 midterm. I eagerly volunteered for the latter, not only to get out of what was sure to be a really boring lecture, but also to get an idea of what the midterm would be like. We had a whole new level to master before we would be taking the exam, but every day had gone by so quickly in Level 1, I knew our own midterm would be here before we knew it.

We spent the early morning preparing the classroom, setting out trays of ingredients for each student and checking and rechecking that everything they might need, from kosher salt to fresh herbs to extra pots and pans, was on hand in the room, ready for use. When the Level 2 students finally trooped in to take their practical, all of them nervous and pale, we stayed in the corners of the room, scuttling out to fetch things only when asked by the chef-observers, who lurked around the class like malevolent hot-air balloons.

While we didn't really do very much work, certainly not as much as we were used to, the tension of the Level 2 students had worn off on us, and we were all exhausted from the nervous strain. When at last the exam was finished and we returned to the locker room to change into street clothes at the end of the day, I was not very alert.

Absently I hung my chef's whites on their hook in my locker, returned my red toolbox to its cubby hole, and neatly folded my neckerchief and my paper chef's hat, ready for tomorrow. I even gave the food-splattered toes of my Docs a polish, ready to make a good impression on Chef Pierre. As I gazed into my locker before shutting and locking it, it seemed that something was out of place. But what was it? My uniform was there, my toolbox was in its proper place, its sundry cooking utensils neatly organized. My notebook and new textbook were stacked on the floor of the locker, waiting for the next day. I looked around me, to see if I had forgotten something, but in the crowded confines of the tiny locker room, with almost a hundred students in various states of undress, the floor was a churning vortex of bags, shoes, and sweaty cast-off clothing. None of it seemed to be mine, so, shrugging to myself, I locked my locker and made my way to Toad Hall to meet my new teammates for a beer.

It was only after Tucker had been discussing the new Santoku knife he was hoping to purchase that I realized what was missing. My knife kit! I had forgotten to put my knife kit in my locker! But where was it? I hadn't seen it on the floor when I was leaving, and I certainly hadn't left it in the exam classroom. With a mumbled apology to Tucker, Junior, and Ben, I flew back to school to see if I could track down my missing knives. I had the stomach-churning feeling that something terrible had happened. Sure enough, as I stared at the barren locker room, I knew: my knives were missing. Despite scouring the entire school, from the pastry classrooms to the supply closets, I couldn't find a trace of them, not even the black polyester knife roll they were stored in. What was I going to do?

I trudged home and investigated my knife block, looking for suitable replacements. Suddenly, the knives I had been happily using at home for years weren't going to cut it anymore, literally. While they were perfectly decent, serviceable blades, they lacked the keen edge and beefy heft of the pro models I was using in school. There was no way I could show up at school with my wimpy six-inch chef's knife and try to pass it off—Chef Pierre would spot it right away. I couldn't show up without any knives, either. Coming to class without the proper uniform or equipment was cause for suspension. I didn't know what I was going to do.

Despite Michael's assurances that things had a way of working out, I tossed and turned that night, unable to sleep, worrying about what had happened to my precious knives. I was convinced that someone had taken them, but claiming that they had been stolen would be of little help in the morning. When I finally did drop off to sleep, it was to dream endlessly about being chased down the hallways and stairwells of the school, dropping piece after piece of my *batterie de cuisine* as I fled.

The next morning, I told Imogene and the other girls about the missing knife kit. Imo was outraged, but I was defeated. My knives were lost and gone forever, and there was nothing I could do about it. My only hope of avoiding punishment in class was to try to find another set of knives. I wearily put on my uniform and trudged downstairs, feeling the missing weight of the knife bag where it should have been slung over my right shoulder, banging against my hip. I found Chef Jean by the coffee urn and confided my troubles to him. Somehow, during the trials and tribulations of Level 1, Chef Jean had become my friend, and I often asked his advice about everything from what to stock my home kitchen with to how to brine a turkey to where to find a good conversational French class. As I told him the tale of my missing knives, his already long Gallic face became even longer.

"Ooh la la," he clucked, making that distinctive clicking noise of disapproval unique to the French palate. Chef Jean said that my knives had definitely been stolen, and they were indeed gone for good. It happened every time there was a midterm or final—some student who was missing their own tools simply swiped someone else's to take the test, and then kept them afterward for use in their kitchen career post-school. Chefs, it seemed, were an inherently amoral lot. The realization that someone I knew—and who had probably seen me naked in the locker room—had stolen from me was very sobering. I thought we were all, well, if not friends, then at least good acquaintances. I would have lent my things to anyone who asked for them, but now I wasn't so sure.

Chef Jean patted my shoulder with one of his large, surprisingly gentle hands. *"Vous êtes désolée, ma chérie."*

I was indeed very sad—desolated, in Chef's words. But there was no room in the kitchen for self-pity, and I needed knives right now, not sympathy. Chef Jean, of course, also had some good advice. He directed me to the storeroom, repository for all things sought after in school, from lettuce and eggs to saffron, truffles, and pasta

machines. They might have an extra knife kit left over from an orientation, Chef thought, but I would have to pay for it. At this point,
with only a few minutes before Level 2 was set to begin, I would
have gladly handed over my firstborn child to the guys in the storeroom for a new set of knives.

I hustled to the storeroom window and told my tale of loss once
again to the sympathetic ears of David. David was definitely one
of those guys who "could get things," be it lobsters or otherwise. In
addition to running the storeroom for the school, tales surfaced that
David had a very healthy relationship with various dubious orga-
nizations and black marketeers, and could put his hands on practically any sort of illicit merchandise you could imagine. Despite this
somewhat shady reputation, David was a real sweetheart, joking and
flirting with all of us students, even throwing a game of darts with
us in Toad Hall sometimes. David nodded sagely when I wound up
my story and asked him if he happened to have any spare knife kits
hidden away.

"*Sí, señorita.* I do have a knife kit left over here somewhere, but I
can't give it to you without some major *dinero.*" David shrugged his
massive shoulders sadly. What could he do? Rules are rules.

To say that I was running low on funds would be an understatement. My bank account was hovering on the brink of being over-
drawn, but I needed those knives *right now.* Taking a deep breath,
I asked how much it would take to get some new knives pronto,
knowing that I was about to be put over the barrel.

"Two fifty," said David, with a small shrug of apology. Two hundred and fifty dollars would take every last dollar I had left to my
name, but I didn't have a choice. I wrote out a check and received
my new set of knives.

The new knives felt cold and unfamiliar in my hands as I began
to work with them, but soon they began to take on the battered and
scarred appearance of my previous set of cutlery and were well on
their way to becoming old friends. I kept my new blades under lock

and key, and never let them out of my sight, let alone lent them out. No one touched my blades but me. The old kitchen dictum that no one touches a chef's knife but its owner suddenly made sense, and the punishment for disobeying that rule, a nasty cut from the rightful owner, now seemed a just and fitting punishment.

I hoped that my old set of knives, wherever they were, had cut their new owner good.

CHOUX GOT WHAT I NEED

Tucker, Junior, Ben, and I began our Level 2 efforts in the pastry kitchen. What could be better? With a choice of caramel custards, fruit tarts, chocolate-raspberry ganache cake, lemon tart, apple tart, a classic génoise cake with crème anglaise, or profiteroles with warm chocolate sauce, I thought I had died and gone to heaven. Not only could I sample these mouthwatering desserts during their creation, I would also be able to eat any of the leftovers. Level 2 might not be so bad after all.

All Level 2 students would be making their dishes for the chefs and deans to taste and critique at the chefs' table, a long banquet-style affair set with snowy white linen, crystal, and silver, nicely tucked away in a quiet alcove of the restaurant's dining room. There they would be waited on by the members of my class as they were served a fulsome meal including appetizer, fish course, main course, salad, and dessert. In addition to the fine tableware, the table was also set with pens and pads of paper, on which the chefs recorded their impressions of each dish, complete with a letter grade. These critiques would be collected at the end of the meal and given to Chef Pierre, who would then read them aloud to the class assembled for our lecture, which at this level came not first thing in the morning, but after lunch. As part of the lecture, an example of each dish prepared by each brigade would be plated and arranged on the marble of the pastry station. After all the critiques had been read, the class was allowed to sample the example to see what, exactly, the chefs were complaining about. The only exception was the poor, overworked brigade handling the family meal, that frantic team trying to churn out lunch for the two hundred students and staff in the school. They were exempt from the often stinging commentary the chefs slung at our best efforts.

Tucker, Ben, Junior, and I argued about what dessert we should prepare for the chefs on our first attempt at the Level 2 pastry recipes. After a brief skirmish, we decided to tackle the *choux* puffs with warm chocolate sauce. Tucker thought that making the *choux,* the little round balls of puffed dough, in a uniform manner would be beyond our piping skills, but I argued that everyone loves a good cream puff, and the warm chocolate sauce was sure to win over the chefs.

While we had learned to make the *choux* dough in Level 1, it was merely part of a larger introduction to the many different types of pastry dough and not an intensive *choux* learning experience. *Choux* dough is made with flour, butter, whole eggs, and water. Added salt makes it ideal for a savory concoction, while the addition of sugar instead makes it a perfect dessert. The butter and water are cooked gently in a small pot over low heat until the butter melts and the mixture begins to simmer. Then the flour is added all at once, in a great dusty pile. Using a wooden spoon, the mixture is then stirred, hard, to remove any lurking lumps and coerce everything together in a smooth paste. The paste is then cooked until it is dry and forms a cohesive clump. The pot is then removed from the heat and the eggs are added, one by one. There is no set number of eggs to be added— the number varies from three to as many as six, depending on how well the paste has been cooked, how humid the day is, and how big and fresh the eggs are. It is advisable to proceed slowly, cracking one egg at a time and mixing each egg very well with the wooden spoon after its addition. The dough is ready to be piped when a trench dug through the middle of the dough (good chefs use their fingers to dig the trench, the better to taste the dough as one goes along) fills in, but slowly. There's no very precise measure, but it's one of those things that once you see, you learn to recognize and repeat. This was often the case in chef school—preparing the same recipes in the curriculum over and over and over again would teach us to recognize the proper look and feel of the food we were making, more than merely learning the recipe.

Once the dough is formed, it is transferred to a piping bag with a large tip and piped onto sheet pans covered with parchment paper. The trick to piping even circles is one of practice and mastery of a whole-body motion, a modified crouch garnished with an arm swirl and wrist flick that would take thousands of choux to master. The choux are then baked in the oven until puffed and golden brown. The water and the moisture content in the eggs turns to steam, which causes the dough to puff up, making an air pocket inside that is a perfect nest for a delicious morsel or two.

At least, this is what is supposed to happen. More than one team in Level 1 had turned out something that looked more like pancakes than golden spheres. Lack of puff can mean that the eggs were too old to work with, or that the moisture had already evaporated from the dough before it went into the oven, or that too much moisture was added with the inclusion of too many eggs and the dough was too heavy to rise. There are lots of pitfalls on the road to perfect pastry. I was confident that my team, with Tucker, who was a stickler for following direction, and Ben, who quietly and methodically produced gorgeously plated food, would be equal to the challenge.

Junior, the fourth member of our little crew, was certainly proficient enough in the sauté and vegetable-cutting departments, but too often I noticed that his mind would wander, and he would lose focus, right in the middle of preparing a recipe. At the age of eighteen, Junior was fresh out of high school, and his youth was evident in everything he did. But he was so good-natured about everything, always grinning even when he set his pan on fire, we couldn't be angry with him even if he was constantly a half step behind the rest of us. The nickname of Junior, itself an allusion to his age and his innocence, stuck to him like glue. Junior would need a bit of supervision to keep him on course, but on the whole, I really felt like we were the A-Team and could handle whatever criticism the chefs felt like dishing out. Okay, maybe I secretly saw myself as Mr. T, the ass-kicking, take-no-prisoners leader of our crew. A mohawked angry black dude I am not, but I pitied the fool who underestimated my team's abilities.

With no morning lecture to start our day now, we simply began cooking when everyone had assembled. Chef Pierre didn't even call roll, just stalked among the bent heads of the brigades, mentally tallying up those present. We had memorized the ingredients and the procedure for our chosen recipe, but each of us had copied down the important bits on an index card that we kept tucked into our jacket pocket for quick reference. These index cards were required in class for all the levels, part of our daily homework assignments. By the end of Level 1, though, few people in class bothered with the cards, as Chef Jean had long ago stopped checking up on us. But Tucker had insisted we come to our first class well prepared for anything Chef Pierre might ask, and so we were ready. Good thing we were, too. Suddenly, out of nowhere, Chef Pierre was looming in the pastry kitchen, arms folded over his belly as they had been after he had delivered his first lecture to us, tall chef's hat already slightly askew from his morning's exertions—no doubt of yelling at the other teams in the main kitchen.

I whispered quickly to my teammates: "Eyes down! Watch what you're doing!" We all immediately tried to look even busier than we already were, weighing out butter, measuring flour, organizing pots, pans, and bowls, and generally getting in each other's way.

I tried not to make eye contact with Chef, but I could feel his stare boring into each of us in turn—it felt like my back was on fire, and I kept messing up the scale, my shaking hands unable to set the weights to zero before adding the flour. Finally, I looked up to meet his eyes, blurry behind the incredibly thick glasses he wore—forget Coke bottles, these were more like the reinforced glass on the bottom of champagne bottles.

"Oh, hi," Chef said, super casual. It was obviously a trap. We didn't fall for it.

"Good morning, Chef!" the four of us chorused in perfect unison, as if we'd spent hours practicing.

"Oh, such obedience. Not at all what I'd heard about you four from Assistant Chef Cyndee."

Somehow this didn't surprise me. To everyone's chagrin, Cyndee had been promoted from a Level 1 assistant to a Level 2 assistant, and had moved with us to the kitchens downstairs, just when we thought we had escaped the sneers, snide comments, and that horrible, ringing guffaw. It really wasn't fair that she had told Chef Pierre we were less than stellar, but nothing about Cyndee was fair. I made a mental note to clean up Junior a little bit and feed him to the voracious Cyndee like a hunk of man meat. Nothing made Cyndee happier than having a guy flirt with her, and even though she was distinctly less than gorgeous, with her flaccid lips, protuberant eyes, and mud-colored irises, to say nothing of the truly enormous contours of her lower half—her ass was a cautionary tale of what could happen to someone who spent all their time in the kitchen—I thought I could convince Junior to take one for the team. Despite his endless braggadocio about his stud-muffin status back in his rural Maine high school, we all knew that poor Junior was still a virgin. He was pathetically eager to dissuade everyone on this point, and would do anything (or anyone) to prove his prowess to us.

However, there was a more pressing situation to deal with, and I was forced to shelve my plans to pimp out my teammate for the moment. Chef Pierre was still looming uncomfortably large in the pastry kitchen. Now we would have to try especially hard to convince him that whatever he had heard from Assistant Chef Cyndee, it wasn't true. In fact, I was determined to prove that we were the very best brigade ever to storm the Level 2 kitchens. But it was going to be uphill work, and it looked like we were already losing ground.

Suddenly Chef barked "CARDS!" For a moment, I just stood

there, puzzled, and then I remembered the index cards we had written the recipe on. We all yanked our cards out and held them out for Chef's inspection.

"Good, good," he said, not even bothering to scrutinize them. "Now, get going! What are you standing around here for? Go. Go, GO!"

With that bellow ringing in our ears, we galvanized for action. In record time we were fully prepared for our recipe, the ingredients marshaled together in orderly rows like soldiers, while we stood at attention at the stove. Tucker prepared the sheet trays, Ben was in position to cook the *choux* paste, Junior ran the dirty dishes to the dishwashers, and I manned the piping bag, ready to lock and load. We were wheels up, and Operation Cream Puff was a definite go.

Ben was the man in charge of the recipe. We had decided to take turns bossing one another around so that we wouldn't fall victim to the infighting and backbiting that often destroyed the unity of other teams. It is true: too many cooks *do* spoil the soup! Only by working together, as one unit, could we hope to make it through the difficulties of this new level. It was also true that a good team needed a strong leader to call the shots and make difficult decisions in tough situations—a scenario that came up more often than not in the battlefield of the kitchen.

Each of us—Ben, Tucker, Junior, and I—had our strengths and weaknesses. Junior had great knife skills, Tucker was great at "the big picture"—getting us from the recipe on the page to the food on the plate—and Ben was excellent with the small details, making him a natural in the pastry department. Unlike other stations, where cooking is an inexact science full of pinches of this and dashes of that, pastry is the realm of precise measurements. I wasn't really sure what I brought to the team—sure, my knife skills were pretty good, and I was a stickler for the little details, but other than a flair for seasoning and a really competitive drive to get things done, and get them done well, I wasn't sure what I was bringing to the table.

But the fast pace of our new level didn't leave me any time to brood about things. We needed to start the recipe, pronto. Ben added the water and butter to his pan and brought it to a boil. Junior stood by, handing each ingredient to Ben as it was needed. When Ben barked out, "Wooden spoon, pronto!" like a surgeon requesting a surgical implement, it was slapped into his hand with all the swiftness and panache of an ER nurse with twenty years on the job. But when Ben requested, "Flour, sifted, NOW," his hand outstretched, his attention still on the stove, things came to a screeching halt. We hadn't sifted the flour, because none of us had a sifter. The large drum sifters were locked away in the Level 3 and 4 pastry kitchen next door, and would have been too unwieldy for use anyway. What we needed was a small, round-bottomed sieve that could easily fit in our toolboxes. Unfortunately, we didn't have one. We stood, looking at each other for a moment as the butter and water bubbled over on the stove.

"Shit." Once again we had spoken simultaneously, in this way, if in no other, a well-oiled machine. We got out a fresh pan, and fresh ingredients, and started over again, this time with Tucker manning the stove. Butter, water, salt, sugar came to a swift boil, and this time, without a word, Tucker tipped the contents of the measuring cup full of unsifted flour into the pan, and continued to cook furiously. The paste thickened and began to clump together. Tucker whisked it off the flame and began breaking eggs into the dough, stirring with all his might, muscles cording and standing out on his forearms and a fine mist of sweat breaking out on his brow. Four eggs in, the dough had begun to take on a glossy look and was slower to incorporate the eggs—we were almost there. After the fifth egg, we took turns drawing our fingers through the dough to see if it was the right texture and taste.

I have never been a big fan of raw dough, refusing to even nibble the sugar-coated scraps left over from an apple pie, but in my determination to broaden my palate, I took a big swoop through the warm dough with my freshly washed finger, and gingerly crammed it in my mouth. It was good, really good, more like a hot cereal than chilly pastry dough. It had none of that raw mealiness of uncooked flour, only smooth, slightly sweet, buttery paste, made subtly richer with all those bright orange egg yolks. So far, so tasty.

Choux dough must be shaped and baked while it is still warm, so we lost no time loading up a couple of pastry bags with the warm mixture and began piping little blobs onto the waiting sheet pans. Ben and I each began to pipe our circles on different ends of the pan, and when we met in the middle, we realized we had a problem. We hadn't coordinated the size before we began, and now half the *choux* were about an inch big, and half were almost three inches! Another communication snafu.

Regardless, we put the first pan in the oven and began on the second pan, this time agreeing to make the *choux* about an inch big, hoping that this compromise was the right size. We had used up all the dough and were tidying up our station while the *choux* puffed up and turned golden brown in the oven when we received our second visit from Chef Pierre. He definitely had a more laissez-faire style than Chef Jean—*he* would have been at our shoulders the whole time, gently correcting and critiquing as each step was accomplished. Half the morning had gone by, we had completed most of our dish, and we still hadn't gotten any feedback from Chef. Interesting. Maybe we were doing everything right. Yes, and maybe the pork terrines prepared by the garde-manger students could fly.

Sure enough, when Chef looked in on the *choux* rising merrily in the convection oven, he barked out the traditional French exclamation of disgust. *"Merde!"* he spat, and turned on us, the short brown hair peeking out from his tall chef's toque seeming to bristle like a dog's before it attacks.

"Who piped those?" Chef barked. Somehow, I knew it would be all my fault. "They are too big and too small. How did you manage to do that? Not one of those is the correct size! Do it again, and come get me when you are ready to pipe and I will show you how to do it correctly."

Okay. Fine. Hopefully, the third time would be the charm for cream puffs. We began all over again. This time it was my turn to make the dough. As I stirred the melting butter and water, adding the flour in a great dusty cloud, I was suddenly taken back to a long-ago summer afternoon in Virginia. To combat the late-summer doldrums of school vacation, my mother plopped my recalcitrant, bored, eight-year-old self down in front of her extensive cookbook collection. If I was quiet as a mouse while the grown-ups rested during the heat of the afternoon under the soothing swoosh of the ceiling fan, I could choose a recipe from the many books to make with her for the evening's dessert. I spent the afternoon reverently paging through the hundreds of cookbooks, many of them beginning to crumble with age and the inevitable mildew of humid Virginia summers, spotted with grease, spider-webbed with notes in an old-fashioned cursive—the only remnants of long-ago cooks in my family whom I would never know, whose names would be remembered only on the flyleaves of these much-thumbed volumes.

Despite the appeal of these volumes, with the exotic smell of great age wafting from every yellowed page, and with their mystical names of recipes, like Hoppin' John, Yum Yum Pie, and Hummingbird Cake, I found myself drawn to the severe line drawings and exotic ingredients of Julia Child's *Mastering the Art of French Cooking*, Volumes I and II. I was entranced by the luscious depiction of *pâté en croûte*, shivered at the cold-blooded descriptions of how to debone a chicken, and practiced the elegant motions of fluting mushroom caps with a paring knife stealthily purloined from a kitchen drawer.

I chose her recipe for *croquembouche*—a towering confection made from many piped *choux* filled with whipped cream and stacked in a large pyramid, glued together with caramel and dusted with confectioners' sugar. Knowing the mortally sticky nature of caramel on a thunderstorm afternoon in August, my mother suggested a slight alteration to my vision. We made one enormous cream puff—a giant ring of *choux* dough that we baked in the oven, split, filled with vanilla ice cream, and topped with a bittersweet chocolate sauce made in a tiny battered yellow enamel pot with a tin of sweetened condensed milk and big blocks of unsweetened chocolate from the pantry.

We ate it on the porch, after dinner, while we watched a great, gray-black storm tumble down the steep slopes of the Blue Ridge Mountains to settle, with great drumrolls of thunder, in the woods, on the dusty cornfields, and in our little garden. The rain still pounded our copper roof when Eben and I were sent up to bed, and for the first time, as I snuggled into the cool sheets and smelled the wet, fertile smell of the drenched fields drifting in through the window screens, I felt the deep satisfaction of creating something that my family enjoyed. I included Julia Child in my childish prayers, and felt the first scratchy inclinations of my life's passion.

In no time, it seemed, I had finished mixing the *choux* dough and we once again had a warm batch in the pastry bags and ready to go. We sent Junior off to find Chef Pierre, so that we could get these in the oven—suddenly, it was almost eleven o'clock. The *choux* would need a half hour in the oven to bake and another half hour to cool. We would have to have the desserts plated and on the chefs' table at 12:24 precisely, and we were running out of time.

Chef Pierre came bursting in, flexing his wrists and making piping motions with his hands, warming up for the demonstration. He grabbed the bag from Ben's grasp and began churning out absolutely perfect little orbs of dough at a lightning speed. "Watch and learn," he said over his shoulder, piping out several perfect little *choux* without even looking. Was that a teeny tiny grin on his face? Nah, couldn't be. Distinguished chef-instructors didn't grin. In no time at all, he had cranked out an entire tray of *choux* and slammed them into the oven. He made one more on a new sheet pan as an example and then let us try our hands at it once again. None of ours looked quite as good as his, but we were definitely getting better.

At last the *choux* were baked and drying in the gentle heat on top of the ovens. Without this "dry time" any steam still trapped inside the *choux* would condense back into water again and instead of possessing ethereal lightness, the interior would be a chewy, soggy mess. While they dried, we made chocolate sauce, really just equal parts heavy cream and semisweet chocolate heated together; and *crème Chantilly,* whipped cream. Whipped cream was always to be made by hand, with a large balloon whisk over a bowl of ice. This way, we students would learn precisely when the cream had reached the peak of fluffy lightness before it became overwhipped and formed tiny granules of butter.

Though it took merely seconds to make, we always grumbled at this process—we all knew how to make whipped cream! But Chef was immovable on this point, and eventually showed us why. While the whipped cream he made in a standing mixer was perfectly adequate, somehow it lacked the delicate lightness of the hand-whipped version. Forget using those neat stainless steel canisters with the cartridges of nitrous oxide to make instant whipped cream. Those had been outlawed by the school years ago—the students were stealing the gas cartridges and huffing them in the walk-in refrigerator. The parting words from Chef Jean as we stood over my caramel wafted back to me: good things are worth the time put into them, and sometimes perfection can't be rushed.

But it was already 12:22, and Chef was waving his arms frantically at us from the other end of the kitchen, summoning us and our trays of dessert into the dining room for service. Tucker moved with lightning speed, and while I frantically sawed open *choux,* he filled them with the vanilla-spiked whipped cream. Ben plated them and added the perfect dusting of confectioners' sugar to their tops, and Junior filled the little silver serving pots with rich, dark, hot chocolate sauce. We ran through the big kitchen, trays held high overhead, and dashed through the swinging doors and into the dining room. Covered with sweat, confectioners' sugar, and trails of chocolate sauce, we didn't present quite the polished façade I was hoping for, but it was 12:24 on the nose as we began to clear away the salad plates and replace them with our cream puffs. We'd made it.

As we returned to the kitchen, depositing the empty dessert plates, silverware, water goblets, and accrued detritus with the dishwashers, I couldn't help but feel flushed with triumph. While our first effort in the Level 2 kitchen had not gone without a hitch, at least it *had* gone. Chef Pierre was actually grinning when he saw us, exhausted by our efforts, collecting our well-earned lunch from our compatriots running the family meal.

"Not bad," he said. "But wait until tomorrow. You will have to make two desserts for the chefs from now on."

Two desserts? I almost impaled myself on my knife.

Spiced Choux with Calvados Ice Cream, Apple Compote, and Caramel Sauce

For the Calvados ice cream:

8 egg yolks

2 cups granulated sugar

2 cups whole milk

2 cups heavy cream

1½ teaspoons pure vanilla extract

1½ teaspoons vanilla paste

½ cup best-quality Calvados

For the *choux:*

4 tablespoons (½ stick) unsalted butter

½ cup water

¾ cup all-purpose flour

2 tablespoons granulated sugar

Pinch of salt

½ teaspoon ground cinnamon

Pinch of ground cloves

Pinch of ground cardamom

3 or 4 eggs

For the egg wash:

1 egg yolk

1 tablespoon heavy cream

Pinch of salt

For the apple compote:

4 apples (see Notes)

¼ cup water

½ cup light brown sugar, or a bit more or less (see Notes)

1 teaspoon ground cinnamon

¼ teaspoon ground cloves

⅛ teaspoon ground cardamom

For the caramel sauce:

1 cup granulated sugar

2 tablespoons Calvados

½ cup heavy cream

Confectioners' sugar, for garnish

1. To make the ice cream: In a bowl, whisk together the egg yolks and sugar until the mixture is a very pale yellow.
2. Heat the milk and cream in a large pot over low heat. Stir in the vanilla extract and paste and the Calvados. Once the mixture begins to steam, remove it from the heat.
3. Temper the yolks and sugar with the hot cream and milk. Add the tempered mixture back to the milk and heat gently, stirring with a wooden spoon, until the temperature reaches 180°F. Strain through a fine-mesh sieve into a stainless steel bowl placed in an ice water bath. Chill.
4. Follow the directions for your ice cream machine. Once the mixture has been spun, remove it from the machine, pack into a covered container, and freeze to firm and ripen for a few hours.
5. To make the *choux:* Preheat the oven to 400°F. Cover a sheet pan with parchment paper.

6. In a small saucepan over medium heat, bring the butter and the water to a boil. Add the flour, sugar, salt, cinnamon, cloves, and cardamom all at once. Stir vigorously with a wooden spoon until the mixture is well combined. Continue to stir over medium heat until the mixture is smooth and dry.

7. Remove from the heat and quickly stir in 1 egg, making certain to incorporate it before the egg cooks. Continue to add eggs one at a time until the texture is correct—a paste should form, but it should not be too firm. A finger drawn through the mixture should leave a deep furrow that slowly fills in.

8. To make the egg wash: In a small bowl, whisk the yolk with the cream and salt.

9. Using a piping bag or two spoons, pipe (or scoop) about a tablespoon of dough into small circles on the sheet pan. Brush with egg wash and bake until golden brown and dry, about 20 minutes. Turn off the oven, crack the door open, and leave to dry for another 15 to 20 minutes.

10. To make the apple compote: While the *choux* are baking and drying, peel, core, and dice the apples. In a small pot over low heat, combine the apples, water, brown sugar, cinnamon, cloves, and cardamom. Cook slowly until the apples are completely cooked through and broken down. The time will vary from 20 minutes to an hour, depending on what sort of apples are being used. The water should be completely evaporated, and the compote very thick. Keep warm until needed.

11. To make the caramel sauce: In a medium saucepan, stir together the sugar and Calvados. Add enough water to make the sugar the consistency of wet sand. Cook over high heat, wiping down the sides of the pan occasionally with a pastry brush and some fresh water, until the mixture comes to a dark golden brown. Remove from the heat.

12. Immediately add the cream all at once. Be careful! The mixture will bubble up violently and spit hot caramel. Stand back! Stir briskly with a long-handled wooden spoon until the caramel has dissolved into

the cream and a thick, sticky sauce has formed. Keep warm until needed.

13. To assemble: Split open the *choux* puffs and remove any spongy filling that may remain inside. Spoon some of the ice cream into the *choux* and replace their caps. Place a spoonful of the apple compote in the center of a plate and arrange three *choux* around it. Sprinkle lightly with confectioners' sugar. Drizzle caramel sauce liberally over all.

NOTES: A variety of apples is best here for a more complex flavor. I like to use a nice assortment of tart and sweet varieties. At least one should be a tart variety such as a Granny Smith.

The amount of sugar will depend on the sort of apples being used.

Makes enough for 4, with plenty of leftovers for breakfast!

THE BOWERY

After our first few days cooking in our new level, Junior, Tucker, Ben, and I quickly realized that we would need better equipment if we were going to survive the jungle of the Level 2 classroom. Our knives and the kitchen implements the school provided us on the first day of class were still in great shape; they just weren't quite adequate for the new tasks that we were being faced with. The basic equipment found in all commercial kitchens, like pots, strainers, sauté pans, and Robot Coupes (think food processor on steroids), now served as integral parts of our *batterie de cuisine*. But we Level 2 students shared all of this equipment with the students from Level 3 and Level 4. More senior students always had priority—if someone needed that Robot Coupe and it was full of your pea puree, you'd better empty it out, clean it, and have it on that student's workstation pronto, or the wrath of the chef-instructor would come crashing down on your head and on Chef Pierre's. Chef had made it very clear that he did not enjoy being reprimanded by his colleagues for his students' bad behavior, and woe betide the student who caused such a ruckus.

While none of us thought we really needed a full-scale standing Hobart mixer like the pair that churned away in the pastry kitchen—they are totally gorgeous, but weigh about as much as a fully loaded SUV—we all agreed that there were a few items that we needed to add to our arsenal, and as soon as possible. We decided to take a field trip to the Bowery. Only a few blocks from the back entrance to the school, the Bowery has long been famous for its restaurant supply stores. When a restaurant folds, as more than half do every year in New York City, the Bowery is where most of the tables, chairs, refrigerators, stoves, pots, pans, mixers, and even spoons go to retire.

Like a French market, each vendor on the street sold only one or two specialties. There was a cluster of stores selling only front-of-house paraphernalia, everything from napkin dispensers and silverware to bar stools and hostess stations. Several more sold only industrial mixers, even larger than the ones in school—the huge machines seemed to loom out of the dark interiors like prehistoric monoliths, a culinary Stonehenge. Delivery trucks unloaded enormous refrigerators and stoves that still had parts of the walls they were attached to trailing from them.

None of us really needed a rotisserie oven or an almost-new deli case, tempting as all that stainless steel was, so we decided to concentrate on the smaller stores. Dented stockpots shared dusty shelves with extra faucet handles, giant fry baskets, and the occasional pan, whose burned-out bottom had seen better days. In a locked case at the back of one store were a few huge cleavers and what looked like a chain saw—I couldn't imagine what purpose that had served in the kitchen. There were sieves, spoons, and squareboys, all things we needed in class, but none of us had room for this equipment in our tiny lockers at school, and I couldn't imagine showing up to tutor with a big conical sieve under my arm, or riding in a crowded subway car with a ten-gallon stockpot wedged between my knees.

A beautiful set of old-fashioned scales sat in one corner, but even secondhand they were out of my price range. While it was fun to look at all the wonderful culinary toys for sale, it was also difficult. All of us were on student budgets, with tuition, rent, and bills to cope with. Tucker and Junior were roommates in the school's dorm out on Roosevelt Island, and often took home leftovers from the school lunch for their dinner. Ben, a native New Yorker and the son of hardworking first-generation Korean émigrés, still lived with his family in the Bronx to save on rent. I was lucky—Michael and

I agreed that while I was in chef school, he would handle the rent and I would handle the food bills. It was good training in more ways than one. School had taught me how to get more out of the raw materials I was buying, such as breaking down a whole chicken and using the meat in three different preparations—even using the liver to make rustic pâté, and the bones for stock. I had also learned to turn vegetable scraps into lovely soups and soufflés. In class, nothing was wasted, and I was quickly putting this lesson to use in my own life. The classes we had on calculating food costs and pricing had also come in handy, and I found I was quickly honing my mental math skills with the help of the grocery store's sale circular. None of us was going hungry, but we weren't exactly rolling in dough. The green kind, that is.

We decided that each of us would spend some of our hard-earned money on one piece of equipment that we could share. Tucker and Ben found a box full of unusual cooking utensils, some of which looked more like surgeons' tools than something used to make dinner. Ben was hefting a giant pair of tweezers, while Tucker made appreciative noises at a smallish double strainer. Both were useful pieces of kitchen gadgetry that we would use often in class. I, on the other hand, was smitten by a line of deli slicers gracing a window display. Ranging in size from a civilian toaster to an army jeep, they promised to reduce everything from pineapples to pig thighs to translucently thin slices. Like a mandoline equipped with a circular saw, these pieces of weaponry were made to slice your hand off. And like a bad boyfriend you just can't seem to get out of your system, I thrilled at the danger of it.

"I really, really need one of these," I said to Tucker, as I stroked a brushed aluminum handle.

Tucker, the voice of culinary reason, gently pried my hand loose from the slicing plate and firmly steered me away from certain mutilation and back toward the more useful, if slightly more mundane, utensils. At this point, Junior was careening around the store,

banging on a stockpot with a metal spoon. We had to buy something and get out of there before Junior broke something, or before I
bought something ridiculous. Ben bought his giant tweezers, Tucker
a strainer and a stockpot for his personal use. So far, I was empty-
handed.

We made several more stops as we wandered uptown toward
Houston Street, but we still hadn't been able to locate a good electronic scale, or any more wooden spoons to replenish the ones we
had been issued on the first day of class. With proper care and
handling, a wooden spoon can last for years and years. My mother's
wooden spoons were old friends of mine, and had populated her
kitchen for as long as I could remember. My wooden spoon, on the
other hand, had been through a hard few months and was ready for
retirement. Once I left it too close to the high flame beneath a simmering stockpot and once I let it get way too close to the blades in
the blender. My battered spoon looked more like a piece of kindling
than something to cook with. Chef Pierre had recently inspected all
our equipment and found my battered spoon to be cause for alarm.

"Darling. What have you been doing to that poor spoon? It is
black! You can't make food with this thing! It is *dégueulasse*. Disgusting!"

He pitched my spoon into the closest garbage can and ordered
me to find a replacement. Once his back was turned, I rescued
the poor thing from its grave among the potato peelings and tomato seeds and stowed it away in my toolbox. My spoon may have
been unsightly, and possibly unsanitary, but it had already seen me
through a lot in the trenches of cooking school and it didn't deserve
its unceremonious end in the trash. But I hadn't managed to replace
it yet, and it was becoming a critical situation. We used our wooden
spoons for everything in the kitchen, from stirring soup to sautéing
vegetables to slapping each other on the rear end. I couldn't keep
borrowing Junior's spoon forever. Eventually, he would realize I had
it. Also, at the end of this level we would be taking our midterm

exams, and we had already been warned that borrowing equipment was not allowed. We would be on our own with only the chef's jacket on our backs and the utensils in our toolbox.

Still, I had no luck at the stores on the Bowery. Tucker and Ben seemed to be snapping up the most useful and exotic tools, and Junior and I lagged behind, ogling impractical bits of machinery and getting in the way. We were at the end of the road, literally. The Bowery dumped a ceaseless stream of cars onto Houston Street, and we stood on the sidewalk for a moment, blinking in the late-afternoon light as heat waves rolled off the tarmac and the hoods of passing taxis. I still hadn't gotten a new spoon, and we were still missing some critically important equipment. The prospect of tomorrow's work loomed up before us—yet another day spent waiting in line to use the school's old and inaccurate scales, or frantically searching for a clean strainer, all the while listening to Chef Pierre telling us *"Vite, vite!"* was not appealing. By unspoken agreement we turned left and headed back downtown to regroup at Toad Hall. Surely something useful would occur to us after a couple of pitchers of beer.

There we met almost half our class, nursing beers and in similar states of dissatisfaction. We were only a few weeks into our time in Level 2, but already it felt as if we had been at chef school for years. We had all settled into a comfortable routine, shuttling back and forth to and from school, our jobs, and our regular table here at Toad. We had all learned a lot during Level 1, and we were continuing to expand our knowledge and expertise rapidly in the high-pressure environment of Level 2. But we had reached an awkward teenage stage of our development as chefs, eager to try new things, break some rules, and stun and impress the chefs at lunch with dazzling culinary exploits. This was heresy, of course. We were having a hard enough time pleasing the chefs with our efforts with the curriculum recipes.

Every day, we threw ourselves into preparing the recipes we

had chosen from the curriculum. Every single person in class was focused on making the very best seared salmon, green salad, or chocolate roulade that the chef-instructors had ever tasted. Every day, every single one of us waited with fingers crossed and bated breath to hear the meal critiques from the chefs' table. Every single day, we were disappointed. Our very best efforts were never good enough—the comments weren't always all bad, but no dish received good reviews from all the chefs. If the crust of the lemon tart was a good texture and baked well, then the lemon filling was bland or the candied lemon peel garnish was bitter. The veal stew might have a good flavor, but the presentation looked like a piece of *merde de chien*. The niçoise salad might be gorgeous to look at, but the boiled eggs were ever-so-slightly overdone. On and on it went, an endless torrent of criticism that swamped our classroom in invective.

I wasn't sure how much longer we could go on. Yes, we were certainly better cooks than we had been when we started out in Level 1. The recipes were no longer intimidating lists of unfamiliar ingredients, measured out in the bizarre shorthand of the metric system (we could now easily eyeball 10 grams of fresh chervil, or 35 milliliters of vanilla paste), and the French vocabulary of the kitchen was now our own familiar vernacular ("*Blanchir* me six yolks with 250 grams of sugar!" or "I need some *ciseléd* shallots for the *poulet* pronto!"). But we were no closer to being Chefs with a capital "C," the well-known gods of the Food Network and best-selling cookbooks, churning out original recipes to the "oohs" and "aahs" of a studio audience—we couldn't even make the chef-instructors happy with a simple cream puff.

FAMILY MEAL

At last it was our turn for the trial by fire—the next three days would be spent in the family meal rotation, fixing lunch for the 250 students, kitchen staff, faculty, and administrative support who kept the school humming each day. Lunch for two hundred is quite a daunting prospect, especially if the largest dinner party you've ever thrown was for eight.

Complicating the issue was the fact that the entirety of the waitstaff at the school was comprised of devout Hindus, whose religion forbade them from indulging in certain beastly delights. This meant that in addition to the green salad that was always on offer, there must also be enough side dishes of a substantial enough nature to provide these men, and any closet vegetarians (there were a few in addition to Marita, though they mostly were in the pastry program), with a hearty lunch.

Even more burdensome than these dietary restraints on our potential family meal planning were the cost prohibitions placed on each serving. Because the school paid for these meals, we were obliged to make them as cost effective as possible. Each serving should cost between $2.00 and $2.50—less than a venti drip coffee from Starbucks. For this reason, things made from ground beef were a popular choice: we had eaten everything from spaghetti Bolognese to meat loaf to some truly unique casseroles that could only have been dreamed up by the students from the Midwest. Chicken was also popular, because the "industrial" chickens ordered by the school were incredibly cheap, and they were easy to prepare in bulk— roasting fifty chickens in the convection ovens was a snap compared to some of the more labor-intensive recipes we had learned to prepare. Time was the final burden placed on students in charge of family meals. Class started promptly at nine o'clock each morning, and the first staff began to line up for lunch at quarter to twelve. Even with the most simplistic recipes, the sheer bulk of food requiring at least a minimal level of preparation—from washing salad greens to chopping tomatoes to trussing chickens—took at least a few minutes apiece. Multiplied by the hundreds of vegetables to be washed, diced, and cooked, the dozens of chickens to be prepped, and the meatballs to be formed, that meant a lot of man-hours were needed to get everything ready in time. Want to serve barbecue? No slow-roasted pork shoulder here—no time. How about a cauldron of chili? No time for that, either. We needed something cheap, quick, and filling.

As usual, our little band of four was going to find the rotation through family meal to be particularly stressful since we were short-handed. Despite a spirited pep talk from Chef, we were glum as we perused the order sheets and tried to come up with something quick, tasty, not religiously offensive, and cheap. I suddenly began to understand why working parents so often feed their children frozen dinners or simply order out—not even a pan to clean up! It was starting to sound like heaven to me. I am not sure if that's what the rotation in family meal was meant to turn us into—enthusiastic proponents of the Kentucky Fried Chicken family meal bucket—but I was definitely becoming a convert.

Thoughts of ordering in for 250 were reluctantly shelved as we began to discuss what we should prepare. Like every other station, we knew that family meal was a secret test of our abilities, a competition among the students to see who could churn out something even more delicious and inventive than the brigade before them. It was an Iron Chef competition on the grandest of scales. No kitchen stadium, but performing in front of everyone was even more of a challenge, especially on a tight budget.

After much discussion, we decided to eschew pasta on our first day, as the brigade before us had made nothing but macaroni and cheese, baked ziti, and a truly awful rendition of tuna casserole. Making a selection of cold cut sandwiches was frowned upon, as it didn't give us nearly enough to do, but component meals, where the hungry masses were able to pick and choose among various things to create their own individual version of lunch, had proved extremely popular. It was a useful lesson in giving people what they want—they crave something tasty, of course, but they like to fine-tune the details themselves. For this reason, taco day had been a particular success, but since Imogene's group had done this less than a week before us, it was definitely out. We had to find a crowd pleaser, especially for our first day.

We finally decided to make spicy sausage heroes with sides of gooey melted cheese, grilled onions and peppers, lettuce, and red, ripe tomatoes. September is the season for street fairs in the city, and every weekend my classmates and I scouted out a new venue at which to gorge ourselves. The "street meat" featured at these festivals ranged from pepperoni pizza to hot dogs to lamb souvlaki and corn on the cob with lime and *queso fresco*. But the biggest and best street fair in Manhattan had just begun—the Feast of San Gennaro in Little Italy, just a few blocks from school. In addition to all the T-shirts proclaiming Italian pride and shoot-the-freak games, there were stalls selling everything from prosciutto with melon to veal parmigiana to *fritto misto* (clams, oysters, and whitefish dusted with flour, fried, and served with big lemon wedges) to zeppoles (sweet yeast dough balls fried and dusted with confectioners' sugar—divine). But everyone's favorite was the sausage hero with all the fixings—a delicious, intestinally challenging mess of spicy pork sausage heaped with charred sweet peppers and onions and smothered in melted provolone. Sinus-clearing hot sauce was available upon request. We had a secret weapon: we had conned the bread kitchen students into making our sub rolls for us. The prospect of hot, freshly baked bread was a sure winner—starch gets them every time. A big, greasy, gut-busting hero (the vegetarians could have the grilled veggies on a roll with cheese), plus a big green salad and maybe a dessert or two donated by the pastry students, and we would be golden. It was a natural choice for our debut at family meal. It had everything: it was sure to be a major crowd pleaser; it was cheap; the ingredients were within our budget; and we could get everything ready in the time we had. It was also a quintessentially New York meal, a conglomeration of flavors and textures that screamed "Little Italy," the neighborhood crammed with delicious eats only blocks from school. Perfect.

We blithely put in our order for two hundred Italian sausages (one hundred hot and one hundred sweet for a nice balance), ten pounds of cheddar and Monterey Jack cheeses, three dozen tomatoes, a case of peppers, a few sacks of onions, and a lot of lettuce. The rolls were free. We were way under budget and thrilled. What could possibly go wrong?

Our first day in family meal saw the four of us washing vegetables at eight o'clock in the morning. Not even the chef-instructors were in the kitchens yet—just us and the guys in the storeroom. We were way ahead of schedule, making more than a gallon of salad dressing in the industrial blender, when Assistant Chef Cyndee finally showed up. Since coming with us to Level 2, Cyndee's main job, other than to make our lives miserable with her nasty comments and her howling laughter, was to help run the family meal station. Tucker and I shared one long look as Cyndee began poking her fat finger, which bore a striking resemblance to the sausages we would be serving for lunch, in our work so far.

"You know, you shouldn't have started without me" was the most scathing comment she could come up with.

Ben, Tucker, Junior, and I shared a big, happy grin. Things were going well. Then Cyndee began unpacking the rest of our order, which had just arrived in the kitchen on the broad back of David. That's when the shit really hit the fan. A piercing shriek rent the quiet air of the kitchen that sent shivers down everyone's spine. Cyndee was screaming at us, her mouth opened so wide it was easy to see every single one of her graying smoker's teeth as she waved our order form around like she was learning to semaphore in a high wind.

"Who did the order?" she crowed, unable to modulate her voice into anything other than a booming death knell.

Somehow, whatever had gone wrong, I knew that it was going to be my fault.

"I did," I said, furious that I was unable to keep the slight quaver from my voice. She smirked, little knowing that my voice cracked from building rage, not fear.

"Well, *smartass*, it looks like *you* totally fucked everything up." It was hard to take insults from Cyndee, especially since I was dealing with someone who had a total of three brain cells, but there was nothing I could do about it. I was still clutching my paring knife, covered in the bloodred pulp of the tomatoes I had been dicing. For just a fraction of a moment I let my mind ponder the statistics of how many obnoxious and overbearing chefs had been stabbed in their own kitchens, but I let that thought go quickly. The cleanup would be horrendous.

Tucker must have caught the passing homicidal gleam in my eye because he quickly moved between the two of us and tried to steer the conversation back to whatever had gone wrong. Using his most ingratiating voice, he asked to see both the order sheet and the order itself, still in its crate. Calling out everything in methodical order, Tucker made his way down the list of supplies for lunch, crossing things off the list until we came to the last, the most important part of lunch—the sausage. What if the meat men hadn't gotten us the sausage? We would be sunk for sure—we couldn't have sausage sandwiches without the sausage. No fear, we got the sausage. Oh, man, did we get the sausage. But instead of the links we had ordered, we had seventy-five pounds of ground sausage, in one very large plastic bag. Crap. This was a mistake, a big mistake. The meat purveyor that filled the school's order didn't have Italian sausage links in stock, so they sent what they had. Cyndee was actually right for once—we were in deep shit. My God, seventy-five pounds of loose sausage, all (metaphorically) on my head. "Fucked up" was putting things mildly. What were we going to do?

"Use an ice cream scoop." In a stroke of brilliance I didn't think he was capable of, Junior galvanized us into action. Using all our combined brawn, we emptied the huge sack of sausage into the biggest stainless steel bowl in the kitchen. Battered from use, the bowl was big enough for me to take a bath in, and easily contained the wad of sausage now huddled in the bottom of it. Using big handfuls of salt and pepper, chili flakes, and dried oregano and thyme, Ben and I seasoned the meat, up to our elbows in ground flesh as we mixed in a few dozen egg yolks to bind it all together. Junior returned from the pastry kitchen, where he had borrowed four large ice cream scoops. With them we began to make hundreds of balls of sausage, the size of a hefty snowball, but much more delicious. We filled tray after tray after tray with the sausage balls and slotted them into the monstrous convection oven to cook as we kept going, churning out spherical hunks of sausage like demented automatons in a Jimmy Dean factory.

They weren't very gorgeous, but they were tasty, and as we sandwiched them between halves of the crusty, still-warm rolls delivered from the bread kitchen, I thought our sausage balls would probably pass muster. We wouldn't win a James Beard award, but we did manage to feed several hundred people on time. And Junior saved my ass. Wonders would never cease in the kitchen.

HORS D'OEUVRES

While every morning of Level 2 was nothing less than all-out war against the clock and sometimes against the recipes themselves, after the stress of preparing and serving the chefs' table lunch, or the even more grueling family meal, the afternoons were more relaxed. Instead of preparing for an evening meal, as would be traditional in a real restaurant kitchen, we peons in Level 2 were in charge of preparing hors d'oeuvres for the dinner service. Because the school ran two shifts of students a day—the day shift that ran from around eight-thirty in the morning to three in the afternoon, and then an evening shift of students from five to ten at night—each shift prepared only one meal. Because we had more class time each day than the night students, we were able to learn a bit more of the esoteric tricks and tips from our instructors. One of these things was the hors d'oeuvres course from Chef Pierre.

After serving lunch to the chefs' table and making certain our workstations were spick-and-span, we were allowed to have lunch. Once our lunch break was over, we reconvened for our afternoon lecture, where the critiques of the dishes we had prepared for the chefs were read aloud and further commented on (read: ridiculed) by our fellow students. After this ritual had been performed, and everyone had had their fair share of embarrassment and praise, we moved on to discussing the art of the bite-size morsels we would be learning to construct for the evening's dinner patrons in the restaurant. Chef Pierre eulogized what he believed to be a lost art, before launching into a truly passionate discussion about the art and architecture of a proper hors d'oeuvre, or just plain hors as we called them for short.

The concept of hors d'oeuvres was hijacked, like so many other gorgeous French ideas in food, by the nouvelle cuisine movement of the 1980s. While the movement itself was French in origin, Chef Pierre admitted, he faulted the American chefs of the New York restaurant scene and the yuppie clientele they served for the perversion of French ideal concepts. The cocktail parties catered by these same chefs were the true culprits in the death of the proper hors. During the decade of excess, these little bites had grown far too large, far too filling to be anything less than a legitimate course at the dinner table, and it was therefore inappropriate to eat them standing up, with one's fingers.

In the early nineties, the fashion for overblown hors became a passé habit of the outgoing Republican regime and the parties they threw for their friends. No longer would filet mignon on potato crisps be a staple of political fund-raisers. Beef was so un-PC, as were seared foie gras on figs and braised pig jowls on tiny cheddar biscuits. It was an era of earnestness in both the political sphere and the kitchen, as chefs began to pare down their ideas and their imagination, and served hors only reluctantly and then with a heavy sauce of irony. The horrifying appetizers from fifties cocktail parties made a heavy reemergence, and upscale caterers would often serve pigs in a blanket as a deliberate tongue-in-cheek reference to a more halcyon era. Chef Pierre shrugged his shoulders sadly. There was a time for irony in food, but not perhaps before the guest has had a chance to sit down and fully appreciate it, *non*?

Chef continued, his agitation mounting ever higher as he came down the home stretch in his discourse on the rise and fall of the hors d'oeuvre. We were now in the age of the techno-hors. Chefs seemed to think that if it could be served in a glass beaker or perhaps with a syringe, then it must be magnificent. Flavored foam has become an hors d'oeuvre now, as have the smoked remains of a vanilla bean, kept in a tightly sealed vial and then inhaled. Chef shook his head. Things were indeed in a sad state. But, he said, raising his head, the light of a true zealot evident in his stare, we were here to save the hors d'oeuvre from itself. We would be taught the dying art of constructing something delicious, stable, and economical, or he would die trying!

We were in a state of awe at this speech. It was not unusual to see our instructors worked up, but rarely did they actually come to the brink of declaring a holy war, especially after lunch. But Chef's zeal seemed only to burn more brightly the later in the afternoon it got. I knew things were truly serious when Chef pulled out a dry erase board and began making what looked like architectural drawings on it, complete with mathematical equations detailing load balances and stress factors. I believe he may even have said something about cantilevered suspension, but I may have been wrong. We studiously took notes in a state of silent bewilderment. I had come within an acute angle of failing geometry in high school and had never bothered to take physics—was it finally going to come back to haunt me? I snuck a glance at Tucker, but found that he was already deeply diverted, and was sketching what looked to be a miniature ziggurat made from toasted pita and cucumber rounds in his notebook.

Chef managed to rein in his drawings and his mumbled calculations and begin at the beginning. We must first learn the construction of a proper hors. All hors should be small enough to fit neatly in the mouth in one bite. A lengthy bit of chicken tenderloin threaded on a skewer was *not* a proper hors, no matter how delicious or unusual its flavor, as it required more than one bite to ingest and the use of more than one hand to eat. This brought up the other key point of construction. The hors must be well constructed, with a stable base on which the flavorful components must be securely perched. To this end, cream cheese is often used as edible cement, stabilizing errant bits and pieces so that the whole may be conveyed to the mouth without danger to the diner's outfit. Chef paused for a moment here to discuss the recent fad of foods on skewers. While so deeply ingrained now as to be acceptable, ideally an hors should be made from only edible ingredients. A skewer that could be theoretically eaten was acceptable, like a sprig of rosemary or even sugar cane. A bit of sharp bamboo was not—too much like a weapon, Chef said, and, besides, what to do with it when one was finished? Stab fellow guests? Better to learn the proper way of doing things— the refrain we heard over and over again at school.

Secondly, every hors d'oeuvre must be beautiful to look at, as well as delicious to eat. There must be a good use of color—ideally at least three of the five or so colors found in nature should be used in the tiny morsel, even if it is merely the tiniest hint of red from finely diced red pepper or pomegranate seeds sparingly arranged as garnish. The cool, elegant celadon green of a tiny cucumber cup could be enhanced with a minute scoop of red from tuna tartare, perhaps, and a splash of bright acid green from a spear of fresh chives. The golden yellow of a small corn fritter would pop against the deep green of a bell pepper, the subtle pink of caramelized red onion, and the snowy white of a liberal crumble of *queso fresco*.

Most important, a good hors is boldly flavored. It should, in the words of Chef, "really make the taste buds say *'Bonjour.'*" An hors d'oeuvre should not be merely filler before a meal, or, even worse, be eaten instead of a meal. It should merely prepare the diner, prime his taste buds, and give him some hint of the delights yet to come. Because it is bite size, a mere morsel of food, the flavors and their combination together must be big—all the power of a well-hit bass drum, a resonating note of tantalizing deliciousness that lingers on the palate after the food has been swallowed. To make such a small thing so delightfully memorable, a deft hand must be used to season and balance the flavors. Unusual herbs and spices are in their native element here, as are delightfully unctuous flavored oils and tangily unusual vinegars.

Here is the perfect stage for a single, highly flavored ingredient, like a wafer-thin slice of truffle balanced on a Parmesan crisp, with no other distractions. Here also is a chance for the chef to try out various flavor combinations on a small scale before attempting to create an entire dish around them. Do dried cherries sing when dusted with Hungarian paprika, or are their chewy texture and hint of sourness muffled? Would a creamy dab of mascarpone add richness to the austere toast and prosciutto with tiny slices of candied kumquat, or would it overwhelm the bright citrus flavor?

For the first time in chef school we were being given a bit of free rein, a creative moment to express our own tastes and thoughts about what would taste good together, and how each little bite should look. It was like a wedding cake competition, each of us madly innovating within the strictures of a tightly controlled medium. The hors d'oeuvre must conform to Chef's idea of what a proper hors should look like, but the garniture was up to us. While we were also free to experiment with new spices and could go as far afield as we dared with ingredients, they must not be too expensive, and we must also incorporate some of the scraps left over from the kitchens, in order to be economical, in the hors d'oeuvres tradition. So seared foie gras was definitely out, no matter how delicious a nibble it would make, and cured salmon was only possible if there were sufficient trimmings left over from the fish station. The Level 3 and Level 4 students would often swing by the Level 2 kitchens to drop off the leftovers of one of their specials from lunch that hadn't sold out, and we also benefited from frequent donations from the bread kitchen. All of these goodies went into a large plastic tub that was hauled out every afternoon. It was very reminiscent of a dress-up box, crammed with unexpected pieces of clothing, except we would be using these edible odds and ends—the leftover quail, the crispy salmon skin, the excess roasted pineapple flowers—to deck out our little creations.

Sometimes inspiration simply refused to strike, or, while we had myriad suggestions for fantastical creations, Chef vetoed them all. This usually happened when there was something we had to use up lurking in the box on the edge of funking, and Chef had his own ideas about how best to utilize it. A large jar of rosy pink salmon eggs was reaching the end of its usefulness, but there was still an ocean of it left. We all made suggestions for new creations— I thought a wafer made of crispy salmon skin, topped with a tiny sliver of our own house-cured gravlax, garnished with a piped rosette of crème fraîche, and topped with the eggs would be just the ticket, but Chef only shot me one of those powerful X-ray looks of his, and I quickly fell silent. Finally, Chef decided we would beat cream cheese until it was soft and then fold in the eggs, which we would then use to top dark pumpernickel toast rounds. We would add a garnish of tiny fronds of chervil and that would be it. Repeated sixty times and labeled and wrapped and stuck in the giant fridge for the evening classes to serve to the dinner patrons in the restaurant, and we would be done for the day. Sometimes it was nice not to be trapped in the mire of a creative idea that didn't have a lot of practical application, and so my group volunteered to churn out this easy, if unimaginative, hors d'oeuvre.

I should have noticed the wicked glint in Chef Pierre's eye, but I was intent on getting the cream cheese and salmon mixture properly mixed and seasoned and on the toasts and out the door. The afternoon was draining away and we had had a difficult time in the *saucier* station earlier—our chicken *au sauce diable* had been roundly criticized at the chefs' table, and the comments about our lack of technique and taste were still ringing in my ears. So I wasn't at all prepared for what happened. My attention was far away from what I was actually doing, which is why Chef Pierre chose such a moment to strike. We had called him over to taste the cream cheese and salmon egg mixture for proper seasoning before we began smearing it all over our prepared toasts, set out in even rows of ten like a well-ordered Roman legion. Ben had prepared the chervil, and sixty minute, perfect sprigs stood at attention next to the toasts. The cream cheese was the last thing. Chef picked up the extra-large industrial spatula I used to fold together the ingredients and took a big whiff.

"Ooh la la," he said, the French verbal equivalent of a disappointed head shake.

Uh-oh, I thought to myself, *the salmon eggs have already spoiled and I have just ruined two pounds of cream cheese. I am definitely in for it this time.* With a pronounced expression of distaste, Chef held the spatula, loaded with the mixture, up close to my face so I could smell it, too. Without thinking, I bent close, inhaling deeply, trying to get a whiff of the distinctive funk of old fish. WHAP! Chef hit me on the nose with the spatula, spreading cream cheese and salmon roe all over my face. Tucker, Ben, Junior, and Chef exploded in great gusts of laughter, while tears welled up in my eyes—that blow to the nose had hurt!—and I tried to expel the squishy eggs and slippery cream cheese from my nasal passages. I could feel everything sliding off my face and dripping onto my chef's jacket, leaving long, faintly pink trails before dripping onto the floor.

Yuck.

Cheddar Biscuits

These biscuits make great hors d'oeuvres spread with spicy whole-grain mustard and topped with some Bayonne ham, or a dab of crème fraîche topped with tart Granny Smith apple slices. In fact, these tasty biscuits make a perfect base for any number of toppings. And served hot from the oven with even more cheese melted on top and a smear of spicy mustard, they are a perfect midwinter meal paired with some saucisson sec, a simple salad, and a pint of extra dry hard cider.

For the egg wash:

1 egg yolk

1 tablespoon heavy cream

Pinch of salt

For the biscuits:

2 cups all-purpose flour, plus extra for shaping

1 tablespoon baking powder

1 teaspoon salt

½ teaspoon baking soda

½ teaspoon dried thyme

5 tablespoons unsalted butter, chilled

¾ cup shredded sharp cheddar cheese

¾ cup buttermilk

1. To make the egg wash: In a small bowl, whisk the yolk with the cream and salt.
2. To make the biscuits: Preheat the oven to 400°F. Line a sheet pan with parchment paper.

3. Combine the flour, baking powder, salt, baking soda, and thyme in a bowl. Cut in the butter with a pastry cutter (or use a mixer fitted with a paddle) until the mixture resembles coarse cornmeal. Add the cheese and mix well to distribute evenly. Add the buttermilk and mix just until combined—the less the dough is handled now, the lighter the biscuits will be.

4. Pat the dough very gently on a well-floured work surface until it is ¾ inch thick. Cut out 20 small or a dozen large biscuits. Place the biscuits on the prepared pan, well spaced, and paint the tops with the egg wash.

5. Bake for about 10 minutes, until mightily risen and golden brown. The little biscuits will take a bit less time to cook, the larger biscuits a bit longer. Let cool on a wire rack.

For a delicious variation of this recipe, replace the cheddar with ¾ cup of crumbled blue cheese. Omit the thyme and add a healthy pinch or two of coarsely ground black pepper. Top with some Onion Marmalade (page 194).

Makes about 1 dozen large or 20 small biscuits

Onion Marmalade

This is a wonderful condiment to have on hand. After the onions are cut, the marmalade requires very little work other than an occasional stir with a wooden spoon. It keeps for weeks in the fridge in a tightly sealed jar.

2 tablespoons (¼ stick) unsalted butter

1 medium yellow onion, chopped or sliced (see Note)

1 medium red onion, chopped or sliced

1 small Vidalia or other sweet onion, chopped or sliced

2 medium shallots, chopped or sliced

Salt and freshly ground pepper

1 tablespoon dark brown sugar

2 tablespoons balsamic vinegar

Leaves from 2 sprigs fresh thyme

In a large saucepan, heat the butter over gentle heat until just melted. Add all the onions and the shallots and stir to coat evenly. Brown gently over low heat, stirring occasionally. Be patient and let the onions caramelize fully—the slower the better. Add salt and pepper to taste, and toss in the brown sugar. Once the onions are fully caramelized and soft, remove from the heat, stir in the vinegar and thyme, and let cool. Store in a tightly closed jar in the fridge. Let come to room temperature before using.

NOTE: I like to chop each type of onion a little bit differently, to give the marmalade an interesting texture. If you want something a little more homogeneous, feel free to chop everything fairly small or cut into thin slices.

Makes about 1½ cups

LEFT OUT AT LE CIRQUE

As we soldiered on through the long days of our second level of chef school, everyone began to get a little closer. We were all passionately interested in food, and while we came from many wildly divergent backgrounds, cooking played a big role in them all. The difficulties we faced every day, from the oppressive heat of the kitchens to the complexity of the recipes we prepared to the emotional hardships we endured as the butt of the chefs' never-ending sarcasm, all made for a strong bond between everyone in class.

And then there was Mimi.

Mimi was older than the rest of us students, but was loath to admit it. She kept her black hair long, in a swingy ponytail like a teenager, and her café au lait complexion was clear and totally unlined. She wore only the latest trends from Diesel, Marc Jacobs, Miss Sixty, and Chanel, and carried a real Hermès Kelly bag. The rest of us shopped at Old Navy or thrift stores and carried shape-less totes, the better to squeeze in all the paraphernalia we needed for our jobs after school. Mimi didn't need an after-school job—or a job at all, for that matter. Word leaked out that she was actually a member of the ruling family of a small Middle Eastern country, one whose oil assets and ruthless oppression of its subjects were equally infamous. She was in chef school only in order to stay in the country, to fulfill the requirements of her student visa. At thirty-eight, Mimi wasn't really the typical picture of a student, but she was part of our class, for better or worse.

Midway through Level 2, it definitely began to seem like worse.

With our new, larger groups, there was a new social dynamic—people were suddenly tossed together and expected to work seamlessly, without disagreements, distractions, or discord. New social groups were forming, while old partnerships were lost. It was very much like being a high school freshman all over again—suddenly it was cliques, hazing, and gossip about who was sleeping with whom.

I was lucky to be working with a bunch of guys. There were none of the tense social niceties to be performed with them, which would have been totally lost on them, anyway. We were all out for the same thing—graduating first in the class—but with the guys there was no pretense, no need to cloak ambition behind politely bitchy conversation. Tucker, Ben, and Junior were just as single-minded as I in their devotion to the work. When we weren't going full tilt at the stoves, we spent a lot of our time trading stories back and forth, divided equally between great places we had eaten, dishes we had dreamed up, and sex. Well, mostly we talked about sex, partly because it seemed to be fading into a distant memory for all of us. Tucker had left his wife back in Michigan, working in a refrigerator factory; Junior *still* hadn't gotten laid; and Ben's girlfriend was spending the summer in France. Michael and I were still living in sin in our little apartment on Thompson Street, but pressure from school and the stress of renovating our new place a few blocks away were taking their toll, and there wasn't a whole lot of sinning going on. Not to mention that planning a wedding is hard work, and we seemed to have very different ideas about what we wanted. Michael wanted to trot down to City Hall and get it over with, and while I shuddered at the thought of a huge froufrou affair complete with a dozen bridesmaids in hideous dresses, I did want to have a little celebration. And wear a really pretty dress and drink Champagne, of course. We had had several arguments about it, culminating in Michael slamming the door on his way out of the apartment, leaving me fuming. I had seen photos of NATO summit meetings that were more amicable than some of our dinner table discussions.

We were all so tired at the end of the day that sex seemed like yet another fancy French recipe to prepare—lots of prep work, a few exciting minutes over a high flame, and then the inevitable cleanup. Between the jobs we all worked after school—Tucker had scored a paying gig at a restaurant downtown; Ben was interning at the famed Blue Hill restaurant outside the city; Junior helped out at a local bistro; and I spent my afternoons and evenings tutoring private school students and wishing I could escape the mind-numbing boredom—and the homework we did every night (memorizing and re-creating the dishes cooked that day and preparing for the next day's work), there wasn't a lot of free time for sleeping, let alone more active pursuits. So we talked.

There was something about all the heat, sweat, and hard work that made it easy to share confidences, and soon I was privy to Tucker's marital problems—he missed his wife and two little kids, and worried about leaving them home alone for so long. Ben was more circumspect in his feelings for his girl, Renee, but his stories were always very funny, and usually involved a self-deprecating (forgive the pun) climax. Junior's stories were always long, involved, and improbable. They were unintentionally hilarious as he bragged about exploits that we all knew he hadn't done, some of which weren't even physically possible. (I know, I tried.) So when we weren't frantically working or cleaning up, we were talking, getting to know a hell of a lot about one another. While we were friendly with everyone, helping out when it was needed or just generally chatting, we were our own little social island, independent of the rest of the class. This was one of the consequences of working in a brigade—much like a military unit, our loyalties were now more to each other than the class as a whole, like the Marines' motto of loyalty: "Unit, Corps, God, Country." Ours was quickly becoming "Brigade, Class, Chef, School." This is one of the reasons why I was unaware of the social machinations of Mimi until it was too late.

CR

We were just back from running in our dishes to the chefs' table and were beginning the long cleanup before we could have our lunch when Imogene came rushing toward me. Imo and I had been friends since orientation, when we had found ourselves standing side by side, sipping Sancerre and ogling Dean Jacques Pépin. It turned out that we were both from Virginia, she from the suburbs immediately outside D.C., and I from a bit farther outside the Beltway. Though Imo had a few years on me—her two girls were in high school and college already, and she had already concluded a successful career as a computer programmer—we hit it off right away. Both of us were already firmly anchored to our lives outside chef school, and while we both loved it at The Institute, we were well aware that one day soon we would graduate and have to return to our lives out there in the real world. We would be chefs, with all the authority and ability that entailed, but someone would still have to do the laundry, walk the dog, and make the beds.

Though we were not above a spot of gossip about our fellow classmates, rarely did it escalate to the level of actually running to share a juicy tidbit, but here Imo stood, actually panting from her exertions. She was clutching a Diet Coke from the bodega across the street from the back entrance to the school, a popular spot for the students to hit during lunch—their cold sodas were half the price of those from the vending machines in the school hallway— and while Imo caught her breath, I eyed that icy can with envy. Because our brigade was short one member, we were often scrambling to finish our work on time, and rarely had a moment to wolf down lunch, let alone amble across the street for a cold drink. Before my thoughts could turn from merely envious to outright larcenous, Imo had pulled herself together and begun to speak.

"You'll never guess what's going on," she whispered loudly, drawing Tucker and me into a huddle with her.

"Hmmm ... Keri is pregnant with Junior's love child?" I hazarded, making a gentle jab at Junior's most recent dating fiasco—asking Keri, the straight-arrow Mormon, out on a date to a bar.

"Please, old news already," said Imo sarcastically, rolling her eyes.

"Just spit it out," Tucker said. He was—he claimed—uninterested in gossip, but like most men, he secretly reveled in it.

"Mimi has made reservations to have dinner at Le Cirque 2000!" Le Cirque, the well-known warhorse French restaurant on the Upper East Side of Manhattan, was regarded by most of our chef-instructors as the most polished temple of haute cuisine in New York at the time. Le Cirque 2000 was its most recent incarnation.

"Well, lucky Mimi," I said, trying to keep the tinge of envy out of my voice. Mimi had money to burn, literally. In spite of her Muslim upbringing, Mimi had taken up smoking cigarettes since starting chef school, and would often buy cigarettes by the carton to give to our classmates—at more than ten dollars a pack, this was not an insignificant gesture, and one that had won her more than a few fast friends. Le Cirque was famous for its excellent food, incredible wine list, and truly spectacular bills. Mimi would definitely need her daddy's money for this jaunt. Still, as envious as I was about Mimi's trip to the temple of French food in America, I didn't think it merited Imo's exertions or the air of suppressed emotion still evident on her face. I was right, there was more—much more.

"She isn't going alone," Imo said, her face now twisting in a grimace.

"She has a date?" Tucker asked, his face not quite able to conceal his disbelief. Mimi looked pretty good for her age, but it was definitely a case of mutton dressed as lamb, as my mother would have said.

"Well, in a way," Imo said.

I was losing patience—I was hungry, tired, and hot, and we still hadn't finished cleaning up. If Imogene didn't stop being mysterious, I was in danger of losing my already frayed temper.

"Dish it. NOW!" I shout-whispered.

And so Imo told us.

Turned out Mimi was going to Le Cirque with eleven of her
friends from school, precisely half our class.

Imo, Tucker, and I were not in the half that had been invited.

That was enough for me, and I lost the tattered remains of my
once-sweet disposition.

"BITCH!" I shouted, too worked up to mind the warning look
Chef shot me from across the room. Since beginning chef school, my
vocabulary had gone from Ivy League to Teamsters convention, but
in this situation, no other word would have sufficed. I really couldn't
believe it. It wasn't so much that I hadn't been invited, though that
slight did sting. It was more that Mimi was deliberately dividing our
class into two groups, those who belonged at the table of popularity
and hipness, and those who didn't. As far as I was concerned, no one
in our class deserved the title of hipper than thou, and most especially
not Mimi. She tried too hard, a cardinal sin for coolness. Still, why
hadn't she invited me? It wasn't as if I disliked her, or even that the
two of us didn't get along. I got along with everyone in the class, even
Penny, who seemed to have a burgeoning persecution complex and
would often complain to me that other students in the class were out
to get her. Apparently I could befriend someone with a mental disor-
der, but not a social climber. It was too much—too much drama and
hurt feelings for a group of people who were supposed to be adults.
Looking at Imogene's downcast face, I resolved that I was going to do
something about all this foolishness, and the sooner the better.

So when Mimi sauntered back into class after lunch, her chef's
jacket still redolent of the smoke from all those free cigarettes she'd
handed out, I politely asked if I could have a word with her. Instead
of retiring to the recycling closet where the school kept all its cardboard, cans, and paper and where most private conferences were
held by our fellow Level 2 students, Mimi wheeled around with a
hostile look in her eye. This was not the best beginning for a con-
frontation, but I wasn't one to run from a war of words, especially
when we were quickly drawing a clutch of onlookers from the class.

Looking down at her (thank God I had the advantage of height, at least!), I cleared my throat and began.

"Ummm, hey, Mimi, I heard you are going to have dinner at Le Cirque with a bunch of people. That sounds like so much fun. Mind if Imo and I come?" I could almost hear my grandmother rolling over in her grave. Her rules of etiquette, which she drilled into me from a very tender age, were written in stone and absolutely immutable. Where I came from, people did not invite themselves to a party. Of course, where I came from, excluding people from parties in the first place wasn't done, either. Hoping that mine was the lesser of two mortal social sins, I sent a mental apology to my ancestors and waited for Mimi's response.

It was much more brutal than I had anticipated. Flipping her long black hair over her shoulder, she hissed, "Yes, I have a table for twelve at Le Cirque. It is the private chef's table in the kitchen. Unfortunately, I have already invited people, and you two didn't make the cut. Now don't make such a big deal out of it, crybaby."

With that, she turned on her heel and left me standing there, trying to hold my guts in place with both hands after that violent social evisceration. She'd actually called me a name! That hadn't happened to me since the eighth grade, when, cursed with the dork trifecta of glasses, braces, and brains, I'd had a sign saying "Nerd Alert" taped to the back of my shirt.

Angelo tried to comfort me, his beefy paw patting my shoulder with all the gentleness of a black bear savaging an apple tree. "Darling, it's okay. You wouldn't have wanted to come anyway."

Wait. A. Minute. I looked at Angelo in disbelief. "You're going?" I spat out, unable to hide my chagrin. Angelo was *my* friend. Mimi could invite some people in our class to her little party, but not *my* people. This was shaping into a social war of attrition, and I was standing on the deck of my sinking battleship. The only thing worse than inviting Angelo would be inviting one of my own little brigade.

Realizing that I had been outgunned and outmaneuvered, I wheeled away from Angelo's embarrassed explanations without another word and retreated to my brigade, hoping to cut off a sneak attack from the rear. I was too late; there was already a spy in my midst. I knew Tucker wasn't going, and I was certain that Junior wouldn't have made the cut, either—his puppyish antics were a source of amusement and gentle derision from everyone, but Mimi's scathing comments about Junior were well known. That only left Ben—quiet, unassuming Ben, whose sly humor often kept a smile on my face through the grimmest morning prep work. Ben, whose running social commentary on our classmates had often found an easy mark in Mimi's blatant pandering. He wouldn't defect to the other side, leaving his comrades in arms out in the cold, would he?

For the promise of a meal in the hallowed halls of one of the city's sacred temples to gastronomy, he would. Everyone has a price, and for Ben, it was the promise of a private dining room and the chef's tasting menu. I wanted to be angry, to rage against him for going to the other side and breaking the code (not to mention our earlier truce)—brigade first, stomach and classmates second—but I knew, deep down, that there was a part of my chef's mentality that would have done the same—selling out my family for the elusive number to a top-flight restaurant's private reservation line, making excuses to friends for holding back that truly superb bottle of Champagne. In our gluttonous heart of hearts, all chefs are the same—we are all chasing that perfect meal, and we would do anything, *anything,* to have our chance to sit at the table.

I could smell the acrid scent of defeat clearly. I knew I was beaten; my own men turned against me. I was loath to fall on my sword, however. I wanted to live to fight another day against Mimi, my new nemesis. One day, I was certain, I would have the opportunity for a rematch, and I was going to be ready.

The night that half the class trooped uptown to Le Cirque 2000 to eat, drink, and be merry, I invited Imo and Tucker over for some wine. I opened a very nice Chablis Premier Cru that I had been holding on to for far too long. What good was a nice bottle of wine if I had no friends to share it with? The little meal we put together from the leftovers in my refrigerator was not star worthy, but it was very good, the wine was great, and the company of friends was without price.

ASSISTANT CHEF CYNDEE

No one deserves this, I thought to myself, as once again I had earned the unwelcome attention of Assistant Chef Cyndee. It always seemed to happen on those mornings that were particularly hectic, or when my whole team was hungover. Or worse, when things were hectic *and* we were hungover, which was pretty often. Suddenly, just as Ben was dicing leeks a micrometer too big, I had let the stock boil over on the stove, Tucker was at the storeroom requesting more potatoes, and God alone knew what Junior was doing, in would sweep Cyndee, her pug nose almost twitching with anticipation. I was never certain if she could actually smell the mounting fear or panic when the team was going slightly off the rails, but it never failed that she would be there, waiting to draw Chef Pierre's attention to the nascent disaster, if she wasn't actually spurring the disaster itself along.

I know that everyone suffered under those protuberant gimlet eyes, invariably ringed in heavy black eyeliner, which seemed to see every unofficial trip to the bathroom, every small slipup and meager mishap. Her large ears seemed tuned to catch every muttered aside, to hear even the briefest of pauses before a student could muster the obligatory "Yes, Chef" to every command. Of course, none of these venial offenses went unremarked on, even in passing, by Cyndee's acid tongue, caustic as freshly squeezed lemon juice in a new cut.

While none of the students escaped from Cyndee's evil eye, somehow I always managed to be the one whose most minor transgressions brought a wicked smile to her face. While Tucker or Ben might get away with a brief reprimand for their lack of attention to detail or momentary lapse in discipline, if I even seemed to be thinking of a quick retort to one of her many needling questions, she would smile that serpent's smile and raise her voice to call "Chef!" Chef Pierre would always appear, listen to Cyndee's gratingly nasal voice complain about the real or imagined infraction I had committed, shrug his massive, bearlike shoulders, and say, "*Tant pis pour toi. Tout le monde!* Back to work!" Roughly translated, his comments meant: "Big deal. Let's move on." It always seemed to please Cyndee, though, and it took me months to realize that despite the fact she was a member of the faculty (a junior member, but still a member), she could not speak or understand a word of French, even though the school sponsored French lessons for all the teaching faculty, free.

We all complained about Cyndee, but she wasn't totally without admirers. Cyndee was a chain smoker, and at every opportunity she could be found hovering outside the students' entrance, taking a long drag off a cigarette. Mimi's habit of giving away packs of Marlboro Lights ensured that the two were soon thick as thieves, a situation that could not have been more ominous for me. Ever since our tangle over dinner at Le Cirque, Mimi and I had been rivals, engaging in periodic social skirmishes in which no clear winner was ever apparent. With a chef's assistant on her side, though, Mimi was beginning to consolidate an unfair advantage.

But Cyndee's enmity toward me needed no encouragement. It seemed that her eyes were always on me, waiting hungrily for some mistake. It could be hard to work while worrying about whether or not Chef Pierre was going to suddenly materialize at my elbow to point out some flaw in my efforts. His comments at least were always geared to be instructive and helpful, if not necessarily gentle in their critique. It became almost impossible to work smoothly and efficiently while knowing that at any moment the slightest fumble, the merest wrong twitch of a spoon at the stove, would bring Cyndee, the evil harpy, down on my head.

Michael thought I was imagining things. I was just being too sensitive to criticism. That was partly true. It *was* hard for me to take criticism, as Michael well knew, but I argued that it would be hard for anyone to take criticism well all day, every day. No one in the world could be that nasty, he told me. Maybe not in the world Michael lived in, but in the world of the kitchen, I knew it was all too possible.

Cyndee's principal job at school was to supervise the students preparing family meals, ensuring that things went smoothly and there would indeed be a hot lunch for two hundred people at noon each day. Her afternoon was spent creating new ideas for the hors d'oeuvres selection we prepared for the evening meal in the restaurant. This meant that my orbit would rarely intersect with hers—only when we were in the family meal rotation, once every ten days or so, would Cyndee and I have to interact. Somehow, though, Cyndee always managed to be around, in the doorway of the pastry kitchen as I rolled out piecrust, in line in front of me at the storeroom window, washing her knives at the sink just as I was draining a steaming cauldron of potatoes. Coincidentally, this was also when I was doing something wrong. The potatoes were too done, or too raw. The piecrust was too cold to be rolled out and would crack, or I had overworked it already and it was too warm. I couldn't win. This was the way things were, day in and day out, in Level 2, until the day I got the phone call.

Phone calls at chef school were strictly prohibited during class. During lunch and after school, cell phones could be used, but never in the kitchens, only in hallways, the locker room, or any other corner where you were unlikely to be caught by a visiting dean. That said, ever since the cataclysmic events of September 11, which occurred less than a half mile from the plate glass windows of the school's restaurant, all of the chefs and students carried their cell phones with them at all times, just in case. Like everyone else, I carried my cell phone tucked away in the deep pockets of my chef's pants, and lived in fear that one day I might inadvertently forget to set the damn thing to vibrate, not that anyone ever called me. I had warned Michael and my family that I was never to be reached during school hours unless it was a matter of life and death, and while I had had an occasional phone call that set my pants vibrating, it was always a wrong number.

So when my pants began to ring loudly one Wednesday morning in August, I knew it was bad. For once in my life I had forgotten to put my phone on vibrate, and who could possibly be calling? Without checking its display I reached into my pocket and switched it to manner mode, thankful that just this one time, Assistant Chef Cyndee was not lurking in some corner of the classroom to witness my most recent faux pas. But the damn phone kept ringing and ringing and ringing and ringing. It became impossible to concentrate on poaching eggs for the garde-manger dish we were working on, and the buzzing was so loud and so continuous that even Tucker finally said, "For God's sake, Katie! Just run to the bathroom and see who it is!"

Whipping off my apron (we weren't allowed to wear our hats or aprons anywhere but the kitchen, to cut down on cross-contamination), I made my excuses to Chef Pierre and ran for the ladies' room. I was angry—no one needed to call me fifty-six times in a row for any reason that I could think of. I checked my long log of missed calls. They were all from Mom, Dad, and a number I didn't recognize. Flushing the toilet and running a torrent of water into the basin to cover any telltale sounds of conversation, I called my mother to see what the fuss was all about. I imagined my brother might have finally proposed to his longtime girlfriend, which would be fantastic news, but not something I couldn't live without hearing before we broke for lunch. I could hear the long pause before it began to ring, a strange blip in technology that told me Mom was out of her cell phone carrier's range—odd. No answer. *Typical,* I thought, my mild annoyance at being bothered turning to a tiny flame of anger. The least they could do was pick up the damn phone! I rang my father, to no avail. This was getting ridiculous! I had already been gone too long from my station, and I hadn't come any closer to finding out what the heck was going on. I crammed the offending lump of plastic and technology back in my pocket, whipped open the door to the ladies' room, and prepared to stomp back to my station. What a waste of time that had been. Inevitably, halfway down the long corridor, the phone began vibrating yet again. Without thinking I snatched it up and shouted, "What do you want?"

Big, big mistake. There was a moment of stunned silence on the other end, and then my grandmother's quavering voice.

"Honey? Is this Katie? It's your grandma. Your grandpa has had a heart attack and is in the hospital. Your mom and dad are here, and we think you should come home, if you can. We don't think Pop-Pop is going to make it."

Oh, Lord. I knew that my grandfather had not been well for a long time, but I hadn't been expecting this. His support had meant so much to me when I was trying to decide to go to chef school. It wasn't fair—he couldn't die, not yet, not until I had made it through school and showed him I had done it, I had lived up to his expectations. I stood stock-still for a moment, trying to take it all in and decide what to do—my thoughts seesawed between the Amtrak train schedule and the recipes we had chosen to prepare for the rest of the week in class as my body automatically headed back to the bathroom, seeking a safe and relatively quiet haven from the sounds of the lunch rush already coming from the classroom.

I was almost to the door, the phone pressed so tightly to my ear it was actually cutting off the circulation while I listened to my grandmother make the sort of ineffectual conversation people create when they are facing the inevitability of death, when suddenly the phone was plucked from my clenched hand. I whirled around just in time to see Cyndee standing behind me, her pudgy paw clutching the phone, which was still emitting the tiny, tinny sounds of my grandmother's voice, but far off, like the cries of a lost kitten. With a terrible grin, Cyndee casually hung up the phone, cutting off the faint sounds of tears with a flick of one grimy, pudgy thumb.

"You are in so much trouble," Cyndee said, unable to keep the glee from her voice, the malicious giggles contrasting starkly with her usual Texas panhandle redneck twang.

Looking back at that moment, it was really a very good thing that I was not actually in the kitchen when this happened. Since I had originally intended to head to the bathroom, I was completely unarmed, and that is really what saved Cyndee. Otherwise, I am quite certain that in that moment, I would have stabbed her with whatever I might have had handy. Why was she doing this to me? Why did she hate me so much? And why now, when I really, really needed to use the phone?

Shocked with anger and emotion at the sad events unfolding for my family three hundred miles away, I followed Cyndee into the class, my confiscated phone vibrating occasionally in her fist. Instead of presenting me to Chef Pierre, as I had expected, Cyndee led me to the broad back and none-too-clean chef's jacket of Dean Franco. Chef Pierre had been called away and the dean would be watching us for the next half hour. My bad luck. Chef Pierre would have yelled, but everything would have been okay. Dean Franco was another matter. Cyndee handed him my phone and reported my transgression to him.

Without even letting her finish, Dean Franco said, "Suspension. The rest of the day. And I think we should keep this," indicating the phone, "until you can understand how to handle it properly. Not during class. Tomorrow, you may have your phone back, after class."

I was shocked. Suspended? Me? I didn't even jaywalk, and had never ever been in trouble in school. Confiscating my cell phone was unthinkable. I had no other way to contact my family. All I could get out in my defense was a feeble "But . . . but . . ." Even Cyndee seemed slightly taken aback by the sentence Dean Franco had given. Pointing out that my brigade was already short a member and we had not yet finished preparing the first course for the chefs' table, she was able to commute my suspension. I was sent back to my station.

I made it through the rest of the morning, trying not to mess things up too badly while my mind was occupied with thoughts of my family. Suddenly, Chef Pierre was once again at my elbow, a very serious look on his face. I have never been more relieved—I dropped my paring knife and turned to Chef, mumbling incoherently and twisting the French knot buttons on my chef's jacket. I tried to tell my side of the story, hoping that at least Chef Pierre would listen. Chef patted my hand and told me that he had heard about what had happened, and he needed to let Franco know the gravity of the situation and we would see about getting my phone back and getting me excused from class for the next day or so for a family emergency.

He returned from the dean's office with my phone and a signed note excusing me from class, but he needn't have bothered. My grandfather had died that morning.

Apple-Bottom Gingerbread

This is the sort of food you really need in tough times. You can make it with a reasonably well stocked pantry without having to run out for groceries, and the recipe is just enough work to occupy your hands and mind without being taxing. It is wonderful right out of the oven, but if you are like me, and can't even think about eating when you are very upset, this actually gets better the longer it sits, so when you wake up hungry in the middle of the night, this is the perfect thing—not too sweet, with a comforting, squishy texture and delightful spiciness. Perfect with a dollop of vanilla ice cream or a big, frosty glass of cold milk.

For the apple bottom:

2 tablespoons (¼ stick) unsalted butter

2 tablespoons dark brown sugar

2 apples, peeled, cored, and cut into ⅛-inch-thick slices

For the gingerbread:

Nonstick cooking spray or butter, for the pan (see Note)

2¼ cups all-purpose flour

1 teaspoon ground ginger

1 teaspoon ground cinnamon

⅛ teaspoon ground cloves

⅛ teaspoon ground allspice

1 teaspoon baking soda

⅓ cup dark brown sugar

2 tablespoons freshly grated ginger

1 cup dark molasses

1 egg

¾ cup hot water

½ cup vegetable oil

1. To prepare the apple bottom: In a saucepan over low heat, stir together the butter and brown sugar until the butter melts. Add the apples and cook gently until the apples soften and caramelize slightly but still retain their shape, about 15 minutes. Remove from the heat.
2. To make the gingerbread: Preheat the oven to 325°F. Thoroughly grease a 9-inch round cake pan or ovenproof glass baking dish.
3. In a large bowl, combine the flour, ground ginger, cinnamon, cloves, allspice, baking soda, and brown sugar. Stir in the grated ginger and the molasses, then the egg. Once the egg has been fully incorporated, add the hot water and oil. Mix gently until everything is well combined.
4. Spread the apples and their caramel in one layer in the prepared pan. (I like to arrange them in a roughly circular pattern, but it doesn't really matter.) Gently pour in the gingerbread batter.
5. Bake for 45 minutes to 1 hour. The gingerbread is fully baked when a toothpick comes out clean.
6. Let cool in the pan for 5 minutes and then invert the pan onto a large plate or platter. Everything should come out beautifully.

NOTE: To grease a cake pan, I like to use Baker's Joy, but Pam would work and butter is just fine.

Makes one 9-inch cake, enough for 6 people

THE OTHER WHITE MEAT

I went home to Virginia for the funeral. Even though I wanted to stay, to hold my grandmother's small, gnarled hand, to cook comforting food for my father, whose quiet devastation shook me more than tears, within hours of the service I was on my way back to New York. The midterm exam was coming with the first cool days of fall, and I couldn't afford to lose more than one day at school. So of course my train broke down and had to be pushed into the Wilmington, Delaware, station and I ended up taking a bus back into New York. I emerged from the Port Authority Bus Terminal onto Forty-second Street in the middle of a windy night—not good timing, but I didn't even register the seamier side of big-city nightlife as I hailed a cab and made my way downtown. Being teased by the tranny hookers on Forty-second Street was the least of my problems. At last I turned the key in the apartment door and slipped into bed next to Michael's sweetly sleeping form. It was well past midnight, and I would need to be at school in a few hours.

Things were more and more hectic in the Level 2 kitchens, as we were fully occupied not only with our own daily tasks, but also with preparing as much as possible for the midterm. Not actually studying, but starting to prepare all the little things that would be needed in the heat of the test, like bread crumbs, veal stock, and chicken stock, and replenishing the kitchen with fresh containers of kosher salt, peppercorns, vegetable oil, and vinegar. We started cleaning the Robot Coupes, industrial blenders, food mills, and large ladles and spoons to a high polish. The Level 4 students were doing the same thing, but on a much larger scale. Because of the more complicated nature of their recipes, they had already begun to make their more elaborate stocks and freezing them, portioning meat, and preparing the odds and ends that would be needed for their final.

There was just one small problem—the school had not been designed for so much stockpiling of ingredients, and everyone was running out of places to put things. The Level 4 students did not have large industrial refrigerators in their kitchen, merely little under-counter lowboys that needed to be cleaned out every afternoon so that the night-shift students could use them. The colossal walk-in refrigerator, the size of a studio apartment, was almost always full to bursting with plastic buckets full of congealed veal stock, five-quart cans of mustard, trays of bizarre experiments the chef-instructors had made and then covered with foil and forgotten about, and anything else that might come in handy sometime. This left space only in the large Level 2 refrigerators and freezers, space that we were already using for our own midterm exam materials and our daily allotment of ingredients from the storeroom. Things were getting messy, and the door of the refrigerator often opened to reveal an incredible muddle of leeks, carrots, bits of lamb, veal bones, potato scraps, and celery leaves all jumbled together, garnished with a disk or two of chilling puff pastry. It was only a matter of time before Chef Pierre noticed and exploded, which he did one hectic morning as we frantically tried to start our two recipes for *saucier*.

KABLAM! The door of the refrigerator banged shut like a gunshot, and Chef's face went through its now familiar transformation from pink to fuchsia to beet red to a deep magenta before he began the now familiar refrain—"What the fuck eez this? What is going on here?" It was so familiar by now that it no longer caused me to tremble in my chef's clogs—I barely registered it, actually, as I bent my head over my cutting board, minding my own business as much as possible. I had learned not to make eye contact or involve myself in these volcanic eruptions unless it was specifically targeted at my brigade. This seemed more of a general, whole-class condemnation and nothing to worry about. Until the ingredients for our two

dishes—roasted chicken *en sauce diable* and a *blanquette de veau*—
began pelting our workstation and ricocheting into our faces. It was
very unlike Chef to throw food—ingredients were a precious commodity that should be treated with care and respect. Chef must have
been feeling the pressure of the upcoming exams, too.

Now was the time to get involved. Motioning to my teammates,
we stashed our cutting boards, complete with vegetables mid-mince,
under the workstation and dove into the fray. Junior neatly fielded
a head of lettuce that seemed to be aimed at the students in garde-
manger and began stacking a small pyramid of vegetables together in
the family meal workstation. I started to pull out the trays of ingredients that were stacked haphazardly on top of one another in one walk-
in, labeling them by their dish (it was easy to tell what tray belonged
to what recipe, and what brigade, as we had all made the same recipes
so many times by now) and consolidating them into one corner in a
neat stack. Much better. Angelo and Jackie had repacked all of the
mise en place we had prepared for the midterm in a neat arrangement
in another fridge, and all that was left was to sort out the remaining
ingredients that littered the kitchen and get back to work. Chef had
backed off from his impression of a major-league pitcher and watched
us put everything back with his hands folded across his chest in classic
Chef Pierre posture. When we had almost finished, he said, "*Merci.
Allez!* Back to work!" Merely asking us nicely to clean up the kitchen
wouldn't stir us into action; it took an act of God, or Chef.

We returned to our station, our ingredients out now in a pile. The
vegetables had been dealt with, for the most part, which just left the
garnishes and the meats themselves. The chickens had been separated from their fellows and stored in a large bowl over ice, which
was standard procedure. This left us only a large plastic bag of pale
pink meat scraps, already roughly cubed. This was not that unusual—
if a brigade had recently done the same recipe, they would have been
faced with an entire breast of veal to debone, and the extra meat not

used in their recipe would have been carefully wrapped, labeled, and set aside in the fridge until the next group came along. One thing was strange, though: this package was unlabeled. This was (yet another) cardinal sin in the kitchen. Without a label clearly describing the contents of the package, to whom the package belonged, as well as the date on which it entered the refrigerator, things would often go missing—thrown away, stolen by another student (or instructor) for their own use, or sucked into the void where stray socks and car keys go. There was a moment's hesitation as I hefted the package of pink meat in my hands, wondering where its label had gone. *Probably got lost in the scuffle,* I thought, adding it to our little pile and getting ready to begin.

Ben and Tucker would be working on the chicken *au diable,* a quartered roasted chicken liberally laced with fiery hot mustard and seasoned bread crumbs and napped with a tart vinegar and tarragon sauce enriched with a powerful demi-glace. Junior and I would be tackling the veal stew, made by the cooking process known as braising—in which the meat is first seared, then cooked gently in a small amount of liquid—a wonderful technique for cooking especially tough cuts of meat. The long exposure to low heat, gentled by the addition of a bit of liquid, causes the fibrous tissues to slowly break down, yielding an exceptionally soft, almost buttery texture. The liquid is enriched by the juices from the meat released during cooking, and the whole is fortified with a bit more highly flavored liquid (usually wine and stock), reinforced with some well-cooked and seasoned vegetables, and it all comes together as a whole infinitely more delicious than its parts.

Braising is a cooking technique that also allows a degree of latitude in its preparation. While it is possible to overcook the meat, making it tough and stringy, in general, the longer the cooking time, the more tender the meat will be and the more delicious and rich the braising liquid. But this *blanquette de veau* was for the chefs' lunch, and so we had only a little less than two hours to let the veal cook. After searing the veal, the meat must also be blanched twice to remove any lurking impurities in the flesh. These impurities take the form of an ugly grayish scum that rises to the surface of the water and must be removed before the meat can be added to the stew—otherwise the grayish scum will discolor the distinctive white sauce the blanquette is known for. This is a laborious process, taking on all the frustrating aspects of watching water slowly come to a boil not once, but twice—the slime must be skimmed, the meat drained and examined thoroughly for any clinging bits of albumin (as the scum is technically called), and then returned to a large pot called a *rondeau* to begin its braise.

As Junior and I patiently seared, then blanched, drained, and examined our bits of veal, it occurred to me that this veal was not as scummy as usual. Perhaps it had been washed before it was put away, I thought, and it had affected the veal in a good way. I didn't have time to ponder this aberration long, as we were going to be pressed for time, as usual. Braising can be done on the top of the stove or in the oven; in general, because ovens are able to sustain a low and even temperature, chefs prefer to braise in the oven. It makes a better stew, but it does take significantly more time—something we didn't have. We placed the veal in the pot and added a creamy velouté we had made. A velouté is a rich sauce made from a mixture of white veal stock and heavy cream or milk and thickened with a roux. We covered everything tightly with two layers of foil and stuck it on the back of the stove over a low flame while we got on with the garniture. A classic *blanquette de veau* is a creamy white color, broken only by the pale chunks of the meat and flashes of green from peas, brilliant orange from tournéed carrots, and the translucence of lightly sautéed mushrooms and pearl onions. All of these vegetables are prepared separately and added to the stew only when the meat has reached the proper consistency. While we peeled mushroom caps, cut carrots, and peeled pearl onions (one of the most thankless tasks in the kitchen), Junior and I would swoop by the gently simmering stew to check on the meat.

Taking a spoonful of the sauce and inspecting it for proper color and flavor went well, but the lumps of grayish meat didn't seem to be getting any more tender. In fact, the meat seemed to be going in the other direction, becoming progressively tougher each time we tested the stew. I kept hoping that at any moment the fibers would relax, the veal would become buttery soft. Once again, we were running out of time, and for once, Chef Pierre was too busy to rescue us. We had a whispered conference with Tucker and Ben, whose chicken was turning out beautifully, of course, blast them. We really had no choice, we had to add the garnish and send it out as it was. In large soup bowls we placed small mounds of molded rice pilaf, and surrounded them with odd numbers of carrots, onions, mushrooms, veal pieces, and peas, heavily sauced with the velouté. Then we prayed that somehow, between the kitchen and the dining table, the veal would magically become tender.

We gathered in a little cluster for the afternoon lecture, waiting to hear the comments of the chefs on our efforts. This was never a happy time for us students, as Chef Pierre read the often insulting comments out loud for the rest of the class to hear. No one escaped without some cutting comment, and frequently these judgments were so amusing in their phrasing that a student could be dogged by a new nickname for weeks—nothing could be worse than the nickname given to Wendell, a boy in our class who had royally messed up the recipe for coq au vin (use your imagination). I kept my head down and my fingers crossed.

As we progressed through the dishes prepared by the garde-manger and the fish station, it seemed as if perhaps we might escape a verbal thrashing—there were no terribly cutting comments so far. Perhaps the chefs had allowed themselves a bit of wine with lunch? Then Chef turned a page and began the comments written about our efforts in *saucier*. The chicken received high marks, and Ben and Tucker were rightly proud of their work.

On to the blanquette. Instead of reading out the commentary, though, Chef began to read out the recipe, word for word, beginning with the ingredient list. The class waited in silence as Chef then went through the procedure, emphasizing words at random with his strong French accent. I could feel myself going red with embarrassment—this was excruciating. Finally he reached the end of the recipe. Silence descended. At last, he began to read the comments. The rice pilaf had been well cooked, as had the vegetable garniture. The presentation on the plates had been quite correct. The velouté had been well seasoned and was the proper creamy consistency and color. However, *blanquette de veau* is always made from veal, hence the *veau* in the recipe's title. We had used some pinkish meat, but it certainly wasn't veal. Perhaps Chef Pierre should once again demonstrate the difference between a calf and a pig to us?

The room exploded in laughter. Chef Pierre's eyes twinkled briefly behind his glasses, then he shouted for silence. He chastised us all for the sloppy way we had been keeping the refrigerators, and then apologized to us for giving us that bag of meat. It turned out that we had commandeered the scraps of pig meat the Level 4 students had been saving to make stock for their final exam. We would have to replace it before the final, but we were excused for our innocent error.

But our mistake was not soon forgotten. A week passed, and as we busily began yet another day in the kitchen, checking our tray of ingredients, gathering together all our pots and pans, and teasing each other, Chef Pierre staggered into the room. He was bent over in a modified crouch and seemed to be having some trouble walking. He barely made it to our station before collapsing. "Chef!" I shouted, dropping the plum tomatoes I had been holding to rush over to him. "Are you okay?" I asked breathlessly. Chef Pierre was leaning up against the stainless steel table for support, his hands clenched together underneath his apron. Suddenly, he flung the apron aside and flopped a large, long, very pink hunk of meat on my cutting board. It was a whole pork tenderloin, but the way he was holding it between his legs, it sure seemed like something else. He and the boys in my brigade were howling with laughter. "So now you know what real pork looks like," guffawed Chef. Tucker snickered. Faster than I could say *"merde,"* I had a new nickname, one that was going to haunt me for the rest of school: Miss Piggy.

I vowed revenge.

Rabbit Ragoût

Rabbit is the other other white meat, and, frankly, better than veal, pork, or chicken. Because it is so lean, it does not require the long braising time that veal does, and it has a much better flavor than chicken. If you have a hard time tracking down rabbit (and don't feel like ordering it online), you can substitute stew veal or skinless chicken thighs.

One 3-pound rabbit, cut into serving pieces (have your butcher do this if you are uncertain how to do it)

Salt and freshly ground pepper

2 tablespoons all-purpose flour

2 tablespoons olive oil

2 ounces bacon, diced

12 ounces mushrooms (button, wild, or a mix), quartered

1 medium carrot, peeled and finely chopped

½ medium yellow onion, finely chopped

1 stalk celery, finely chopped

3 cloves garlic, finely chopped

1½ cups dry white wine (I have even used dry vermouth in a pinch)

1 ounce dried porcini mushrooms, rehydrated in 3 cups hot water

1 bay leaf

½ cup heavy cream

Cooked Fresh Pasta (page 225), for serving

1. Preheat the oven to 325°F.
2. Pat the rabbit dry with paper towels and season very lightly with salt and pepper. Sprinkle 1 tablespoon of the flour over the pieces. In a medium ovenproof pot or Dutch oven, brown the rabbit pieces

over medium-high heat in the olive oil. When the pieces are nicely browned on all sides, about 5 minutes, remove them from the pot and set aside.

3. Wipe out the pot and return it to medium heat. Add the bacon. When the bacon begins to render its fat, add the mushrooms, carrot, onion, celery, and garlic. Sift the remaining 1 tablespoon flour over the vegetables, season lightly with salt and pepper, and cook until the vegetables are soft and lightly colored.

4. Add the rabbit pieces to the pan and cover with the white wine. Add the porcini mushrooms and their soaking water, being careful to leave behind any dirt that has settled to the bottom. Add the bay leaf.

5. Cover and cook in the oven until the rabbit is tender, about 1 hour. Remove the bay leaf.

6. Over medium heat, reduce the liquid in the pot by half (if this has not already happened in the oven). Add the cream and cook for 5 minutes more to thicken. The sauce should be thick enough to coat a spoon. Taste and adjust seasonings.

7. Serve piping hot with wide ribbons of fresh pasta.

Serves 4

Fresh Pasta

Nothing tastes quite as good as fresh pasta you have made yourself. It is very easy to make, especially if you have a pasta machine, and takes almost no time. I have even made this in the food processor—a must if you are tripling or quadrupling the recipe, as we often did for the restaurant in school. For the rabbit recipe on page 223, I like to roll out the dough by hand, without using my machine, and cut it into wide, irregular ribbons. Somehow this rustic touch makes it taste better to me than the precision-cut, mass-produced varieties in the supermarket, though if you are pressed for time, or are just plain unwilling to make pasta yourself, store-bought pasta is fine.

2 cups all-purpose flour, plus extra for dusting

1 teaspoon salt

4 eggs

1 egg yolk

1 teaspoon olive oil

Cold milk (optional)

1. To make the dough in a food processor: Put the flour and salt in the bowl of the food processor. Give it a quick blitz to blend. Add the eggs, yolk, and olive oil, and pulse on and off until the dough comes together in a ball. If the dough doesn't come together, add a teaspoon or two of cold milk, just until the dough combines. Remove the dough from the processor and knead it for a few moments until it is smooth and soft, like a piece of vintage Italian leather luggage. Wrap securely in plastic wrap and let rest for at least 30 minutes at room temperature or up to a day in the refrigerator.

2. To make the dough by hand: Sift the flour and salt together into a large pile on your work surface. Make a well in the dry ingredients

and add the eggs, yolk, and olive oil to the well. Using your fingers, stir together the wet mixture, slowly incorporating more and more of the flour until it is all combined. Add a few teaspoons of milk if the mixture is too dry to work. Knead strenuously until a supple dough has formed. This may take as long as 10 minutes, depending on how much oomph you put into your kneading. (I like to really work out my aggression by kneading, so bear that in mind. If you are a gentle kneader, it will certainly take you longer.) Wrap in plastic wrap and let rest as in step 1.

3. To roll out the dough: Segment the dough into four pieces. Either use a pasta machine, following the manufacturer's instructions, or roll out by hand: Dust the work surface with a whisper of flour. With a heavy rolling pin, use even pressure to roll out one piece of the dough as thin as possible without tearing it. Cover with plastic wrap and set aside. Repeat with the remaining dough, covering each piece with plastic wrap.

4. Return to the first piece of dough. Again roll it out as thin as possible. It should stretch a bit more this time around. Once the dough is ⅛ inch thick or a little less, it can be cut into shape. If not, put it aside and repeat rolling out the rest of the dough before rolling out the first piece one more time. Once the dough is thin (⅛ inch), cut it into the desired shape.

5. To cook the pasta: Bring a large stockpot full of well-salted water to a boil. It should taste like the sea. Once the water is boiling hard, add the pasta. Cook for a scarce 2 minutes, until the pasta is al dente and just floats to the surface of the water. Drain and serve immediately.

Makes 1 pound of pasta, enough to serve 4 generously as a main course or 6 as a first course

WINE CLASS

When we were not deeply engaged with our pursuits as budding craftsmen in edible art, one afternoon a week we were treated to wine class. Wine class was another special perk for the day students, one that the night students didn't get to participate in. While our tuition was slightly higher, I really didn't mind so much on that first afternoon of class, as Chef Pierre brought out several bottles of frosty cold white wine for our first adventure in palate education.

Wine has always been a particular passion of mine, ever since I worked at a small winery during college. Granted, the winery was tucked away in the foothills of the Blue Ridge Mountains of Virginia, an area known more for its spectacular views than for its *terroir*, but I caught the wine bug nevertheless. I was lucky enough to work for a man who loved wine tremendously and wanted everyone to love it as much as he himself did. During business hours I was busy preparing plates of hot baguettes and rare, runny cheeses, and keeping the wine refrigerator stocked with chardonnays, seyvals, and rieslings and the bottles of cabernet franc and cabernet sauvignon just this side of cool. After work I was allowed to sit in on the late-afternoon discussions between Jim and his fellow grape growers, usually over some dusty, exotic bottle of wine. They talked about the weather and its effect on the upcoming harvest, and what flavors and textures they could detect in the wine they were drinking. Shrouded in a paper bag, the wine's origins and varietal were a mystery, and they would all try to identify the grape, the wine, the country of origin, even what vineyard and year. It was fascinating instruction in the subtle tastes, textures, and nuances possible in wines, and also a great education on how much was possible to tell about a wine with the proper palate.

So I was thrilled that along with my culinary education, I would also be getting further education of my wine palate. Not that I had not been working on it pretty diligently, but it would be so nice to have an official guide, a chef, no less, on my personal adventure. There was just one tiny snag: Chef Pierre was a recovering alcoholic.

This was not a totally shocking discovery. Chefs are, by their very natures, a hard-living breed. They are famous for working late into the evening and womanizing early into the morning. Booze and drugs just seem to be the lubrication that keeps the creative (and other) juices flowing and the candle burning at both ends. It was slightly unusual that Chef was on the other end of the spectrum, having discovered this unfortunate aspect of his personality and taken steps to curtail its effects on his life. It can't have been easy, as the kitchen is often awash in alcohol, even if you are just counting what is used in the recipes. Everything from sauce for lamb to fish fumet may have the aromatic and powerful addition of wine, and ice creams, chocolate sauce, even pastry cream, are often fortified with spirits of a harder nature.

We all learned about Chef Pierre's abstention from alcohol through a mistake. This was not unusual. We made mistakes all the time, and had come to the happy conclusion that if we learned something from them, they were not a waste of time or ingredients. This particular mistake was one of Penny's many, many disasters, also not an unusual event in the kitchen. This time, Penny had been in charge of preparing a batch of pastry cream for the *bande de tarte aux fruits,* a summery confection made from a rectangular base of baked puff pastry dough, slathered with pastry cream, and then smothered with the freshest fruit of the season, all neatly laid down in rows of stark precision and made shiny with a liberal application of apricot glaze. It was not a difficult dessert to create, once the puff pastry had been properly made and rolled out to the correct size, with the help of a yardstick and a razor-sharp knife. By this point in Level 2 we had all made pastry cream so often that I could make it in my sleep and thought nothing of whipping up a batch of my own at home to serve as a light dessert with summer's bounty of fruits and berries.

Penny, however, seemed to have forgotten the injunction laid down by Chef Jean in the days of Level 1: "It doesn't matter what the recipe says—if I say to leave it out, then leave it out." We had been instructed never to add Kirsch, the strong, cherry-flavored brandy, to our batches of pastry cream. None of us ever had, mainly because it would mean a special trip to the storeroom. I didn't care for the taste of cherry brandy, anyway. But somehow, Penny managed to make the pastry cream, go to the storeroom, request and receive a double measure of Kirsch, and add it to the cream without anyone else's knowledge. So when Chef Pierre checked on the progress of Penny's brigade, there was no one to warn him that Penny had slipped him a Mickey, and none of us knew yet what disastrous consequences the seemingly innocent pastry cream would have.

With his characteristic lack of pretense, Chef Pierre began by tasting all the component parts: blueberries, kiwis, strawberries, a tiny hunk of puff pastry, a heaping dollop of pastry cream, scooped up on one hairy forefinger. Suddenly Chef Pierre gagged in a most spectacular fashion, spewing the cream down his pristine shirt front and making a running dive toward one of the giant sinks. Without even bothering to remove his chef's toque, he stuck his face under the faucet and ran water into his mouth. We stood around, stunned, unwitting spectators to a poisoning.

"Holy shit!" shouted Chef, as soon as he could talk again, water from the faucet still clinging to his chin. "Who made zat?"

Penny reluctantly raised her hand, asking innocently, "Did I do something wrong?" We all gaped at her. We had all done something wrong at some point, like oversalting the salad dressing or undercooking the chicken, but none of us had actually poisoned a chef before. It was awe-inspiring. I just wish she hadn't chosen Chef Pierre as her victim—I was getting very fond of him, in spite of the ribald jokes he was always telling and his tendency to shout insults at us from across the crowded kitchen. Chef Pierre was talented, and watching the easy confidence with which he moved about the kitchen, instructing when necessary and demonstrating technique with a swift and steady hand, was a privilege. Chef knew how to teach us without words—a rare talent. And now, it looked as if Penny had managed somehow to incapacitate him in one small bite of pastry cream. I wheeled on her.

"Penny, what did you do?" The class turned on the budding Lucretia Borgia like a wolf pack on the lone sheep in their midst.

"Oh, I'm in trouble. I'm definitely in trouble" was all Penny would bleat, over and over again, clutching her hands and rocking back and forth, her eyes darting wildly around the room, looking for an escape. There would be no help for her. We were all a little reluctant to approach the bowl of cream, which sat ominous and undisturbed on the marble of the pastry station. The furrow made by Chef's meaty forefinger was still clearly visible in its pale yellow surface. Finally, Angelo stuck his own paw into the bowl and tentatively took a small lick of the goop with his pierced tongue. We leaned forward, in fascinated horror, waiting for the terrible fate that would befall him. His face wrinkled up; eyes screwed tightly shut, he swallowed slowly. We held our collective breath. Suddenly, Angelo's eyes opened and he shrugged. We let our collective breath go in a gust. Not poison, then. But what?

Angelo began to talk. "It's not nearly sweet enough, and kinda grainy from the overcooked eggs, but not awful. It does have a funny aftertaste, though, like fermenting cherries."

Uh-oh. We knew what Penny had done now, but why had Chef reacted so violently? It was definitely not the pastry cream we were supposed to make, but Kirsch was called for in the recipe, after all.

Surely he wasn't allergic to cherries. Sensing the mounting confusion of the class, Chef pulled himself together and then told us all what had happened. Chef was an alcoholic, and not even a trace of booze could touch his lips. Some people could give it up with relatively little effort, but Chef just couldn't come close to it without falling back to his old habits. He apologized, herded us all back to our stations, and worked us for the rest of the afternoon as if the incident had never taken place.

We students couldn't stop discussing it, however, over drinks that very afternoon at the bar in Toad Hall. The consensus seemed to be that we all admired Chef for his courage in admitting his alcoholism to all of us, and we admired him even more for working around temptation without giving in.

Days passed. I eagerly awaited our first wine lesson and volunteered to set up the glasses for the tasting. Since Chef would not be participating, that meant even more for the rest of us. But who would lead the class through the four *S*'s of tasting wine: seeing, swirling, sniffing, and sipping? I fervently prayed it would not be Assistant Chef Cyndee. I did not respect her palate and doubted whether she would know the difference between a cabernet sauvignon and a cabernet franc. I needn't have worried. Cyndee would not be running the tasting for the class.

I would.

Chef approached me during lunch, calling me over to his makeshift office, which consisted of his grade book, his lunch, and a grease-splattered, tattered copy of our course curriculum. Expecting a reprimand for some mistake, I racked my brain trying to think of some recent mishap I might be culpable of. Nothing was coming to mind, for once. Talking around a large hunk of well-dressed salad he had just inserted in his mouth, Chef casually asked me about my wine experience. I waxed enthusiastic about my time at the winery, slightly embellishing my role from that of kitchen wench to something a little more dignified. Cutting me short in the middle of a rapturous description of my first experience with dessert wines, Chef merely said, "You'll do. Here are the keys to the wine closet. Bring two bottles of the Sancerre out, and pour everyone a taste. I want you to run the tasting with them. Here are the official notes on the wine, in case you get stuck." With that, he handed me the keys to the kingdom, a battered set of handwritten notes, and excused himself from the room, taking the remains of his salad with him.

Intoxicated by the first heady whiff of power I had ever known, I regarded my role as sommelier to my fellow classmates as a sacred trust, handed down from on high. I wasn't about to mess this up. As the bottles of Sancerre chilled in an ice bath, I read through the official notes on the wine and practiced my pouring technique. Thumb pressed firmly in the dimple at the bottom of the bottle, fingers splayed out in support, I poured imaginary glasses and raised my eyebrow, perfecting my professional sommelier's arch look. I needn't have bothered with the subtleties.

Everyone streamed back into class, fresh from the lunch break and full of excitement at the prospect of the first wine class. I was arranging the tasting glasses in even rows around the marble island, practicing my spiel so that it would come out perfectly in front of my classmates. I had just poured the last drop of honey-colored wine into the last glass. Already droplets of condensation were frosting the bowls of the filled glasses, as the heat and light of the afternoon wafted into the kitchen on the backs of my friends. Before I could begin my now carefully rehearsed patter about how to properly taste wine, and what notes they should be able to detect in this wine, Angelo wrapped his huge hand around a glass and threw its contents back in one mighty swallow. "Ahhhh. Thirsty," he said, beckoning me back to fill his glass again. Oh, no. This was not the way I had imagined things going. I resolved to nip this unruly behavior in the bud.

"Wine is supposed to be savored! It is a gift from the gods!" Admittedly, it was probably not the best argument to make. We worked hard in class, and when class was over, we partied pretty hard, too. I could understand why my fellow students were more anxious to get their swerve on than discuss the possible aromas of honeysuckle and wet dog (a terrible way to describe a wine's bouquet, but it had been done), and it would be hard to explain to them that learning to taste wine really had little to do with the sloppy happy hour drinks we had so often shared together. It was an uphill battle, but I was determined to share my enthusiasm with them.

I demonstrated how to judge a wine's body by determining how colorful it was—light-colored wines are usually light on the palate, without the power of the darker, more opaque wines, which have also usually been aged longer. I showed everyone how to hold the wineglass by its stem, so that body heat wouldn't warm the wine too much. I didn't think I had the chutzpah to insist everyone try the wrist flick that would swirl the wine, eliciting the smells and flavors locked in the wine's structure for proper sniffing, but I did insist that everyone first dip their noses deeply into the glass for a good sniff before finally giving the wine a taste. I am not sure how many of them could taste the crisp apples in the finish or detect the delicate perfume of acacia flowers in the bouquet, but at least I had managed to get them to hold the glass properly before quaffing its contents down. For a first lesson, I thought I did pretty well.

I returned the keys to the liquor closet to Chef as he strode back into the classroom to dismiss us for the afternoon. Pocketing the keys, he asked me how it went, a smile just barely kicking out from his eyes.

"It's harder than I thought," I admitted, hoping that candor would perhaps earn me a bit more credit for my performance.

"Good," said Chef. "Then everyone learned something today."

A Few Wonderful Wines

Michael and I both enjoy buying new wines, collecting special favorites, and, more than anything, drinking great bottles with our friends. We have sampled everything from a screw-top white that was so good we bought six cases (and counting!) to a Premier Cru Chablis that we first had at Bouley the night I graduated from chef school. We bought a case of that as well, but only break it out on very special occasions.

Michael has a soft spot for big, beefy red wines, everything from the Super Tuscans of the Piedmont region of Italy to the velvety smooth pinot noirs of Oregon.

While we never shrink from trying a bottle of something new and different, especially from an unusual location—we have sampled bottles hailing from the North Fork of Long Island, Virginia, Peru, New Zealand, Portugal, Greece, Turkey, and even Canada—we find ourselves returning again and again to the wines of France. While some people complain that "Old World" wines are thin, lacking the heft of "New World" wines from California, South Africa, or Australia, I find that the complexity of French wines is unmatched. Furthermore, many wines from the warmer New World climates pack such a heavy wallop of big, bold fruit flavors (in the case of red) or creamy, oaky notes (whites) backed by a high alcohol content that they overwhelm many foods.

The best way to find out what wines you like is to try as many different ones as possible. Experimentation is a must. Sample wines whenever possible—many shops run regular tastings, often with the importer or even the vintner on hand to answer questions and provide commentary on the wines. Establish a relationship with a wine merchant. They can help you focus on what you like and suggest different wines to try. Research is also an important part of educating your palate. While it isn't necessary to take sommelier courses or stay up late at night trudging through the *Oxford Companion to Wine,* learning a bit of background can help make a more informed choice. If you are building a wine collection, research is even more important, if only to ensure that the wine you have fallen in love with will age gracefully and taste as good to you in two years as it does today. The best piece of advice for aspiring oenophiles is this: keep track of the wines you like and the interesting information you have gathered. A small notebook you can fill with tasting notes, labels, a good vintage you have run across, even the name of an importer of a favorite bottle, is indispensable. I have found keeping track of importers can be very helpful. When I tasted the Chablis at Bouley, I knew I had to track down more bottles of this fabulous wine. The restaurant was able to give me the name of the importer, whom I contacted when I was unable to track down the bottle in any of my regular stores. The importer was able to tell me precisely where to find it. I even got a discount!

Everyone has a list of desert island discs, music that they can't live without. I have a desert island case: twelve bottles that would make my exile on an island paradise. I have broken my case into three whites, three reds, three rosés (I couldn't stand the desert heat without the refreshing, easy-drinking rosé; it is happiness in a glass), two sparkling wines, and one dessert selection.

WHITE

Château Bonnet Entre-Deux-Mers 2005

A lovely, crisp white Bordeaux that costs about $10 a bottle and has a screw top. Deliciously dry but nice notes of crisp Asian pear. Very quaffable. I drink it with everything from figs stuffed with goat cheese to a crispy crunchy BLT to rabbit in mustard sauce.

La Moussière Sancerre Alphonse Mellot 2004

Flinty flavors and aromas pervade every tasty sip of this white. A whisper of grassiness, like a newly mown field after a rainstorm, complements the citrus flavors perfectly. Excellent with spicy hot Asian fare or a simple piece of steamed fish. About $27.

Christian Moreau Père et Fils Chablis Premier Cru Vaillon 2005

A masterpiece of subtle oak and cream, with tiny hints of vanilla and honeysuckle. Unparalleled smoothness with a nice balance of acidity that stands up well to almost anything thrown at it, especially a creamy lobster bisque or a juicy pork chop with apples. About $50.

RED

Alain Jaume & Fils Lirac Clos de Sixte 2004

Aromatic berries add nice balance to a hearty full-bodied red with medium tannins. Perfect to serve at a dinner party with red meat and thirsty friends. Steak frites and this bottle were made for each other. About $18.

Llewelling Willamette Valley Pinot Noir 2003

An explosion of fresh fruit—blackberries, wild raspberries, and currants—is tempered by a nice bite of tannins on the back of the palate. The most velvety smooth finish I have ever experienced in a pinot noir. There is a surprising whiff of violets in the glass—delightful. Marvelous with cedar plank–roasted salmon or balsamic-roasted duck breast. About $40.

Château les Barraillots Margaux 2003

A Bordeaux lover's dream, this wine is *the* man—lots of body with intense, smoky aromas. The tart kiss of dried cherries marries a hit of tongue-prickling pepper with a nice long finish. I love to pair this with game meats—bacon-wrapped venison tenderloin, elk bourguignonne, or squab stuffed with bitter greens and shiitakes. Lots and lots of bang for the buck at about $35 a bottle.

ROSÉ

Château de Pourcieux Côtes de Provence

Lovely, light, easy-drinking rosé with the crispness of a Gala apple. A bit of acid gives this wine a nice backbone, making this more than just adult Kool-Aid. There are nice notes of citrus and apricot. This wine is delightful with everything from a rustic tomato tart to a bowl of blackberries dressed with brown sugar and lemon. About $13.

La Bastide Saint-Dominique Vin de Pays des Portes de la Méditerranée 2004

A very bright, tart taste of fresh cranberries gives way to the mild sweetness of ripe strawberries. Quite simply, summer in a glass. Delicious with a plate of cheddar, crackers, and sliced pear, and divine with a lobster roll. About $14.

Chateau Peyrassol 2006

A great spicy rosé from a vineyard specializing in reds.

SPARKLING

Veuve Clicquot Ponsardin Brut Rosé (nonvintage)

What's not to love? All the characteristics of Veuve—dryness tempered with a nice, toasty hit of yeast, small, uniform bubbles that just won't quit, and a nice long, creamy finish—with that romantic, pale pink hue that just screams out "Drink me!" Who am I to argue with perfection? About $80.

Moët et Chandon Cuvée Dom Pérignon Brut 1998

This is the sort of wine to pull out to really celebrate that special occasion. I would drink it every day if I could (damn those student loans!). The right amount of zing, with a dry, but not too dry, bite to it, the smallest bubbles in the biz, and (to me) a faint whiff of honey. Gorgeous. About $140.

DESSERT

Windsor Oaks Estate Late Harvest Zinfandel 2003

Lovely, leads with an intense, jammy flavor of cooked fruits and a delicate, honeyed sweetness. Rounds out the end of a meal perfectly—I really like to serve it with the cheese course. Perfectly balances a nice, creamy-tart piece of Bucheron. $15 for a half bottle.

MIDTERM

As in all things both eagerly anticipated and morbidly feared, the actual day of the midterm was the epitome of anticlimax. Weeks of preparation and a steady diet of nothing but the possible dishes on the midterm ensured that at least most of us knew what we were doing, but there was always the looming specter of something going wrong at the last minute.

In my case, something went wrong the night before. Despite the fact that I had made it very clear (I thought) that this midterm was the most important thing in the world, and my entire life would be sacrificed on the altar of studious endeavor, there was a slight problem. Michael, my darling lamb, had scheduled an important business dinner for eight o'clock the night before. Unfortunately, all of my pleading, whimpers, and frosty resistance did nothing to wear down Michael's determination that this was an evening the two of us were required to attend.

Not only that, but he had volunteered me to make dessert.

This was an opportunity, I told myself, as I frantically whipped together yet another piecrust, to assemble the latest in a long line of practice *tartes aux pommes*. One more chance to perfect my technique before the exam. But I was secretly furious. How could he? Didn't he know how important this midterm was to the rest of my career at school? I silently raged around the kitchen as I rolled out dough and diced apples, my knife a dangerous blur of motion as I thought about how my preparations for the midterm had been going.

The midterm was *the* most important day of school so far,

because for the first time we were all being tested and graded and ranked as individuals within the class. All of the infighting and skirmishes and aggressive cooking would pale in comparison to actually having the top spot, ahead of everyone else—friends and enemies alike. Tucker was determined to be number one, and so was I. Ben was much quieter about his desires, but the steely glint in his eye spoke louder than words. For all we knew, Junior could want the top spot as well, but recently the redolent and distinctive odor of herb, and not the kind we cooked with, seemed to follow him everywhere he went. Junior had also started oversleeping, and had appeared almost an hour late for class three times in the last few weeks. When he was in class, he had become more difficult to control—letting the crème anglaise burn on the stove, cutting the bread for the minuscule garlic croutons we used as garnish far too large, and generally being a waste of space. Long talks with him did no good, and both Tucker and I were on the verge of consulting Chef. But our concerns about Junior's possible burgeoning drug dependency would have to go on the back burner—for the time being, at least. We couldn't afford to waste the last few days before the midterm babysitting; we needed to learn the final touches that would put our dishes first. This became terrifyingly important when Chef disclosed the possible dishes for the midterm and we realized that our little team hadn't prepared even one of them.

The trout *grenobloise* was a dish that had somehow escaped our attention the two previous times we had been cooking at the fish station. The fillet of sole *bonne femme* (literally, sole made by the good wife—good wives in France apparently use a lot of heavy cream) that we had cranked out had been very good, according to the chefs, and so, flushed with our success, we had prepared that dish twice more, instead of venturing into the unknown territory of preparing the *beurre noisette* that was the central aspect of the trout dish.

Beurre noisette (hazelnut butter) is a delicate sauce that, in its most basic, pure form, is merely butter that has been heated in a pan over a high flame until it melts and the proteins that precipitate out of it turn a lovely golden brown. The butter takes on a heavenly, nutty aroma and flavor. At this moment, the sauce is finished, and must be pulled quickly off the heat and served before the browned bits go from perfectly browned to burned beyond repair. It is very hard even for a top chef to gauge precisely when to pull the sauce at the moment before it is golden brown and then correctly time the carry-over heat so that as the sauce is napped on the fish and the plate travels to the diner, the sauce remains hot and brown without burning or cooling and congealing. A fraction of a second too long over that high flame and the sauce will continue to cook, even after it is on the plate.

In this recipe, timing is everything. Of course, timing was the one thing that seemed to escape my team over and over again. It was always a struggle to meet our deadline to have the plates for the chefs' table on the serving trays and out the kitchen door on time. I knew that every team felt the stress of the clock, but my brigade seemed always to be battling the clock in a titanic struggle. Every morning, Chef would point to the large clock over the doorway in the kitchen.

He would say, "I am not your master. The clock is your master, and she's a bitch. Me? I am here to make sure you are listening to her."

It was true—every morning I would check the time as we began our preparations and feel that this was definitely the day we would be able to finish with time to spare. Every day I would glance up at the clock, ticking off the steps of a recipe in my head, happy to be halfway through our labor, only to see the monstrous hands denoting hours and minutes sweeping madly across its face. There was no possible way that it could be 11:15 already! We weren't going to make it—we were still braising veal for the blanquette, and it would need at least another hour before it was ready. Where would we find the time to plate properly? Or it was 12:08, and we hadn't made the vinaigrette for the chefs' green salad, which had to be plated and out in six minutes precisely. It always took longer to plate than we had time left, and there were many times when Chef hollered out the seconds ticking away as we bent over the plates, frantically arranging vegetables in a decorative pattern.

So with all the pressure to make eight examples of the perfect plate, coupled with the ominous ticking of the clock, it was no real surprise that Ben, Junior, Tucker, and I hadn't chosen to make the trout *grenobloise*. It combined too many elements of the unknown. But this wasn't going to do—Chef was looking squarely at us as he read out the list of dishes.

We were not the only brigade to feel less than prepared for the midterm. Imogene's group hadn't prepared the roast chicken grandmother's style at all in Level 2, though we had all given it a try in Level 1 when we were learning about poultry. Angelo's group hadn't prepared either the apple tart or the lemon tart yet, despite the very broad hints dropped by Chef that a *pâte sucrée* of some type would *definitely* be on the midterm. And I happened to know that Mimi's group hadn't tried to make the *goujonettes*—refined fish fingers served in a little basket made from *gaufrette* potatoes formed into a flower shape and then deep-fried, sauced with a red pepper coulis. We had made the *goujonettes* a couple of times already, and while I was praying that I wouldn't end up having to prepare those fragile potato creations, I was confident I could do it. My wicked side was hoping Mimi couldn't.

As I dumped the cooked apples into the tart crust and quickly arranged apple slices in my apartment's tiny galley kitchen, yet again racing against the clock, this time trying to get this dessert and myself ready and out of the house in time for our big business dinner, the day's events at school played out before my eyes. Tucker, Ben, Junior, and I were in the kitchen extra early, waiting for the fish delivery so that we could practice filleting the trout and finally begin to master this dish. Of course, this was the only day all term that the fish and meat deliveries were late. My classmates were milling around the classroom restlessly, for once with no preparation to do. Chef was herding us around like chickens, waving his arms and shouting, "Check your order! What about the vegetables! Make sure you have everything else you will need!" His efforts at distraction were useless. We all knew that if we were short a potato or a few ounces of bacon, the storeroom would be open for more. The important thing was the protein, and it was nowhere in evidence. We saw David hustling through the back hall and began fussing for him to get us our meat, and pronto! That was it for Chef. None of the students were allowed to be anything but respectful and perhaps mildly flirtatious with the storeroom guys. They were, after all, in charge of the precious raw materials we were learning to create masterpieces from. Yelling at the storeroom guys or even ordering them around was a definite no-no. Chef ordered us to our workstations and we stood in silence with our heads bowed as we were lambasted by Chef's acid French tongue for being so ungrateful. As punishment we were all set turning vegetables into various sizes—which was fine for my brigade, since the trout was to be served with precisely five perfectly turned potatoes cooked *à l'anglaise*. Quiet descended except for the occasional muttered swear word as a paring knife missed its mark by a millimeter and someone would have to start over again.

At last, the people from Western Beef and Fish Importers International took pity on us and our provisions were delivered. David, saint that he was, brought our orders to us first, instead of filling the Level 3 and 4 orders, as was protocol. Our trout arrived in a giant waxed cardboard box filled with briny-smelling ice and fish so fresh I could swear that one of them was still quivering. Not for long, though.

As a lifelong fisherman, Tucker, of course, was the best of all of us at filleting the trout, quickly reducing his specimen to a few beautiful, perfect fillets. Even though we hadn't had that much practice with trout, as each of us grabbed the superfresh, slightly slimy specimens and began surgery on them, I felt confident that with a bit of a trim here and there and the judicious use of my fish tweezers, I would be able to churn out decent-looking fillets for the midterm, even though I was still praying not to have to perform this particular dish.

While we all managed to fillet our fish in a relatively respectable manner, it took us significantly longer than the twenty seconds it would have taken a real chef to reduce the same number of fish to neat piles of fillets. The clock's hands swept forward, edging us closer and closer to lunch for the chefs, and we still had no really good sense about what to do next. We stood and waited, the fish chilling in a squareboy over ice. The potatoes were perfectly tournéed, the lemons and capers used for garnish stowed in the *mise en place* tray.

Everything was ready except Chef Pierre. We couldn't begin cooking the fish until he was ready to supervise us, orchestrating the timing so that we would not begin too early or too late, and generally yelling and screaming an equal mix of insults and directions to get us through the preparation. At the moment we could hear his voice bellowing from the pastry kitchen, and I didn't envy whoever had made the pastry crust for the *tarte aux pommes* in Angelo's brigade. I was certain it wasn't Angelo—for such a big, beefy guy, Angelo had the lightest touch with pastry I had ever seen. After an unfortunate first attempt at pastry in Level 1, when he had borne the brunt of Chef Jean's wrath, Angelo had turned out ethereally light, gorgeous crusts. For a self-described "pizza-making Guido from the Jersey shore," Angelo had talent coming out of his fingertips, and he was never again on the wrong end of a chef-instructor's wrath.

Finally, Chef Pierre's shrieks quieted into spirited orders, and he emerged from the pastry kitchen, wiping his sweating brow with a fresh white kitchen towel. Shouting really seemed to take it all out of him. I attempted a small, subservient smile.

"What are you so happy about?" Chef asked. Uh-oh. "What is all this shit? Where is your *mise en place*? Why are you not ready for me?"

This was merely the opening volley, an obligatory greeting that Chef said to each of the brigades before commencing his instructing. Ben mutely pointed to our bowls and squareboys full of prepared ingredients, and I silently ran a kitchen towel over our already sparklingly clean station. Chef was clearly stressed out about the midterm, possibly even more than we students. For the first time I realized that our performance might be just as important to Chef's standing among the other instructors as our individual scores were to us. The intense competition of the kitchen was not solely for class rank and grades, but simply to be the best of the best. Maybe the instructors felt the same. It would certainly explain why Chef Pierre's shouting seemed to have reached a higher octave.

With a Gallic sniff for which there is no English translation, Chef Pierre inspected our efforts. Poking a long finger into the carefully cut garniture, inspecting the lemons and the toasted croutons, Chef had no comment, the highest praise possible from him. Turning to our labored fish fillets, he ran a practiced thumb across the pale flesh, checking for stray bones and ensuring that the fish was firm and fresh and very cool to the touch. Chef was a maniac for making certain that the fish we used for each dish remained as fresh as when we received it in the morning. This meant that the fish spent as little time as possible on the cutting boards and as much time as possible in squareboys over trays of crushed ice in the refrigerator. Even over ice, the fish should not be left out for more than the bare minimum of time to be sufficiently filleted, boned, or otherwise prepared before returning to its icy home.

Sadly, we did not completely evade a scathing tongue-lashing by Chef, and it was all because of Junior, whose efforts with his trout had taken on the operatic physicality of a WWE wrestling match. After all that prolonged scuffling with fish and knife, Junior had stacked his fillets together not flesh to flesh and skin to skin, as we had been taught, but in a mishmash of flesh to skin and vice versa. While not as unpardonable as leaving fish unchilled, this was almost as bad. The tender flesh had been compromised by its contact with the skin, which could impart all manner of impurities, not the least of which was an errant scale or two.

Chef ceased his ministrations to the fillets and raised his hands to give more breadth and emotional range to his indignation. "Idiots! Morons! Boobies!" he raged, as errant scales flew through the air and then settled gently on our chef's jackets like iridescent, slightly fishy snowflakes. At last, the fillets were deemed by Chef to be acceptable and we were able to move on to the actual cooking.

Cooking in the sense that for this first run-through, as with all the other recipes, Chef would cook and we would watch, gape-mouthed like country bumpkins at the state fair, making notes of the correct way to do things, which often had little in common with the recipe steps we had all carefully copied down on our index cards and memorized the night before. Chef Pierre felt strongly that a recipe was a fine way to list ingredients and amounts, but it had little to do with technique. Technique was learned by watching and doing, not by reading.

Chef brought out four large sauté pans and explained that since the timing of this dish was so important, we would be using two sauté pans to prepare the fish and two to prepare the *beurre noisette* sauce—a slight change in how the classic recipe is prepared.

Traditionally, the fish is cooked in the hot pan until its skin is crisp and browned. It is then flipped for a brief moment or two to ensure the flesh is cooked through on both sides, and then removed from the pan and left to rest on a warmed sheet pan or hot plate while the sauce is prepared in the recently vacated, but still sizzling, hot pan. Because we would be making more than one or two servings of trout, we would break down the preparation into two separate pans so that we could be both more efficient in preparation and have more control over the ingredients as they crept toward doneness, a key advantage for this dish.

Without further ado, once two pans were hot, Chef tipped a

mere whisper of vegetable oil into each and then, as the oil began to shimmer, a sure sign that it was searing hot, with lightning speed Chef dredged the fillets one by one in seasoned flour and slid each carefully into the waiting pans, making sure to shake the pan gently after each fillet hit the hot surface. By shaking the pan gently, Chef was making certain that the skin was not sticking to the hot metal. This way, the fish would cook, and the skin would brown nicely in the vegetable oil with no fear that it would tear or be left behind entirely in the pan when the fish was done. As he used both hands to gently prod one fillet while sliding another expertly into the second pan, all without even the smallest splatter of oil, Chef kept up a running commentary on what we should be doing, what we should under no circumstances be doing, and what would get us thrown out of the midterm for doing to the dish.

As all the fillets neared doneness, he segued smoothly to the second set of pans he had waiting on the back burners. He didn't say a word, but merely by grabbing Ben's chef's jacket in a death grip and handing him the fish spatula, Chef charged Ben with overseeing the final moments of the fish preparation and we huddled over to watch Chef make the *noisette*.

Making *noisette* is hard, making two batches of it in stereo on two different (highly temperamental) burners while explaining the whole process to a bunch of neophytes is even harder, but one wouldn't know it by watching Chef. Like a conductor leading a difficult and headstrong orchestra, Chef used his hands to guide chilled hunks of butter into the pans, bring up a timid flame, and draw out two long sustained arcs of kosher salt and pepper that fell like the last gentle notes of an aria over both pans. All the while, he explained his every move to us, even occasionally humming snatches of song under his breath as encouragement to the sauce.

Without taking his eyes from his work, Chef began shouting orders: "Hot plates! Warm the potatoes! Is the fish finished cooking? Where is the garnish?"

We fled like ants before a rainstorm, scurrying around the work-station, fetching and carrying and making certain the last-minute preparations were ready. The potatoes, all exactly seven centimeters long and turned into perfect little footballs, were immersed in a pot of boiling salted water on the back of the stove to warm before being plated with the fish. Ben pulled the pans full of cooked fish fillets off the flame, and Junior lined a sheet pan with paper towels to blot any lingering oil while the fish were arranged on the tray skin side up to rest.

Tucker stood at Chef's right hand, handing him the requested ingredients Chef snapped out. What was I busy doing? Taking notes, watching, and writing down in chef shorthand every single move Chef made so that we could all reproduce it, down to the last fingertip flutter, tomorrow. At last, we were ready, and just in time: the butter had melted, and the milk solids had settled to the bottom of each pan and were just beginning to turn brown. "NOW!" shouted Chef, and he pulled both pans off the heat simultaneously, while also somehow managing to add exactly the right amount of lemon juice to each. A swirl to incorporate it into the melted butter—Chef Pierre is the only person I have ever met who could swirl two hot pans full of scorching hot butter in opposite directions without spilling a drop—and then the lemon dice and capers were added. Another swirl, and then a tasting spoon was dipped into each pan to ensure the proper balance of seasonings, and we were ready to plate. First, two fillets were piled, again skin side up, on the plate in a pointed, pyramidal shape, and then the potatoes, precisely five, were arranged artistically in a semicircle around the trout, somewhat like a child's splayed fingers. With a large soupspoon, the *beurre noisette* was then gently napped around the fish in a generous but not unruly puddle. The capers and lemon dice would have to be counted and arranged in an even but seemingly perfectly haphazard manner, and the fish would be gently dusted with parsley *haché*. That was it. Chef held up one of the finished plates for a moment, so that we could admire his dexterity and artistic flair. "Simple," he said.

It was far from simple, but at least we had gotten through it, I thought to myself as I reached into the oven to retrieve my beautiful apple tart. It was almost seven o'clock and Michael was home. *Perfect timing*, I thought, as the kitchen timer made bleating noises, right on cue. Unfortunately, though the tart was ready, I was not. Still in my street clothes (what I had struggled into early that morning before heading off to class) and extremely sweaty from a long day's labor over the stove, I looked like a Gorgon. Not exactly a yummy piece of arm candy.

"Aren't you ready yet?" Michael asked, his face a frozen mask of dismay at my dishevelment, as I was still squatting over the stove, pulling the tart toward me. Galley kitchens don't even have enough room to turn around, let alone stand in front of an open oven door, so I was reduced to a prone crab-walk to retrieve things from the hot oven. This was particularly unfortunate, as I was in a hurry and not paying much attention to what I was doing. As I turned away from the heat of the open oven door to save my eyelashes and tell Michael I wouldn't be a moment, I absentmindedly slid the bottom of the tart onto my oven mitt and lifted it out of the oven.

Big mistake. Tart pans come in two pieces, a flat disk that is the removable bottom and a ridged circular ring of steel for the sides, with a lip to keep the bottom in place. When force is applied to the bottom of the pan, without any support on the sides, the two pieces will separate, especially if well buttered and floured. I still held on to the bottom of the pan, and the tart was still sitting squarely on top of it, but the very hot circular ring, freed from its anchor, slid down my bare arm to rest against my elbow, leaving neatly scalloped burns all down my arm. For a moment, I stood there, unwilling to confront the sheer idiocy of the situation, but the tender flesh on the inside of my elbow was beginning to make a soft, sizzling sound. I knew I had about two seconds to put down the tart before my arm rebelled and dropped everything, and I really didn't want to let that happen. All that work! And it looked so pretty! What would we bring to the dinner instead? Carefully, I lowered the tart to the counter, and then removed the ring with a kitchen towel. As Tucker was so fond of saying after a vicious tongue-lashing from Chef, that was definitely going to leave a mark.

No time to work up a full-scale snit, however. We had thirty minutes to get ready and get through heavy traffic to Battery Park City. My closet does not really run to evening wear with long sleeves, but I threw a shawl over the empurpled burn marks, boxed up the damn tart, and headed downtown. We made it just in time for the tail end of cocktails. *What a good idea,* I thought, *just a quick little one to take the sting out of the burns. Nothing to distract me from my goal of going to bed early and being fresh for the exam tomorrow.* However, the vodka martini I quaffed on an empty stomach did nothing to allevi-ate the sting of the burns, but it did seem to cause the dinner table to sway back and forth in front of me in a rather nauseating fashion, like a ship loosed from its moorings in a savage storm. I switched to a glass of white wine or maybe two or three—anything to chill the fire spreading up my arm. At last, dinner reached its conclusion, and we were ready for dessert. My beautiful tart was passed around the table, accompanied by a small bowl of fluffy whipped cream. No one took any. Our hostess, who had shown unabashed and greatly unre-strained enjoyment of the calorie-laden spaghetti carbonara that had been served as our main course, declined dessert, saying that she was watching her figure. Even Michael passed on it, and when I turned my gaze on him in mute appeal, he merely said, "Too full," followed by a soft belch. *Traitor.* I was heartbroken, burned to a crisp, and already working on the beginnings of a wicked hangover. I glanced at the clock, a habit from battling it so often in school, and was dis-mayed to see that it was past midnight. I had to be up in a few short hours, preparing for my big day. I managed to drag Michael out the door before cocktails could begin flying once again, and we made it back uptown into SoHo to collapse into bed at last at half past one in the morning.

As I drifted off to sleep, aided with a Tylenol PM to combat the throbbing pains in my arm and in my head, I kept thinking that I was forgetting something, something very important. I ran through the steps of making a *pâte brisée* again, poaching an egg, trussing a chicken, and, of course, filleting and preparing the trout. Nope, I couldn't be forgetting anything. It was all there. I just had to relax and cook it all tomorrow. I finally surrendered to sleep, confident that just this once, the jittering little voice of warning that was my subconscious was wrong. But I *had* forgotten something.

I had forgotten to set my alarm clock.

AND THEY'RE OFF

I was the last one to arrive in the kitchens for the midterm, breathless, sweating, and nervous. A skull-cracking hangover didn't help, either. At least I was ready for whatever came my way . . . I hoped. I patted down the pockets of my wrinkled chef's jacket and pants, checking to make sure that I had everything—pen and paper to take the written test with, new kitchen timer, thermometer, ruler, and, of course, my knife kit and toolbox. My little paper chef's hat was perched on my tender and aching head, and I was as ready as I would ever be.

As I took my place with my team, Tuck wordlessly handed me a cup of black coffee. The first sip was strong enough to take paint off the walls and did wonders for clearing my foggy brain.

"Boy, Darling, you look like shit!" Tucker said cheerfully.

"Yup, definitely," Junior chimed in.

I am sure I did. When I finally woke up in the morning, the sun was ominously high in the sky. I lazily stretched and tried to remember what it was that I was going to do today. The realization that today was the midterm and that the clock read 8:15 was enough to send me into warp speed. Michael was still yawning and fumbling his way out from under the blankets as I threw on random bits of clothing and sped from the apartment, pelting my way through the streets of SoHo as fast as my legs could carry me. I didn't have time to stop for a cup of sorely needed coffee, but I didn't have time to worry, either. I was the only one in the locker room, and I was so frantic that I couldn't button up my chef's jacket, my fingers trembled so badly with the rush of adrenaline. I grabbed my knives and my toolbox, slipped my new kitchen timer in my pocket, and headed downstairs.

Thank God, Tucker had that cup of coffee. I greedily swallowed every steaming, battery acid–infused drop and felt better. It was a good thing, too. As soon as I threw the crumpled Styrofoam cup in the garbage, Chef Pierre called us to order and announced the start of the written test. This was it!

As I breezily wrote down the ingredients and procedure for preparing *pâte sucrée*, I breathed a sigh of relief. I was prepared; I could handle anything thrown at me, even the trout *grenobloise*. Which was, of course, the dish I wound up with when we finally trouped into the test kitchen and found our assigned places. I would be sharing a kitchen island with Wayne, a quiet kid from Dallas whose incredibly detailed tattoos had caught my eye at orientation. Wayne's wide blue eyes gave him an air of intelligence, as if he was taking it all in, but I quickly realized that intelligent or not, he had no idea what to do with the chicken carcass nestled in his *mise en place* tray. He was assigned the *poulet au sauce grandmère*—roasted chicken with pearl onions, lardons, and mushrooms in a rich reinforced sauce. It was a dish we had made countless times in Level 1 and Level 2, and the easiest of the dishes on the midterm. I was determined to mind my own business and let Wayne sink or swim with his chicken, and for the first half hour everything went perfectly.

The trout was paired with the apple tart, so I went to work preparing the crust, peeling and dicing the apples, and preparing the compote. As I checked things off my mental to-do list, I scanned Wayne's work area. It was a mess, with ingredients from the two dishes he had been assigned, the roasted chicken and a *niçoise* salad, littering every surface. I tried to look away, but found myself staring, fascinated, as Wayne wrestled with his chicken. He was trying to truss it, but had only succeeded in getting his fingers hopelessly tangled in the kitchen twine. I shook my head as I finished assembling my apple tart and placed it lovingly into my preheated oven. I carefully set my timer and slipped it into the pocket of my pants. I wasn't going to forget about this tart and let it burn. As I returned to my station, I couldn't help but notice that across the aisle, Angelo had already put his tart in and was halfway through filleting his trout. I was behind! The smoldering embers of competition, like persistent indigestion, caught fire deep in my stomach, and I redoubled my efforts.

As we worked, Chef Pierre and chefs from the more advanced levels strolled around the kitchen, poking into each student's workstation, clicking their tongues and making notes on the clipboards they carried. I did my best to ignore them all, concentrating instead on each step of my recipes and making sure my station and my tools were clean and neat. I was midway through filleting my second trout when I glanced over again at Wayne's workstation. He was *still* fumbling with the chicken! It was looking a great deal more battered, and I couldn't help but wonder how much longer it could sit out on his cutting board sans refrigeration before salmonella set in. Wayne must have sensed my incredulous stare, for he looked up, and our eyes locked. His held an unmistakable message of panic and appeal. Sighing, I looked around, checking to make sure that all of the chef-observers were busy watching other students. I began miming the right way to truss a chicken, using my half-filleted trout and fish knife as props. Wayne watched eagerly, his hands suddenly more certain as he began to trim and truss the poor bird at last. I told myself that I wasn't cheating: I was merely preventing Wayne from flunking out of school.

Halfway through my silent demonstration, an alarm started beeping, its electronic shrieks muted as if buried deep in a trough of mashed potatoes. In the total silence of the room, even muffled it sounded like a shrill Klaxon alerting a defenseless populace of a prison break. I was so busy with Wayne that I barely noticed, other than to pity, briefly, the poor moron who hadn't figured out that their alarm was going off. It was only when I watched Wayne's face go from eager enlightenment to horror that I thought to turn around. There, standing behind me, was Chef Pierre, his face set in a formidable scowl, his index finger waggling back and forth in rigid disapproval.

"No more of zat!" he barked, and then, barely concealing a grin, he added, "Darling, I think your azz eez reenging." He was right. It was *my* alarm that had been going off for the last few minutes, disturbing everybody's concentration and alerting Chef to my little tutorial with Wayne. I could have died, but there was nothing to do but pull my tart out of the oven and keep on cooking.

Finally, it was time to plate everything up and send it all out to the judges, an anonymous panel of former students and local chefs from the neighborhood. As I arranged my trout on four plates, Chef Septimus, a big hairy Frenchman who taught the Level 4 students, orbited by one more time, to ensure I was plating properly. He stuck his bare finger in the pan of hot water where my potatoes were waiting and asked, "Salt?" I nodded yes, I had salted the water.

"You students are so timid with seasoning. *Regardez-là!*" Without even tasting, Chef tossed a large pinch of salt into the water. I was certain that the potatoes were well seasoned before Chef had added his well-meant bit of advice, but there was nothing I could do about it now. My dishes were due in the dining room, so I arranged the salty little potato nuggets, sauced it all with my beautifully brown *beurre noisette,* and sent them out.

And just like that, it was over. We banded together to wash down the whole classroom, from countertops to sinks to floors. I realized the adrenaline rush of the last four hours of frantic cooking had completely washed away any lingering traces of hangover. I was happy with my performance. There was certainly nothing I could do about it now. After Chef Pierre inspected the classroom, we were dismissed to change into our street clothes and report back to class to receive our scores. Imo and I made a beeline for the locker room, talking over each other in our attempts to tell each other about our mornings. While I thought my embarrassment over the alarm was bad, Imo told me she had dropped her entire chicken on the floor when she was trying to put it in the lowboy refrigerator. Scooping it up, she blew on it and stuffed it in, hoping no one had noticed, only to realize that Assistant Chef Cyndee was watching her every move. Imo was certain she was doomed, but we both had to laugh over our cartoonish mistakes. We could have been extras in *I Love Lucy*, our inadvertent hijinks the stuff of comedy writers' dreams.

Back in class, we lined up and waited as Chef Pierre called each of us up to the front to give us the judges' comments on our midterm dishes as well as our grades. When it was finally my turn, Chef read the comments in his thick accent: "Trout nicely cooked, sauce nicely browned, nice flavor. Garniture well cut. Potatoes . . . way too salty! Apple tart nicely baked. On the whole, good job." I *knew* it! Chef Septimus had turned my potatoes into salt licks! Chef Pierre then showed me my midterm grade: 92. It was okay, better than I thought I would do, but not as well as I had hoped. I knew that grade wouldn't put me in front of my classmates, a place I badly wanted to be. I thanked Chef and turned to go, but Chef had one more thing to say.

"You would have done better, Darling," he whispered, pulling me close so that I could feel his breath against my ear. "I had to subtract points from your grade for helping Wayne. You know it is not allowed."

"But, Chef!" I wailed. "I just didn't want you to fail him."

Chef shook his head. "I wouldn't have failed him. *Pauvre petite* Darling. Do you think he would have done the same for you?" With that, Chef let me go, saying "good job" one more time as I left the room. I was so deep in thought, I almost didn't hear him. It seemed that in the merciless world of the kitchen, no good deed goes unpunished.

Mahi Mahi with Lime-Cilantro Beurre Noisette

Once I got the hang of making a beurre noisette, *I started playing around with different flavors. On a fishing trip to the Florida Keys with Michael, I caught my very first mahi mahi—a firm-fleshed white fish that puts up quite a fight in the water but yields moist and tender fillets once you've wrestled it into the boat. This recipe is a result of that trip—I used Key limes, but regular limes work just as well.*

8 ounces orzo or other small pasta

Olive oil

2 pounds spinach, well washed and shaken dry

Salt and freshly ground pepper

2 limes

Four 6-ounce skinless mahi mahi fillets

¼ cup all-purpose flour

2 tablespoons finely chopped cilantro

Vegetable oil or nonstick cooking spray

8 tablespoons (1 stick) unsalted butter

1. Turn on the oven to its lowest setting. Line a baking sheet with paper towels.
2. Bring a large pot of well-salted water to a boil. Cook the orzo according to package directions. Drain, toss with a little olive oil, and transfer to a baking dish to keep warm in the oven.
3. Heat a large sauté pan over medium-high heat. When it is hot, film lightly with olive oil. Add the spinach and sauté, tossing occasionally, until it has just wilted. Season with salt and pepper, transfer to a baking dish, and place in the oven to keep warm.

4. Juice one of the limes. Peel the other, cut the flesh from the membranes, and finely dice the flesh. Set the juice and dice aside.

5. Pat the fish dry with paper towels. In a shallow bowl, combine the flour with 1 teaspoon salt and 1 teaspoon pepper. Dust the fish with 1 tablespoon of the cilantro, then with the seasoned flour.

6. Heat another large sauté pan over medium-high heat. When it's hot, pour in a dollop of vegetable oil or spray it lightly with cooking spray (to keep the fillets from sticking). Carefully place the fillets in the hot pan, skin side down. Flip the fillets when they are well browned, about 2 minutes, and cook on the other side for about 2 minutes more—the fish will flake easily when prodded with a fork. If your fish is done before you have finished making the sauce, move the fillets onto the baking sheet and keep warm in the oven until you are ready to plate.

7. While the fillets are cooking, melt the butter in a small saucepan. Watch the butter carefully. It will foam up after it has melted, and when the foam subsides, it is almost ready. Once the butter has begun to brown and smells faintly like toasted nuts, pull the pan off the heat and add the lime juice. Taste and add salt and pepper as needed.

8. To plate: Arrange a small mound of orzo on each of four plates. Top with the spinach. Rest a fillet against the spinach and orzo and sauce liberally with the *beurre noisette*. Divide the diced lime among the plates and dust with the remaining 1 tablespoon cilantro.

Serves 4

❧ LEVEL 3 ❧

A LITTLE SLICE OF LEAVEN

W e had all made it through the midterm more or less intact. I had been penalized five points for helping Wayne truss his chicken, but I didn't regret it, not really. Wayne would surely have failed without the whispering encouragement I had given him, and while I did not nab the top honors, my 92 final grade had placed me squarely in the middle of the top few of us in class. Good enough, especially with the wicked hangover I had been battling that day.

We were to begin Level 3 shortly, which meant both new brigades and a new curriculum. At long last we would be cooking for the school's restaurant, aptly named L'Ecole—two dishes every day, one from the advanced course book and one of our own choosing. This opportunity to stretch our wings a bit and use our culinary imagination was beyond exciting, and many of us had been planning our meals in each station for weeks. But before we were assigned our new brigades and stations, we would all be spending a week in the bread kitchen taking an intensive course in artisanal baking.

The bread classroom was across the hall from our old Level 1 kitchen, and I remembered how eagerly we had observed the "bread students" in our early days—it seemed like years ago. They always seemed to be making something delicious, and the intoxicating scent of just-baked baguettes wafting down the hall every morning drove us all to distraction. Now at last it was our turn.

I couldn't wait to feel the leavened dough squish between my fingers, to taste the sturdy, dark brown crust from a *pain de seigle* of my own making. We had moved, in our last level, from merely relearning the basic skills of the kitchen to becoming extremely proficient at them. While I could dice a carrot into minute cubes with a few expert whacks from my knife, and I could even debone most of a lamb's carcass without the flicker of an eyelid, these tasks had quickly become monotonous routine. My soul was yearning for something more creative, more comforting, closer to fulfilling the basic needs of why we cook in the first place. The visceral pleasures felt from making and eating bread, that most elemental of foods, would surely give my soul the respite from routine it so badly craved.

The bread program at school was run by Chef Helmut and Chef Tina. Chef Helmut—or Chef Hel, as he was called—was an extremely taciturn man who wore not the traditional toque of a classically trained French chef, but a small cotton cap that fit snugly over his salt-and-pepper hair. His chef's jacket was dusty with flour, and the sleeves were always rolled up to the elbow, a startling informality that suggested that Chef Hel's work was manual labor, another difference between him and our other instructors. On the inside of his forearm was a large tattoo, an intimidating-looking thing that only seemed to reinforce the steely aura surrounding him, from his erect posture to his bushy mustache, which seemed to be in a state of permanent bristling. I found out later that the tattoo and Chef Hel's rather military bearing came from the same place—Hel had spent most of his youth shipping around the world with the German navy, returning to his father's small bakery to learn his trade only when he had been mustered out. The tattoo was a German compass, so that Hel never lost his way home.

Chef Tina, on the other hand, was all rounded curves and smiles to Chef Hel's stiff angles and lines. This was a woman who enjoyed carbohydrates, who reveled in their doughy appeal. Chef Tina was always nibbling on a bit of something, from a crust of the morning's freshly baked *boules* slathered with creamy unsalted butter to the crispy tail of a croissant that had not been quite beautiful enough to be served. There were often crumbs nestled in the folds of her chef's jacket, and her dimpled smile was warmer than the heat of the ovens. Chef Tina wasn't fat, not even excessively padded—it was just that she reflected so exactly the appeal of the dough she spent her time with, even down to her coloring, a rich, burnished tan, like the crust of a *pain de campagne,* and eyes of a warm caramel, so much like the warm puddle of melted butter and caramelized sugar on a plate of hot sticky buns.

The week in the bread kitchen was not going to be a piece of cake precisely, but it was regarded by everyone, even the faculty, as a bit of a breather for the students after the rigors of the midterm had passed and before we buckled down once again for the second half of our schooling. Everyone knew that it was going to be quite a leap from Level 2 to Level 3, especially after hearing the stories about Chef Robert, our new instructor for the advanced level. He seemed particularly fierce, and though we were all hoping that it was a case of the bark being worse than the bite—as had been the case with our other instructors—my own experience with "Bob the Bastard" at Toad Hall had not been reassuring. As a matter of fact, I couldn't think of a more unpleasant person I had met at chef school—and that included Mimi and Assistant Chef Cyndee, and that was truly saying something. So our week in the bread kitchen would be especially sweet, if Chef Hel wasn't as mean as he appeared.

We needn't have worried. Though his countenance was forbidding, and his German accent lent a faint ambience of rigid discipline to all our lectures, Chef Hel was a total pussycat. Like Chef Tina, Hel loved, loved, loved his métier. Bread was Hel's passion, his joy, his entire life. He loved the dough, the soft, yielding feel of it in his hands, the slightly tangy taste of it before it was baked. He loved the powdery softness of the refined white flour, the gentle coarseness of the rye and wheat flours, the sound of the giant Hobart bread machines churning away, the damp clamminess of the "proof room" where the racks of formed loaves went to rise before being baked, the heft of the giant wooden peels used to pull the just-baked loaves from the heat of the ovens. Most of all I think Chef Hel loved his state-of-the-art, steam-injected, superpowerful bread ovens. Two banks of them took over an entire wall of the classroom and were the pride and joy of Chefs Hel and Tina and the whole school. They were prominently displayed, with a grinning Chef Hel off to the side (he could smile!), in a large, glossy photo in the promotional materials the school put out.

All of this bounty would be ours to share in for the next week. And all the bread we could eat, too. Heaven. My very best intentions in those dark days of carbohydrate consciousness was to be obdurate, to stand firm against the tide of crusty warm baguettes that emerged from those lovely ovens in a delicious flood every few hours or so. Not to let myself be seduced by that heavenly yeasty aroma of loaves ready for the ovens. Not to even look at the gorgeously pale glistening hunks of melting butter smeared so suggestively on the chins of my companions. This willpower lasted all of fifteen seconds after I walked into class—Chef Tina chirped an obscenely happy hello for a Monday, and handed me a hunk of fresh baguette, saying, "Welcome to Bread." It *was* heaven, and Tina was an angel.

Both she and Chef Hel had already been at school for hours, getting the ovens revved up for the week and proofing this first round of baguettes. Bread makers get up early—Chef Hel told us that he would regularly be at his ovens before four in the morning to prepare for the morning rush, filling large orders for restaurants and getting the first batches ready for impatient, bleary-eyed housewives. The steady pace of baking would continue for most of the day until the afternoon began to wind down.

Bread, and particularly baguettes, when made in the time-honored way with no preservatives, last only a few precious hours before they begin to go stale. A baguette made in the morning must be eaten by lunch. Breads made with a mixture of flours like whole wheat and rye seem to have more backbone and can stay fresh for hours, sometimes even a day or two, before they begin to go stale. But chewing my freshly baked, crusty breakfast, feeling the crackle of the crust yield reluctantly to the tender crumb honeycombed with tiny air pockets, I thought the earlier it is eaten, the better. Bread is infinitely more delicious fresh out of the oven. France's national obsession with the state of bread was instantly clear.

Since the 1970s, France as a government has waged a war of law on the makers of industrial, tasteless, artless mass-market loaves. Led by Lionel Poilâne, now considered the patron saint of the artisanal loaf, a few bread makers began making bread in the traditional way, full of the rich flavor of liquid *levain*, natural yeasts, and unprocessed flours. Soon the French consumer was once again discovering the joys of a proper loaf of bread, and the government took notice and action. Bread is now one of many foodstuffs and agricultural products that are carefully regulated by the French government, from chickens to fine wines to sausages and salt. I was rapidly beginning to feel the lure of a more socialist approach to government—anyone who wanted to make it harder to produce things like the abomination of Wonder Bread was fine with me.

This we learned in our first morning in the bread classroom, as Chef Hel gave a brief lecture on the history of bread making, judiciously sprinkled with anecdotes about his many years as a baker before coming to teach at The Institute and liberally garnished with more servings of baguette with fresh butter. As we put away our books and wiped the crumbs from our chins in preparation for the actual work to begin, I couldn't help the wide grin I could feel spreading across my face. This was going to be wonderful.

That was before the class was divided into two groups. I managed to end up without Imo, Angelo, Tucker, Ben, or even Amanda. Instead I was in the other group, with Mimi, my arch nemesis, and Penny, whose high-maintenance antics were certain to dampen my native enthusiasm for the subject of bread. Oh, well, it wouldn't be all bad—my group also included Jackie, a darkly beautiful girl who spent most of her time in the back of class, hanging out with her Level 1 partner Wendell "call me Wendy," a boy with big brown eyes and blond hair he wore fashionably long, but his handsome face was marred by a weak chin. He was from my home state of Virginia, and he had managed to flunk out of UVA, the Virginia Military Institute, and even community college. Philip, the ex–bond trader fleeing his previous life on Wall Street, was also in my new group, as well as Ravi, a tall, dark, and handsome guy from India via Berkeley. He'd fallen under the all-consuming spell of Alice Waters and Chez Panisse, and after working in several restaurants out west in high school and college, decided to come east, get a *grand diplôme*, and break into the four-star echelons of New York chefs.

Ravi and I had become friends during Level 1, after I had idly picked up his knife from his cutting board one day during break. Big mistake. Chef Jean saw me do it, and before Ravi could snatch the knife out of my hand and replace it on the board, Chef had intervened in the situation.

"Never touch another chef's knife. No matter what!" Chef said, waggling his finger under my nose. "Ravi, you will have to teach her the lesson." That sounded ominous. Reluctantly, Ravi took the knife from Chef's hand and dealt me a stinging smack with the blade of his knife. A tiny line of blood appeared across the knuckles of my hand, and as I stood there in shock that someone had actually knifed me, in chef school, on one of the *first days of class*, Chef chuckled and said, "It doesn't hurt too badly, does it? Ravi was easy on you. Now you will never forget, eh? Never touch another chef's knife!" It was true, I had learned an unforgettable lesson—learning etiquette in the kitchen comes from the teachers and the other students who have spent time in kitchens. Ravi and I became good friends after the incident. I was looking forward to getting to know the other students in the class better—people whom I had never worked with before, and might yet be working with in our new level.

We began by learning to make baguettes—which, along with

the beret, are more than anything else the national symbol of France. They were also a staple offering in the breadbasket at the restaurant run by the school and staffed in the kitchen by Levels 3 and 4. Though now widely regarded as being Viennese in origin, the baguette nevertheless is an integral part of every French meal, and we were going to learn to make them the proper, French way. Aside from the traditional construction of a baguette—long and skinny, with a diameter not much larger than the circle made between thumb and forefinger, with seven long diagonal slashes scoring its golden brown top, never six and never eight—a baguette is distinguishable from other kinds of bread by its ingredients. They are of the utmost simplicity, and therefore uphold a basic tenet of French cuisine: It isn't really what you start off with that counts; it's what you do with it that matters. Baguettes are made with white unbleached wheat flour, sea salt, water, and leavening. That's it.

We would learn to make three types of baguette, and each one had a slightly different taste and texture because, in addition to the fresh yeast that would cause the bread to rise, we would also add one of three other types of leavening as well—liquid *levain, poolish,* or *pâte fermentée.* Each of these leaveners added a different nuance to the finished product, and we would experiment with all of them to see what was more delicious to us, and compare them to the "straight" baguettes we would be making as the control in this delicious tasting experiment. Unlike pastry, bread making is not quite an exact science—there is room for a bit of personal determination.

As we broke into our new groups and began measuring out our dry ingredients, I found myself in line to use the scale behind Ricki, who had earned the official highest score on the midterm. While we had all congratulated her on her fantastic grade, I had noticed that since the announcement, Ricki stood a little apart from the rest of us. Perhaps it was more a case of us all standing a bit apart from her. I tried to decide if I was really jealous of how well Ricki had done. In my heart, I knew I was. I determined not to let that nasty feeling of jealousy get in the way of our friendship. Still, I found I had nothing more to say to her than the occasional "Hey there" or "Are you done with that?" Now was no different. As Ricki gathered up her measured portions of flour and salt and yeast, I failed to make eye contact and only mumbled, "Scale free?" Ricki answered in the affirmative, and as she walked past me, for a moment I thought I smelled, very faintly, the sweet-sour tang of bourbon. Booze? On a Monday morning? On Ricki? I must have been mistaken.

I returned to my little group of Jackie, Wendell, Philip, Ravi, and Penny. We would be preparing the dough for the baguettes made with the liquid *levain*. We stood by our enormous Hobart machines, adding first the flour and water, then a block of soft fresh yeast and the cool, gray slick of tangy liquid *levain*, and finally the sea salt, watching the enormous dough hook, a vicious thing that would have made Captain Hook green with envy, churn the ingredients together and then begin to knead the dough with an efficiency that human hands could not compete with. While it lacked some of the romance of making bread totally by hand, we were working with almost twenty pounds of dough, and it would have taken forever to knead the dough to the correct, elastic consistency. It would also make for a better loaf, in the end. As the dough came together and became more elastic under the punishing spins of the hook, it began to make a rhythmic slapping noise against the side of the enormous bowl.

Wendell grinned and spoke—one of the only times I had heard him talk in the months we had been in class together—saying, "Hey, Ravi, Philip, I know you dudes know that sound! Whoo hooo! Oh, yeah! Sounds like a gooooood time." I looked at Jackie, and she shook her head.

"Wendell has a *quirky* sense of humor," she said, shrugging her shoulders and rolling her big brown eyes.

That was an understatement. In the words of my English friend, Wendell was a total wanker. Literally. I began to understand why Wendell was here, after flunking out of every other institution for higher learning out there. He had finally found a calling where his sex jokes would be encouraged rather than stymied. Wendell began making bump-and-grind motions to further elaborate on his joke, fondling his spatula for good measure. Chef Hel ignored Wendell's antics completely and demonstrated how to check the consistency of the dough—when it is ready, it is springy and elastic, and smooth like a vintage leather handbag—and showed us how to use our large plastic bench scrapers to scoop huge folds of dough out of the machine and into a well-oiled plastic bin. It took some major finesse, which is hard to conjure when several pounds of sticky dough are hanging from your hands, but we managed, though I ended up with my fingers glued fast to Penny's with gooey dough when it was all over. As I unstuck myself, Penny looked up at me with her watery blue eyes and said, with devastating simplicity, "What are we doing again?" Oh, no. Penny was forgetful, but I wasn't sure I could deal with someone who forgot which recipe they were working on, midpreparation. Taking her to the sink to wash her hands, I explained what we were doing all over again to her, and then gave her the notes I had taken during class so far. Penny looked over the pages of writing, mostly from Chef Hel's lecture on the history of bread, and instead of thanking me, merely clucked, like an unhappy chicken. This would be an uphill struggle, I was sure of it.

While we waited for the first rise of dough, Chef Tina lectured us on the importance of temperature and timing for bread making in the kitchen. Bread does best during its long preparation if the dough is the desired temperature of 75°F. In order to achieve that temperature, the room temperature must be measured, the temperature of the flour must be taken, and, if additional leaveners are being used, they must have their temperatures recorded as well. The water that will be added must now have its temperature adjusted so that when all the ingredients come together, they will be at the right temperature. While occasionally, in a very hot kitchen, perhaps, the water could be room temperature, most often the water should be very warm or even hot when it is added to the other ingredients so that the yeast can begin working right away in these ideal conditions.

Timing is critical as well. Dough rises at a fairly constant rate, and while it will rise faster in a warm room and more slowly in a cold room, there isn't a lot of tinkering that can be done with how quickly yeasts work. That said, bread makers develop a certain rhythm of making dough, letting it rise, folding it over, letting it rise, folding it over again, portioning the dough into servings, letting it rest, forming the dough, letting it rise, and then finally baking it, cooling it, and selling it. This rhythm is immutable and informs every other aspect of a bread maker's life, from when he gets up in the morning to when he sneaks an afternoon nap to the last folding over in the evening before bed, preparatory to the next day's fresh loaves.

By the end of Chef Tina's lecture, it was time to fold our own dough over—spilling it out of its large plastic tub, folding its outer edges back to the middle, and tipping it back into the tub upside down for the next rise—all to give the dough a more even structure. Structure is very important to a well-baked, well-formed loaf. Structure technically means the development of small air bubbles in the crumb of the loaf, giving the bread proper texture. A loaf of bread that has not had the right structural development will not rise as evenly, which leads to large, uneven air pockets in the finished product. Some breads are more airy and light, like a baguette or a Pullman loaf, while some are more dense and chewy, like a rustic *pain de campagne* or a pumpernickel, but all share the same sort of crumb, well honeycombed with tiny pockets of air.

Soon it was time to divide the dough and shape it roughly before letting it rest again. Allowing the dough to rest after it has been portioned by weight and preshaped allows the glutens in the dough a chance to relax and the dough to retain its springy elasticity without tearing. Dough that has been torn (rather than cut) causes the yeast cells to stretch and rip, once again impeding the formation of structure and even rising. Chef Tina produced several enormous sets of scales and, using the sharp side of her bench scraper, began to portion out wads of dough, casually flinging them through the air for each of us to field (some more successfully than others) and mold into a rough snakelike shape. Twenty-five snakes later, we once again let the dough rest and began work on lunch.

While our baguettes rested, we learned to make pretzels and bagels. Later on in the week we would learn to make pizza—Angelo volunteered his skills as an ex-pieman, and we were all looking forward to learning how to toss the paper-thin disks of dough into the air and catch them again, without damage to the ceiling. After a lunch of salad and pretzels hot out of the oven, we were finally ready to form and bake our baguettes. Wendell, still obsessed with his anatomical references, quickly churned out several baguettes that, he professed, were modeled on his own manhood and were made to scale, too. The baguettes were at least eighteen inches long. Somehow, I didn't believe him. Chef Hel was not amused and ordered Wendell to re-form the baguettes, this time without adding any unnecessary flourishes—we were all relieved. While the kitchen is a famously bawdy place, and jokes and references to sex were always rampant, there was something unpleasant in the thought of actually having to eat one of Wendell's "special baguettes," never mind serving it to one of the patrons in the restaurant. Without further incident, or inappropriately accurate anatomical renderings, we shaped the baguettes and used slim ash paddles to move them onto the large linen sheets where they would rise one more time before being loaded into the gleaming and intensely hot ovens. After the baguettes rose, we began loading them, ten at a time, onto the broad flat surface of the huge wooden peel, or paddle, used to ferry the loaves in and out of the oven. Once the baguettes were loaded on the peel, the peel was shoved into the depths of the oven, and with a quick yank, the peel was retrieved, leaving the baguettes in to bake.

A quick shot of steam, and a few minutes later, we were once again retrieving our baguettes, only now they were golden brown, fully baked, and crying out for a pat of fresh butter.

There were now dozens and dozens of freshly baked baguettes cooling in the wire racks, waiting for us to try the three different kinds made from the different varieties of leavener. As we went back and forth, checking the crispness of the crusts, assessing the structure of the crumb, sniffing the rich aromas, and, of course, tasting each to detect the slight differences in flavor, I thought how lucky I was to be standing there, munching on the best baguettes in the city, which my new friends (even Wendell) had actually made themselves on a beautiful September afternoon, while my old coworkers were no doubt hunched over their desks, staring at a computer screen. This baguette I held had been made by me—had been formed by my own hands, and would be giving pleasure to diners I would never meet. I loved the feeling that I had actually produced something tangible for someone else's enjoyment, for the first time ever.

This was what being a chef was about, I thought, placidly bundling up a cord of loaves, like firewood, to be sent downstairs to the restaurant. The act of creating something that would give someone else pleasure, whether it is a simple slice of bread or an elaborately constructed five-course meal, is a noble and satisfying thing. There was a sense of immediate gratification in the act of cooking, a happy result that I could see within hours of beginning work, unlike my old job, where results in the form of a published book took months, even years, to see. For the first time, I knew I had made the right decision in coming to school. In the upcoming levels, my classmates and I would be creating, feeding people every day, like actual chefs in a real restaurant. I couldn't wait.

A Bit More About Baguettes

Liquid *levain,* a true bread maker's leavening, is a sort of sourdough soup made from flour and water and yeast in a large machine that rigorously controls the temperature of the mixture within. No commercially produced yeast is added to the mixture; rather, the ambient wild yeasts in the air are utilized to busily work away on the starch in the flour. Baguettes are also made with *pâte fermentée,* another form of natural flavor enhancement and leavening. *Pâte fermentée* is actually just a blob of dough, sometimes called *la mère* (mother), left over from the last round of baguettes baked, added to the new dough in the mixer before it is set to rise. Another sort of natural leavener is called *poolish,* made from a portion of the water called for in the recipe mixed with an equal amount of flour and fresh (not ambient) yeast and left to ferment for a few hours.

The Basic Baguette

9 cups bread flour

3 cups water

2 tablespoons fresh yeast

1½ tablespoons kosher salt

Unsalted butter, for the bowl

1. Mix together the flour, water, and yeast. Once the dough has formed, add the kosher salt and mix well. Turn the dough out on the work surface and knead well, until the dough is very elastic and the texture of a nice leather duffel bag.
2. Let rest in a buttered bowl for about 1 hour and 15 minutes, until doubled in bulk.
3. Divide into six 8-ounce balls of dough and let rest for another 15 minutes. Shape into long batons, as long as will fit in your oven. Let rest, covered, for another hour. Make seven long diagonal slashes in each baton.
4. Preheat the oven to 450°F. Bake the baguettes for 20 minutes.

Makes 6 baguettes

Momma's Rolls

These yummy soft rolls are the best thing since sliced bread. Scratch that—they are miles and miles better than a slice from a generic white loaf. My mother has been making them for every family gathering since well before I was born, and has passed the recipe on to me, but my attempts are never quite as good as hers. Which is okay—we all have different strengths in the kitchen.

½ cup lukewarm water

⅓ cup plus ½ teaspoon sugar

1 tablespoon yeast

7 to 8 cups all-purpose flour, plus extra for dusting

2 cups milk, scalded and cooled

½ cup vegetable oil or 8 tablespoons (1 stick) melted unsalted butter
   (the rolls will keep longer if oil is used)

1 tablespoon salt

Unsalted butter, for the bowl and baking pan

1. In a large glass measuring cup, stir together the water, the ½ teaspoon sugar, the yeast, and ½ cup of the flour and set aside for 10 minutes or so, until bubbles form on the surface.
2. While the yeast is proofing, in a large bowl, mix together the milk, oil, and the ⅓ cup sugar until the sugar is dissolved. Add the salt and 2 cups of the flour. Stir in the yeast mixture and enough flour to make a soft dough that holds together, another 4½ to 5 cups.
3. Turn the dough out onto a work surface lightly dusted with flour and knead until the dough is supple and elastic.
4. Grease a large bowl thoroughly with butter and place the dough in it. Turn the dough over in the bowl so that the top of the dough has been greased as well. Cover with plastic wrap and let rise in a

warm place until the dough is doubled in bulk, about an hour and
a half.

5. Butter a rimmed baking sheet. Roll out the dough to ½ inch
   thickness and cut out rolls with a circular cutter or water glass. Place
   the rolls on the baking sheet and let rise once again until doubled in
   bulk.
6. Preheat the oven to 350°F. Bake the rolls for 25 to 30 minutes. If
   the rolls begin to get too brown, cover the tops with foil. The rolls are
   done when they make a hollow sound when tapped gently. Let cool
   slightly on a wire rack.

Makes about 36 rolls

A WOLF IN CHEF'S CLOTHING

*I*f anyone broke my spirit, it was Chef Robert. He seemed to embody everything that is wrong with the essential nature of mankind. He was, in the words of philosopher Thomas Hobbes in *Leviathan*, "nasty, brutish, and short."

Many of the chef-instructors at The Institute were once impresarios of their own restaurants. But restaurant life is hard, and some of the best instructors had come to The Institute after a long career in their own kitchens. Chef Jean had been in the business for almost forty years before he joined the faculty of The Institute, and he would regularly regale us with tales from the kitchen of the famed La Grenouille—one of the first, and best, French restaurants ever to tame Manhattan's concrete jungle. Even funnier were tales of his time as a private chef to some of New York's most high-society (and high-maintenance) matrons. Chef Jean was a lamb.

Chef Robert was not.

He was, in fact, a virtuoso of several of the seven deadly sins, and even Dante would have been hard-pressed to find a circle of hell big enough to contain him. That's what The Institute was for. A perfect den for the big, bad wolf. And we students were like sheep to the slaughter.

Wrath

He would prowl the kitchens, snatching bits of food off cutting boards and sizzle plates and gobbling them down like a feral dog tearing meat from a cadaver. His muzzle seemed to quiver when he sensed, perhaps by sniffing the air, that somewhere in the kitchen a student might be taking pride in his work. He would circle, gliding slowly closer in his silent black clogs, and suddenly pounce, using one finger to spear the object of pride, and sneer. Then the taunting would begin.

"What is this?"

Only a fool would answer this question. It was, of course, a trick. There was no right answer, so any answer at all would invite scorn. But an answer must be given—no student could be so bold as to ignore an instructor. It was a true catch-22 moment, and I think an opening gambit honed by Stasi interrogators. God knows how Chef Robert got his hands on cold war interrogation manuals, but he certainly put them to good use.

"Carrots, Chef" would seem like a straightforward, safe answer. But nothing in Chef Robert's kitchen was that easy.

"Don't insult me. I know they *were* carrots. I have eyes. What have you done to them? They look like total shit." The vowel in *shit* would become long, drawn out in that utterly Gallic way that combined the word *shit* with the word *eat,* almost as if he was saying "eat shit." Which, in effect, he was.

Then Chef would casually pick up the bowl of carrots that had been carefully, meticulously cut into tiny dice or minuscule, ridiculous footballs and casually dump it in the garbage. Sometimes— and this was even more effective at totally destroying the empty shell that was once your self-esteem—Chef Robert would make you throw away the offending vegetables yourself. Your own hands would then be the ones to consign all your hard work to the garbage, where it belonged. A small but brilliant nuance, leaving one more small part of you dying inside. Genius, really.

Greed

It was said that Chef Robert had managed to spawn two beautiful, sweet children. Such are the mysteries of the genetic code, and a compelling argument favoring neither nature nor nurture. The girls were a favorite of the other chef-instructors at school, while we students never actually saw them. They attained a mythical status among us, like an urban legend. Did they really exist? We were never certain.

One day, while I was in the pastry rotation, Chef Robert sidled into the chill confines of the pastry kitchen. He quickly snagged a half dozen of the delicate almond tuiles we had spent the morning laboring over, and crammed them in his mouth. Through the incipient blizzard of crumbs, he managed to articulate to our pastry instructor that he would like a cake for his daughter—it was her birthday. Chef Paul, the extremely talented and long-suffering pastry instructor, sighed and went to work. While we assembled desserts for the afternoon's service, Chef Paul mixed and baked a beautiful génoise layer cake. We frosted it with mounds of fluffy white chocolate buttercream that seemed like drifts of delicious snow, and Chef was just piping "Happy Birthday" in elaborate script with a cornet of melted chocolate when Chef Robert reappeared.

"Too boring," he said, looking at the beautiful creation. "She likes pink. Make it pink!" With that directive, he was gone again, pausing only briefly to grab a few sugar cookies for the road.

With another, mightier sigh, Chef Paul showed us how to melt scads of white chocolate, which we tinted Pepto-Bismol pink, and pour it out onto the marble counter so that it cooled to a glossy sheet. Then we carefully scored and cut out dozens of pink chocolate buttons, which we then used to festoon the cake. It was a vulgarity—the gorgeous simplicity completely obscured by virulent pink dots of all sizes. But it was a cake that any eight-year-old girl would love.

If Chef Robert managed not to eat the whole thing himself.

Gluttony

Chefs love food. They love eating it, they love thinking about it. They love food in the way that regular people love their pets, or their spouses. Food is that constant companion that never disappoints.

Food never starts an argument. Food never flirts with your best friend. Food never has an accident on your new rug. There are a lot of reasons to love food. But there is also a fine line between loving food and being a glutton. With Chef Robert, there was no contest— he was a glutton of the first order, one of the most impressive I have ever seen. Every morning, he would commandeer a member of my brigade—poor, hapless Tommy, who was eager to please Chef, mainly because he failed every single written test he was given in chef school, and still desperately wanted to graduate—to go up to the bread kitchen and steal one of the freshly baked, fragrant baguettes left cooling on the racks. Then Tommy would be dispatched to the storeroom to requisition a slew of delicacies, from silken slices of prosciutto di San Daniele to tender baby spinach to blocks of salty, nutty Emmenthaler cheese. He would return to his workstation, overburdened by this delicious bounty, and all of our mouths would water. But it was not for us. After whipping up some fresh mayonnaise, Tommy would then proceed to construct a sandwich to shame all other sandwiches in the history of sandwich making. It was always a triple-decker, toasted masterpiece, garnished with a smattering of salty-sour capers.

Tommy would throw his heart and soul into making Chef Robert lunch. This epic undertaking took most of the morning, every morning, and so poor Tommy never had a clue how to prepare the dishes in our curriculum. But Chef Robert never went hungry. In fact, you could actually tell time by the state of Chef Robert's trousers: they started off looking like the innocuous, checked pants we all wore, but as the day wore on, they would creep ever upward in a failed attempt to help cover Chef's expanding waistline. After lunch, Chef Robert often sported what looked like a houndstooth-checked Speedo.

Lust

Evil, like water, must find its own level, and so I was not that surprised to find out that Chef Robert was having an affair with

Assistant Chef Cyndee, she of the big ass, sour disposition, and gimlet eyes. Somewhat appalling, but not altogether surprising.

In the closed society of a school, or a prison, often there occurs the phenomenon known as "desert island syndrome." No one around you is remotely sexually interesting at first, but as the days and weeks go by, suddenly even the most physically repellent specimen of the opposite sex holds some attraction. One expected this sort of thing among the students in the classes, constantly being thrown together in stressful situations, where strong bonds were galvanized by the acidic criticism of the instructors. What was unexpected was an affair between instructors, who presumably had the opportunity and inclination to spend time in more congenial surroundings, with company that had not squeezed themselves into chef's uniforms so tight they could be confused with sausage casings. Even more surprising was the revelation that the affair between Chef Robert and Assistant Chef Cyndee had begun when she was herself a student at The Institute. Yet there were no whistles blown, no official reprimand, not even a gentle reproach for this transgression, one that would surely have ended Chef Robert's career, had he been a professor at any self-respecting college in the country in this litigious age.

No, Chef Robert and Assistant Chef Cyndee were free to, in the genteel words of my upbringing, "carry on." And so they did, at every opportunity. Luckily, I was never one of the few to actually catch them in flagrante delicto, and so am spared from having the image of heaving, sweaty jelly-like flesh seared on my optic nerve forever, like the *quadrillage* (symmetrical cross-hatching) on a piece of grilled snapper.

Chef Robert was a despicable, petty man, one who took immeasurable delight in causing other people emotional pain, but he was truly an excellent chef. He had an eye for presentation—the art of arranging disparate elements on a plate so that it transformed mere food into a work of art. He was also a master at unconventional garniture. He often came up with incredibly inventive, witty riffs on an ingredient—salmon with turnip gratin might be garnished with crisply fried turnip chips dyed a gorgeous purple with beet juice, perfectly setting off the mossy green of the herb emulsion drenching the orange-red flesh of the salmon. Chef Robert was a maestro of a symphony of colors and textures that all worked seamlessly to elevate the experience of dining, without losing sight of the primacy of taste. The very, very best chefs in the world are able to present an ingredient that has been eaten a thousand times in a way that is both visually stunning and gloriously delicious, creating a wholly new experience. Chef Robert could do that, over and over again.

I hated the man, with his cutting remarks and sly wolf's smile ("The better to eat you with, my dear"), but I admired and attempted to emulate his cooking, and will for the rest of my time in the kitchen.

PENNY

As we entered our third level, it was no longer possible to ignore the personality of Penny, whose bumbling shadow and irritating chatter seemed to permeate every moment at school. While we had all been aware of Penny from the very first day, I had managed to keep my interaction with her to a minimum, exchanging groggy hellos across the bench in the women's locker room, and occasionally helping her measure out her ingredients when we were both waiting for a turn at the scales. I could not be accused of being uncharitable, but I was not in chef school to babysit. I was there to be the best chef I could be. That did not entail holding Penny's hand through every simple exercise in common sense. Luckily, in Levels 1 and 2, I didn't have to. Penny was always someone else's problem.

Until the day she became my problem. As we convened in the Level 3 classroom for our first day of work after our holiday week in bread, the familiar buzz was back in the air—people were busy trying to figure out who would be in which brigade for this upcoming session, and the now-familiar social dance of alliances made and broken filled the air. The ultimate designation of the new brigades was a collaboration between our old instructor and our new instructor, and we had no say in who would become our new teammate, but somehow talking about the possibilities made us feel less powerless in the decision. No one was trying to ally themselves with Penny. No one was even talking to Penny, and she stood with her hands clasped in front of her, her chef's hat askew, as always, on her short gray hair. I tried not to think about what it would be like to be in a brigade with her, and devoutly hoped that I would escape her presence, as I had in the previous two levels. Finally, Chef Robert appeared in the classroom, his chef's jacket snowy white and his face set in a forbidding scowl.

After calling roll, he read out the newly assigned brigades one by one. At last, it seemed that Tucker and I were going to be separated, but he would have a wonderful time in the all-boys brigade he was now a member of. Imogene would be joining my new friends Philip and Ravi in a group, while Ben and I would remain teammates, with Jackie and . . . Penny. There was a little hush when Chef called her name, and much as I tried to fight it, I knew my face had frozen into a mask of shocked distaste. Not only would we have Penny all the way through this, the acknowledged most challenging level, but we were also going to be the short-handed group, once again. This was getting ridiculous!

Ben and I tried for a whispered conference before the class broke into its new formations. He was furious—his normally stony face was contorted, and his handsomely tanned skin had turned an ominous, dusky rose color.

"Oh. My. God. Darling!" he wailed. "Of all the people in the class! Holy crap! Penny!"

I shared his sentiment, but even as Ben was speaking, out of the corner of my eye I could see Penny's bulk bearing down on us, her red toolbox gripped tightly in one wrinkled hand. Jackie had already joined our little conference, and her big, liquid brown eyes reflected Ben's sentiments exactly. So what if she was irritating, I thought wildly to myself as Penny loomed closer and closer; we couldn't actually be *mean* to her. She meant well, surely. And she could cook—we were in Level 3 already. It wouldn't be babysitting, not really. I pasted a grin on my face just in time.

"Penny!" I boomed, a shade too loudly. "So exciting to have you join our little group!"

Jackie and Ben were staring at me like I had totally lost my mind. Maybe I had. I was preparing to martyr myself and throw all my ambitions and hard work aside.

"So, Penny, since we will be short one person for this level, why don't you and I work together and Ben and Jackie can work together?" I couldn't stop talking. I wanted to cram something, anything, into my mouth to shut myself up.

The incredulous looks on Ben's and Jackie's faces became even more astonished, and as I heard myself uttering the words, I couldn't believe them, either. What was I doing?

It was too late, though. I had volunteered for the kamikaze mission, and it looked like I was going to go down in flames. I shepherded Penny to our new station and began explaining our assignment. The explanations continued unabated for the rest of the term. Penny couldn't remember how to make an omelet or prepare pastry crust. She swore that she had never caramelized onions, something we had done almost daily since the second day of classes. She couldn't understand the chef shorthand our recipes were written in now, and could not go from one step to another without patient discussion and gentle prodding. Sometimes, the prodding wasn't so gentle. The herculean task of explaining, demonstrating, prompting, and making sure that we made it through each recipe, with Penny intact, was all mine. I didn't blame Jackie and Ben for keeping as far away from the train wreck that was Penny as possible. I would have, too, if she had been anyone else's burden. But she wasn't. She was my responsibility, like a puppy that refuses to be housebroken, and I still felt sorry for her—more so now that I realized how far behind the rest of us she was, and how hard it was for her to perform the simplest of tasks in the kitchen. This feeling of pity lasted for a month, until I finally realized that Penny wasn't the fluffy, harmless old biddy I had taken her for.

It began our first day in the pastry kitchen, while we made Calvados ice cream, apple-laced *pain perdu*, and hundreds of petits fours for a private party in the restaurant. Chef Paul, the chef-instructor in charge of the pastry station in Level 3 and Level 4, led us gracefully

through the recipes and new techniques. Chef Paul was acknowledged to be one of the most talented chefs in the school, and he was
blessed with one of the most easygoing dispositions as well. Perhaps
this was because Chef Paul did not come from France, but from the
black sand beaches and volcanoes of Hawaii. He was also very good-
looking. Everyone loved Chef Paul, except, it seemed, Penny. While
we stood at the stove, poaching tiny apple dice in simple syrup and
flipping the crisp, golden brown slices of brioche soaked in eggs and
cream, Penny began talking to me in what she thought was a whisper. It was more like listening to Mr. Ed when he'd come down with
a bad case of laryngitis.

"Well, I don't like him," she said, using her greasy spatula to ges-
ticulate at Chef Paul's back, clad in a perfectly tailored and immaculately white chef's jacket. I wasn't paying a great deal of attention, as
Penny had let the oil in her pan burn and ignite a small grease fire,
which I was trying to stifle with my side towel. I didn't pay a great
deal of attention to very much that Penny said—mostly because I
realized she often wasn't making any sense—but this time, I finally
took some notice.

"Penny, what are you talking about? Chef Paul is excellent, probably the best chef we'll have! Why don't you like him?"

The wattles that swathed Penny's decidedly undelicious neck
began to shake indignantly and her voice lost any sort of control,
unfortunately. "He's *GAY!*" she shouted indignantly. "That's a sin!
It's utterly disgusting!"

I couldn't believe what I was hearing, and neither could anyone
else, judging by the blanket of silence that had suddenly descended
on the pastry kitchen. You could have heard a grain of sugar drop. I
was appalled—to me, it had been obvious that Chef Paul and several
of my classmates were playing for the other team, and that was just
fine with me. In a million years, it would never have occurred to me
that anyone, even someone who'd spent their entire life in Riverdale,
Indiana, would condemn someone else for their sexual preference,

let alone a talented senior-level chef-instructor. Penny must have been totally nuts.

Jackie strode over to us at the stove and began to remonstrate with Penny in a low voice—for once I was too shocked to play minder to Penny myself. But things weren't going well—Jackie and Penny began to get louder and louder, and the other students were cutting their eyes away from the worsening situation. Chef Paul merely kept instructing the Level 4 students on how to properly roll fondant over a layer cake, a small smile on his face the only indication he was aware of what was going on. I was glad he wasn't taking Penny's ignorance to heart, and even more glad he seemed to know it was not a sentiment anyone else shared. But Jackie and Penny were definitely about to come to blows and Ben and I were going to have to do something.

Just then Jackie said, "You really can't say that sort of thing. It makes you look ignorant! What are you—a total jackass?"

Penny came right back with "Of course, you think it's okay. You're just a nasty little slut anyway!"

Another shocking revelation from Penny—slut? I wasn't even aware she knew what the word meant. But Jackie was enraged now, and as Ben dragged her out of the room to cool off, I could hear her shouts echoing down the hallway—"Slut? Slut? She actually called me a SLUT? I'LL KILL her!"

I turned on Penny, who was now humming tunelessly to herself, a smile on her face as she calmly went back to her place at the stove. But I couldn't let that pass—she had insulted one of my favorite teachers and one of my friends. I couldn't keep sheltering her and doing all her work for her if she was going to act like that. I was going to have to say something.

"Um, Penny? You need to apologize to Jackie. She is your teammate and you shouldn't have called her a name. It's just mean. Maybe you could say something nice to Chef Paul, too? Okay?"

Penny stopped humming and fixed her pale blue eyes on me.

Funny, I had never noticed how predatory they looked before—how brightly wicked they suddenly seemed.

"You, you're just a bossy little bitch," she spat at me, her sharp little teeth resting on her chapped lips. "Well, you can't make me do anything. You're just a little know-it-all trying to push me around. I won't do anything you say!"

Her voice had risen to a high-pitched shriek at the end of this tirade, and then suddenly it was over. She turned and went back to humming quietly to herself, placidly running her spatula around her pan, as if nothing had happened. Whoa. Penny *was* totally nuts. Without a word, I went back to work, finishing up the recipe, tidying the workstation, and getting ready for service. I didn't say another word to Penny, not that day, not for the last two weeks we worked together, and not for the rest of the school year. I was through babysitting.

Months later, I was lunching with a friend who told me about the symptoms her father displayed before he was diagnosed with early-onset Alzheimer's disease. The mood swings, forgetfulness, and abrupt personality shifts reminded me of Penny's increasingly erratic behavior. I found myself wondering whether Penny had been diagnosed in that little town of hers, or whether she was still on the loose somewhere, making people's lives hell.

MONKFISH

The *poissonnier* station was proving to be the most difficult station for me in the kitchen, and nowhere more so than in Level 3. While we had mastered the basic techniques of preparing food in Levels 1 and 2, the recipes we were working on now were infinitely more complex. There were many more flourishes, more elaborate garnishes, more steps in each recipe. Compounding this was the fact that fish is almost always prepared at the last moment, throwing our already frantic efforts into desperate overdrive. Today was even worse than usual.

The dish assigned to the fish station was a monkfish stew with aïoli croutons—a perfect balance of tender white flesh swimming in a light broth flecked with tiny bits of carrot, leek, and sweet celery leaves, garnished with aïoli, that intoxicating emulsion of garlic, olive oil, lemon, and bright orange egg yolk so evocative of the sun-drenched south of France. This is, indeed, the way the final dish appeared to the diners, as an almost effortless mélange of flavors that had been casually tossed together and simmered briefly before appearing, as if by magic, in a cloud of fragrant steam.

This is the prevailing philosophy of most modern cuisine, I think. The appearance of ease is carefully constructed; a cashmere throw tossed seemingly carelessly over exquisitely starched and folded 1,000-thread-count sheets. Old-school French cuisine—poached salmon trapped in a prison of glossy aspic with tiny tomato-skin roses and parsley flowers, *boeuf en croûte* smothered in puff pastry swirls and flourishes, flanked by rows of fluted mushrooms—is now out of vogue. Order was once king, and diners knew they were getting their money's worth by the conspicuous care that went into every detail, every single aspect of the dish receiving an almost obsessive level of attention, made obvious by the elaborate carvings on everything from carrots and celery to tiny radish flowers. Then, the pendulum swung, and the avant-garde regarded this as an unnatural affectation, order imposed by an outmoded technique on the inherently "wild" nature of fruits and vegetables.

The level of effort in these seemingly casual dishes remains the same, though. Carrots, leeks, and celery are still meticulously and obsessively cut into tiny perfect pieces, usually a fine dice called *brunoise,* and there are still many hands at work fussing over a plate of food, trying to give every morsel the appearance of an unstudied, graceful delicacy. Careful carelessness. So it was with the monkfish stew. The tiny, perfect little cubes of vegetables floating so casually in the broth were the result of three failed attempts. The carrots, leeks, celery, and Swiss chard had already been diced, blanched, shocked, and set in the *mise en place* for lunch service when Chef Robert, back from his illicit liaison in the walk-in refrigerator with Assistant Chef Cyndee, casually poked his finger through them and announced in his gratingly high, nasal voice, "*Non.* These are not right. Not at all. Too big. Who was it who cut these? Do you not know what *brunoise* means? Small squares. Perfect squares. Use your ruler. Get it right. Do it again."

This was perhaps the most frequent refrain heard at chef school: Do it again. And again. And again. And again. Hands became fatigued from clenching knives in tense frustration, blisters broke, and calluses formed to the steady refrain of "Again." Jackie was dispatched to the storeroom for another load of vegetables to be peeled, diced, blanched, shocked, and tucked into their stainless steel bowl *mise en place* squareboy yet again. This was a waste of precious time. Lunch service started at 12:30 precisely, and everything had to be in place, stations wiped down, nonessential equipment stashed away, and the brigade at the ready waiting for the orders to appear on the board and fire on the line. Redoing the garniture for the stew meant that instead of being able to move on with the prep work, the brigade was stalled, unable to advance to the next round of tasks, while the others must pick up the slack. On a brigade that was already short one member, this meant that we would not have time to take the half-hour family meal lunch. Work became feverish, veggies reduced again to perfectly even squares, then to perfect matchsticks, and from matchsticks to perfect dice as quickly, and precisely, as possible. We did not have time to begin the dish yet again.

Meanwhile, the monkfish beckoned from the lowboy. Two of the ugliest fish I had ever seen lay nestled nose to tail in a long steel pan over ice. Someone would have to break those puppies down into serving sizes, and then clean the bones and head and get the fish stock going for the broth. That someone was me.

There is a reason that until recently, monkfish were considered garbage fish by fishermen. They are hideous; a huge head with a gaping, slimy maw takes up more than half the body, which seems to taper off behind it. It is also strangely flat, like a manhole cover with fins and a tail. They are the color of sludge, a flat brown shading paler on the underbelly. The eyes seemed almost piggish, and far too small in comparison to that terrible gaping mouth. I am not afraid of gutting fish, and have gone deep-water fishing for mahi mahi many times with Michael, proudly reducing my catch to fillets. But most fish, even after being on ice for hours, have a certain briny beauty reminiscent of their home in the blue waters. Mahi mahi are electric in their shades of yellow and teal, swordfish retain their magisterial purple-blue shading, and even trout keep their shimmering iridescence. Monkfish look like malevolent sea mud, alive or dead.

The phrase "You are what you eat" was coined for these fish. Monkfish will swallow anything, and though they feed mainly on other fish, they are bottom dwellers, and anything that floats by, from used condoms to Coke cans, is fair game. That is why, once I had successfully filleted, skinned, and portioned the meat from the carcass, Chef Robert told me to get out my fish tweezers. Fish tweezers are used mainly for removing the odd bone from fillets. Fine as a hair, each tiny bone must be located by feel, each fillet gently and thoroughly prodded and squeezed with bare hands, as deftly as a doctor palpates a patient for illness.

But that was not the purpose for the tweezers this time. When I asked Chef what he would like me to do next, he grinned, the sly "Oh, what a stupid student" grin I hated, and said, "Look closeleee. What is that in the fish, eh?" As I bent down and peered at the fillets, I saw it. Something was wiggling. Something small and white, like a tiny length of dental floss, was emerging from the flesh and seemed to be waving at me. Worms.

"They have parasites, these feeesh, because they live on the bottom. Find these parasites, these *petites* worms, and pull them out. Then put the fish in the refrigerator for service, okay?"

What can you say to that?

"Yes, Chef."

For the next forty-five minutes, I inspected the fillets and carefully pulled the little buggers out. There was only one or two of them, but I couldn't get the image of the tiny worms, deeply embedded in the firm white flesh of the animal, out of my mind all afternoon.

During service, fish is prepared to order, *à la minute,* while meat dishes (almost always) have been cooked in advance and are quickly heated and plated when an order fires. If a table orders a *filet de boeuf* and three monkfish stews, that means that the plates must all be ready at the same moment, so that everything goes to the table piping hot, which means that the fish station is frantically cooking, sweating, and swearing, while the meat station leisurely rearranges garniture one last time. This is the way it went for us. Despite the heat of the day, unseasonable for October, the monkfish stew was a very popular dish, and we were in the weeds all afternoon, braising the fish, reducing the broth, and arranging the tiny vegetable dice just right, so that everything was casual perfection.

The day wasn't over yet. After service, and the inevitable clean-up, Chef announced we would all need to stay late for a lecture in the Level 2 kitchens with a special guest. Someone would have to stay and peel vegetables for the demonstration. Somehow I knew who the lucky soul would be.

So there I was, peeling the hundredth carrot of my day, when the special guest came in. I was deeply immersed in the rhythm of my task. Wash, peel, drop. Wash, peel, drop. Wash, peel . . . I didn't hear him come up behind me. Suddenly, a gnarled hand shot out and stopped my efforts.

"*Non, non, non.* Gently. Do not try to kill the carrot, it is already dead. Gently, gently. Like this." And with that, the great chef André Soltner took my peeler and the carrot I was brutalizing, and without apparent effort, smoothly skinned it, leaving no bevels from the peeler, just smooth, orange flesh. "See? A nice, clean carrot."

He gave me a spoon and asked me to gently smooth off the edges of all the carrots I had already peeled. I couldn't believe I had failed at peeling carrots, right in front of perhaps the greatest living French chef in the world. My face burned, and I finished the carrots with my head down, willing the tears of embarrassment and frustration not to come.

I shouldn't have worried. Chef Soltner is an incredible teacher. There were no belittling comments about my work, no stupid-student smiles to mark my awkward progress. He calmly arranged his knives from his knife kit and reviewed my second attempt with a smile.

"*Bon.* Thank you." He acknowledged my effort! I was in heaven. *Chef Soltner let me peel his carrots! I am king of the kitchen!*

The demonstration was about the lost art of garniture. We were to learn the secret to the intricately carved and worked potatoes, the carrot flowers, and apples reborn as feathery birds. The same work that was hopelessly unfashionable and would never grace the tables of the most hip New York restaurants. It is surprisingly difficult. Chef Soltner's hands flew over mushroom caps as he spoke of a time in the business when this was something every chef could make, and would make with every spare second, with any odd leftover pieces of carrot or parsnip, or anything that happened to be lying around. This elaborate decoration was a way to make patrons feel like they were getting something truly spectacular with their meal, but it was also a way to keep knife skills sharp. Tiny carrot sculptures were emerging from the man's hands. Potatoes became feathery lattices that were then transformed into deep-fried architecture. An ordinary mushroom emerged with two tiny fish cavorting on the cap, enclosed in a perfect circle of neat, interlocking triangles. A few wedges cut from an apple became, in this man's hands, an exotic bird, a phoenix rising from the ashes of a brunch buffet. We tried to mimic him. Some were more successful than others. I didn't have the knack. The bird I carved looked more like a pigeon that had been flattened by a speeding taxi than a bird of paradise, but it wasn't that important. What mattered was that we were trying our hands at a skill that was soon to be lost entirely. At the end of the lecture, Chef Soltner accepted our wild applause with a small smile and said that he hoped that one day we could make this sort of thing popular once again, so that diners could marvel at a plate made glorious with a few deft flicks of a knife in a skilled chef's hand.

OUT OF THE WALK-IN

or once, we had finished service on time, at 2:30, and managed to clean up our station with relatively little fuss. I
packed up the last of the *filet de boeuf,* the leftover crêpes, the
fricassee of wild mushrooms, and the tiny carrot flans that had been
our assignment for the day in the *saucier* station. Each component
was packed into separate squareboy containers, wrapped in a layer
of plastic wrap, then aluminum foil. A large sticker identified the
contents, the date, the level, the chef-instructor, and the station that
had produced it. All that was left was to run them to the walk-in
refrigerator in the garde-manger kitchen and find a safe place to
squirrel away our leftovers.

We played rock/paper/scissors to see who would have to do
this last chore. I lost, and complained bitterly to Ben and Jackie. I
was still grumbling as I made my way through the main kitchen to
garde-manger. The garde-manger stations for Levels 3 and 4 were
run by Chef Chris, a relatively recent graduate of The Institute himself. Unlike many of the other chef-instructors, Chef Chris was almost always smiling. He patiently explained the steps to the recipes
we prepared for him and never yelled at us. It was always a pleasure
to work in garde-manger. Chef Chris was a huge practical joker,
however, and was constantly playing jokes on the students and even
the other instructors. He and Chef Paul were best friends, and since
the pastry kitchen (Chef Paul's delicious domain) adjoined garde-
manger, the two chefs were always playing tricks on each other or
conspiring together to play tricks on someone else.

As I marched through the kitchens to the walk-in, I passed

Tucker and Angelo. Their brigade had finished cleaning up already and they were packed up, knife kits on their shoulders, red toolboxes and notebooks stacked on their workstations, ready to flee out the door the moment Chef released us for the day. They stopped trading good-natured insults with each other and began to rib me.

"Still hard at work, huh, Darling?" Tucker asked, his wide mouth set in a big grin. "Betcha wish you and me were still partners!"

He had no idea.

Angelo chimed in. "I can't imagine how you do it. I see you working with crazy Penny every day. Why don't you make Ben or Jackie work with her once in a while? You're gonna drive yourself nuts!"

"Too late," I said, trying to play along with them, even though everything they said was true. It was funny to them, but to me, the hard work and long hours causing me to lose my marbles was no laughing matter.

They followed me into garde-manger, still debating whether or not I was going off the deep end or just grumpy. I tried to ignore them, calling to Chef Chris to please hold the door of the walk-in for me as I juggled my heavy armload of leftovers. Bowing deeply, Chef Chris ushered me into the chilly confines of the refrigerator. As I carefully stepped over 25-gallon buckets of cold veal stock and between towering shelves packed with all sorts of vegetables, fish, and meat, I tried to find a spot for my leftovers among the huge tins of mustard and olives, open containers of anchovies, troughs of potato peelings soaking in frigid water, and the piles of foil-wrapped packages left by other stations and other classes. Finally, in a far corner, I found a few inches of shelf space and crammed my left-overs onto it. Done. Just as I was straightening up, ready to pick my way back through the crowded and very cold fridge to freedom, I heard Chef Chris say "Watch this!" and heard Tucker's chuckles and Angelo's loud guffaw, cut short by a loud BANG as the door to the walk-in slammed shut.

And then the lights went out.

The funny thing about this walk-in refrigerator was the fact that the light switch was located on the wall *outside* the fridge, along with the door handle. *Don't panic,* I told myself, as the blackness settled over my face like a shroud. I had never told anyone this, not even Michael, the man I was going to spend the rest of my life with, but I am terrified of the dark. I sleep with the closet light on, not in case I need to get up in the night to pee, but to keep the monsters of my imagination at bay. *Don't panic don't panic don't panic,* I chanted to myself, willing my hands to unclench, my muscles to relax. *Just stay calm, it's just a joke, they'll let you out in a second or two.* I took a deep breath. *Don't panic.* Just then, I heard a scuffling noise coming from another corner of the walk-in, and then a disembodied voice say "Shit!"

I panicked.

I screamed, loud and long, and tried to stampede my way to the door, to light and air and warmth and freedom. I took one step, tripped over a bucket of stock, and sat down heavily in a huge pail of potato peelings. Ice-cold water streamed into my chef pants and soaked my jacket, my apron, even my underwear. I leaped up, screaming every curse word I could think of, and tried to feel around in the darkness for a weapon to defend myself against whatever was locked in this freezing hell with me. I snatched up what felt like a huge carrot or maybe a turnip and, brandishing it in front of me, prepared to confront . . . Philip? I would recognize his voice anywhere. He was the only one in school with that smooth, radio announcer's voice, and that "shit" had sounded pretty darn mellifluous, under the circumstances.

"Uh, hello?" the disembodied voice spoke again. Definitely Philip. "Darling? Katie? Is that you?"

"Oh, thank God, Philip!" I could feel my knees going weak with relief, and I stumbled toward the welcome sound of his voice. He had managed to fight his way to the door, and he began to bang on it with what sounded like a soup ladle.

I threw myself into the approximate region of his arms, desperate for some reassurance that I wasn't going to die here in the freezing dark.

Philip immediately recoiled from my soggy embrace.

"I'm gay!" he yelped, trying to fend me off with the ladle.

"I'm afraid of the dark!" I screamed back at him, trying to parry his ladle with my carrot.

"Oh." Philip stopped trying to bean me with his ladle like some hysterical virgin. "Oh. Well, I guess that's okay then."

Gratefully, I grabbed on to Philip's chef's jacket and hung on for dear life, trying to hold in my sniffles.

"Poor Darling," said Philip, as he resumed his banging on the door.

It seemed like we waited hours in that glacial blackness for someone to let us out. I had begun to think about what we would do if no one came to our rescue and we had to spend the night here. There was no way I could last all night in my soaked outfit without coming down with hypothermia, and I didn't really relish the idea of having to chow down on leek greens and anchovies to keep our strength up, either.

Finally, the door swung open. We had been banging on it so long that we practically fell out of it, right at the feet of . . . Dean Jacques Pépin.

"What zeee hell?" he said, as he surveyed Philip and me, both incredibly disheveled, Philip clutching a soup ladle he had apparently been using to dip up mustard when the door shut, me in my soaking-wet uniform, still brandishing an enormous carrot.

I blinked at the sudden brightness, my joints so stiff with cold I was unable to scramble upright speedily. My mind was completely blank. I couldn't think of any story to cover our ridiculous situation—not one believable, anyway. Dean Pépin would never believe we had been locked in the walk-in against our will by a chef-instructor.

Said chef-instructor finally came to the rescue.

"Oh, thank you for the carrot, Miss Darling," Chef Chris said, winking broadly as he yanked the carrot from my numb grasp, "and Mr. Emerson, thank you for returning that, er, mustard. You are dismissed."

Philip and I didn't need to be told twice. We grabbed our things and skedaddled to the locker rooms as fast as we could go. On the stairs, I grabbed Philip by his knife kit.

"Uh, if it is all right with you, Philip, please don't mention what I said in the walk-in," I mumbled, terribly embarrassed now about admitting my secret fear.

"Uh, sure. No problem. And if you wouldn't mind not telling anybody about what I said, either, that would be great," Philip replied, before rushing on. "I am not ashamed, but some of our classmates might not be so understanding."

I thought about Penny and super-religious Keri and Mimi and was sad to say that I agreed with him.

"Your secret is safe with me," he said, holding out his hand.

"Me, too," I answered, giving him a big hug.

TRUFFLE HOUND

Black gold. Truffles are the little nuggets of fungus that grow under French oak trees and command breathtaking prices in gourmet markets around the world. They are the quintessential embodiment of the *luxe et volupté* ideal of French haute cuisine.

The mushroom of all mushrooms had eluded me. Oh, black and white truffle oil had been a precious commodity in my kitchen pantry for years, and I had often been told by posh and verbose restaurant menus that I was indeed about to enjoy a subtle hint of truffle essence with my risotto or potato gratin or as a finish on my wintry *salade lyonnaise,* but the actual fungus remained aloof.

If I had expected to encounter it during my time in chef school, it seemed that I was out of luck yet again. The truffle season runs roughly from November to January, and while we would be in class for two months of this time, the prospects of the skies opening and showering us with the largesse of the Provençal forests seemed poor at best. This was due in part to the fact that the skies hadn't opened at all the past summer, and a drought both on our shores and in the forests of the Luberon meant that there was not enough rain to ensure a bountiful truffle harvest in the fall. This, in turn, had driven prices up to an even more dizzying height than usual, and the cost of a small plate of pasta with fresh truffle shavings on top fetched the astronomical price of $250 from some of Manhattan's ritzier restaurants.

This wasn't to say that all truffles were totally out of reach of the school or of us starving students. There is always the white truffle from Italy, considered by almost all gourmets to be good, but not in the same league as its darker cousin. There are also canned truffles of both varieties—tiny jars of liquid in which one or two tiny specimens lurk, suspended in their own potent juices. This last variety was the sort that we, with much pomp and circumstance, were allowed to use, very occasionally, in our dishes for the restaurant in Level 3. A formal truffle request had to be made to first the chef-instructor, and a thorough discussion of the recipe would then ensue, after which further proceedings would be taken only if the student, through passionate argument and convincing demonstrations of need, could convince the instructor that truffles, and only truffles, were integrally important to the dish. Once this had been successfully argued—and such cases were very rare—then the lucky student and chef-instructor would both plead their case at the storeroom, where David kept the little jars of truffle safely locked away in a secret cupboard, next to the really good saffron stems. With the authority of the chef-instructor commanding it, the keys would magically appear from some hidden pocket of David's white grocer's coat, and the cupboard would open. The jar would be presented, with great ceremony, not to the student, but to the teacher, who would then take custody of it and supervise its use during service. In Chef Robert's case, the jar and its precious contents would go into his pocket, and only when the student begged, with appropriate accents of groveling, would he then carefully remove a small lump from the cloudy liquid and, using his personal truffle shaver, shave the truffle over the dish before sending it on its way. The students never actually got to touch the jar, let alone the truffle.

We could smell it, though. The second the little jar was opened, a heady waft of scent swept outward, enveloping the entire kitchen in its unique, indefinable aroma—part pungent, part earthy, almost animal. This, it seemed, was as close as I was ever going to get to the real deal—that and fondling the Plexiglas case at Dean and DeLuca, in which rested a few of the specimens, recumbent on a bed of pearly grains of arborio rice, their wrinkled ugliness made even more attractive against their virginal white backdrop.

Not that I was complaining, exactly. I was lucky enough to be part of a team that was blessed with the chance to work with truffles in Level 3: Jackie had used her big brown eyes, long brown hair, and a web of complimentary words to convince Chef Robert to let us make the classic dish of tournedos Rossini—meaty rounds of grilled filet mignon topped with a thick slice of seared foie gras and garnished with a single thick truffle shaving. Overwhelming and decadent, it was a lunch special to end all lunch specials at L'Ecole, coming as it did with flash-fried Swiss chard, all dark green leaves woven through with dark red veins, and potato puree molded around a scoop of tart apple flesh into a perfect miniature apple shape and then deep-fried to a golden brown—excess tempered with whimsy. It was a marvelous dish, and we had many orders of it during lunch service. Enough so that even Chef's most parsimonious shavings used almost an entire truffle. But there was trouble with the fish station during service, as usual (at least I wasn't the only one who was having trouble with *poissonnier*!), and while Chef was distracted by their mishaps, finally leaving our station altogether to threaten the students making a mess out of the monkfish entrée, we were left in charge of the truffle shaver, the jar, and the precious lumps of fungus within. Much as I wanted to grate and grate shavings of truffle over a simple round of buttered, grilled bread and try the real deal right then, we had a bit of trouble of our own.

It was Penny, of course, the human crisis, who had managed to burn three orders of the pork tenderloin we were serving as our curriculum dish. How it happened was a mystery—the pork had been cooked before service began and merely needed a gentle reheating in the oven while the cider-braised cabbage was sautéed on the stove. Ben threw his side towel in the sink in despair—she was hopeless, he hissed in my ear as we traded places, and partners, at the stove. It was true—Penny was turning into a train wreck as we moved through the stations in the Level 3 rotation, not only derailing her own efforts, but plowing a wide swath of destruction every time she went off the rails. Cooking for real patrons in the restaurant seemed to totally undo her. She was like a disoriented deer in the headlights, standing frozen before the high flame of the stove, helpless to stem the disaster before her. Which didn't make it any easier on the rest of us. Penny was especially difficult during service and needed to be guided again and again through the plating techniques we had watched Chef Robert demonstrate to us only moments before. Somehow, though, the salmon was always burned, the potatoes were in the wrong place, and the wrong herb was being used as a garnish. For the next hour of the lunchtime I worked on the pork dish, occasionally catching glimpses of Jackie and Ben working on the Rossini: arranging the adorable potato "apples," searing a mouthwatering hunk of foie gras, shaving truffles with happy abandon. I tried not to be jealous.

Service was over, and we carefully packed up the leftover food in its squareboys and labeled it all before passing it along to the *entremétier* station (the "leftover" station in charge of making a pasta, a salad, and a sandwich special out of scraps from the other stations). The pots and pans used during service were bundled away to the dishwashers, and all of our own tools were waiting to be washed and sanitized in the sink. The stoves were scrubbed down, the prep areas swabbed, and everything put neatly back in its place.

If there was time after making certain the station was spick-and-span and the stainless steel surfaces shone brightly, then we would be allowed to use the few minutes left of class time to work on our own pursuits, whether it was working out a potential plating design for the next day's specials or using the school's electric knife sharpener to put a new edge on our knives. While we were cautioned against using the grinder too often—overuse would wear the knife down completely—an electric sharpener was simply heaven, reducing the hours and hours of laborious back and forth with a whetstone to a few noisy moments. But the sharpener was a bit intimidating: not as scary as the razor-sharp promise of amputation inherent in the deli slicer, perhaps, but still frightening. When my knives were finally so dull they wouldn't pierce the skin of a tomato, I knew I needed to use the big guns. I just didn't want to face the grinder alone. So I dragged Angelo with me, to demonstrate exactly how to use the thing without having to expose to Chef Robert my ignorance of yet another kitchen gadget.

Together we traipsed down the hall to the Level 2 classroom, where the sharpener lived in a dark corner. Taking my battered paring knife, Angelo was in the process of demonstrating to me how to slide the blade slowly through the coarse and then fine grinders when a stranger ambled through the kitchen. This was very odd—a password lock protected the front and back entrances to the school, and so he couldn't have just wandered in off the street. But there was something slightly furtive about him—he cast his eyes around the kitchen as if he had never seen one before, and he was carrying what looked like a bulletproof cooler on a strap over his shoulder. Definitely strange.

"Can I help you?" I said, curious to see who this person was and what he could possibly want with the school.

"I am looking for Chef Robert, please?" His French accent was heavy and unmistakable.

Before I could direct him down the hall to our kitchen class-room, Chef Robert popped out of the woodwork, in that irritating way of his. For a fat man, he sure could move with stealth when it was required. Smiling that wicked smile, he tried to shuffle Angelo and me back to class before dealing with his guest, but I was not to be deterred—I wanted to know what Chef was up to. Brandishing my dull knives at him, I begged to use the sharpener. Sighing heav-ily, Chef turned away and began a rapid-fire discussion with the stranger *en français*—using his broad back to shield them both from my vision.

He couldn't shield my nose from what was coming, however.

While I had noticed a vague aroma that seemed to be emanating from the stranger, in my ignorant American way, I put it down to a more European approach to personal hygiene. I was completely unprepared for the full-on frontal assault to my virginal nasal passages when the stranger shrugged the bulletproof cooler off his shoulder, unlocked its several padlocks (!), and slowly lifted its lid. A tidal wave of some colossal, strange smell swirled out, obviously angry at being pent up for so long in a confined space, and began a full-scale invasion of the room and everything in it. It was more than a smell; it was a wild animal, lunging up my nostrils like an angry elephant bent on destroying everything in its path. The lights suddenly seemed to go dim, my head was spinning. I slumped against the wall, feebly clutching the knife sharpener for support. It was like being hit by an eighteen-wheeler, or jumping out an airplane; it was like falling in love. But, my God, what was it? Had I stumbled into a deal to buy nerve gas and become a victim of Chef Robert's secret terrorist tendencies? Was this freaky French guy carrying around a dead animal in there? It smelled like something passing from one state to another—living to dead, animal to vegetable, mortal to divine.

I wasn't too far off. Through the haze—the smell seemed now to have taken up residence, settling over the room like a Victorian fog—I could just make out Chef Robert and the stranger now fondling what looked like gobs of black earth, weighing each on a tiny collapsible scale the Frenchman had conjured from thin air, and assembled with a few deft flicks of his wrist. Chef Robert drew a fat and impressive wad of bills from the pocket of his chef's pants and started peeling off twenties and fifties and stacking them, like paper-thin sheets of filo dough, on the counter. When the stack was a good three inches thick, the stranger pocketed the money, and Chef Robert pocketed several small black knobs. Truffles! From the furtive nature of the exchange, black market black truffles! I wondered if the man had flown them all the way from France—how had he gotten past the bomb-sniffing dogs? How had he explained the *odeur* to his unfortunate seatmate on the plane? Before I could pull myself together to ask any of these or the million other questions I had swirling around in my head, the little dark Frenchman was gone, seemingly disappeared in his own fragrant cloud. Perhaps Chef Robert had just sold his soul to the devil for a few truffles. If the smell was anything to go on, it was probably worth it.

This exchange left me more determined than ever to have a truffle of my very own, but judging from the stack of bills Chef Robert had had to lay out, I was going to have to sell a kidney or other vital organ to finance a purchase. I returned to class and told everyone what I had seen, and smelled, in the Level 2 classroom, but found that few of my classmates were in the same state of thrall that I was in. Of course, none of them had smelled that intoxicating aroma, or actually seen the little nuggets, either. The temptation to make something with truffles was overwhelming, but no matter how many recipes I researched and presented to Chef Robert as possible candidates for preparing for L'Ecole, all coincidentally with truffles, he would approve none of them. I had come so close that day with the tournedos Rossini, but my silly moral scruples about stealing had thwarted me. If only I had that jar of truffles now!

Resolutely, I put the thought of truffles out of my mind. Like a tragic love affair, it seemed it was just not meant to be. Level 3 finally drew to a close, and as we gathered to get our final textbooks and to hear who would be our new teammates for Level 4, I found myself standing next to Ben, whom I had been partnered with since we were on the same island in Level 1. We had been through three levels together and made a very good team. I felt like I didn't even have to say anything to him anymore—every morning, we would nod to each other and begin working side by side, like an old pair of oxen, used to pulling the plow together. But we would not be together anymore. Level 4 was a shake-up for everyone—we were guaranteed to be in new teams with new people, even as we returned to Chef Pierre for our final, and most challenging, level. As Chef Robert called out my name with a group including Jared, Wayne, Tommy, and Amanda (for once I would not be on the short-handed team! Hurrah!), I felt like it was the end of an era, and turning to Ben, I shook his hand and wished him good luck on this last leg of our journey. Ben reached into his toolbox and came out with a small, foil-wrapped package. Shuffling his feet slightly, he handed it to me.

"Here, Darling. It's a little present from me, a thank-you for putting up with me so long." I was speechless. Ben grinned his sly grin and said, "Don't let Chef see it, though. I nicked it from the storeroom for you."

Looking at the shiny package in my hand, somehow I knew what it was. The smell was a big tip-off, too. One of the canned truffles, all for me.

As I served shavings of truffle over gently scrambled eggs, garnished with a dab of whipped cream spiked with a hit of icy cold vodka, at a posh party I threw after graduation was over, I thought of Ben, and my very first experience with truffles. Love at first sight—or sniff.

LEVEL 4

HALLOWEEN

As we began our fourth and final level, there was a tangible sense of excitement in the air. We were so excited to finally begin our last level (and to have made it through the hell that was Level 3), we were primed to party. Level 4 would be the most challenging level we would face—the dishes we would be preparing for L'Ecole were extremely complicated, with sometimes as many as three or four dozen intricate steps involved in their preparation and presentation, though the recipes themselves had become little more than a simple list of ingredients—we were expected now to know not only what to do, but when, where, and how to do it. Every day would be a test run for our final exam; suddenly the specter of the final, and graduation, loomed large in our future, a mere few months away. But for now, we were just thrilled to be finished with Level 3, out from under the meaty thumb of Chef Robert and back to the familiar, barking demands of Chef Pierre. It was time to celebrate. It helped that we moved to Level 4 on Halloween. The fact that Halloween is one of the biggest parties of the year in the streets of New York was just a boozy bonus.

However, we would need to receive our final marks for Level 3 from Chef Robert before we were at last free to celebrate. A lot of the high spirits and hijinks were due to nerves—it hadn't been the best level for anyone in the class, and we were all nervous to see who would be top ranked after the trials and tribulations we had all undergone. I couldn't imagine that I would have done well during this level, after all the personality clashes I had with Chef, and especially my personal sentiment of being unwilling to buckle under to his vicious taunting. I was very proud of the fact that Chef Robert had never made me cry. I was in the minority, even among the guys. While I had performed well, and my skills had gotten more and more proficient during this level, I was certain that there would be some way for him to dock my grade. Perhaps five points would be deducted for excessive feistiness.

So while I wanted badly to know how I stacked up against my peers, I wasn't anxious to hear my name called in that high-pitched, heavily accented voice and to stand before my little nemesis and hear exactly, in detail, how I had fared. There were also more than a few people whose worries had less to do with how well they would do and more to do with how narrowly they would manage to pass (or not) through the level. Chef Robert had been known to hold more than a few students back in Level 3, some more than once even, until they were judged acceptable to go on to the most advanced level. While several of us sharpened our knives and discussed how we could have improved on our specials throughout the six weeks, there was another, more desperate band of students hovering, chatting quietly among themselves, comparing one failed exam paper after another.

When at last my name was called, I could feel my steps dragging as I approached Chef and his open grade book. Making sure that my hat was straight and my uniform unwrinkled and relatively unstained, I stood before him, twisting my hands together, waiting. He made me wait, too, drawing out his greeting into the longest "Well, well, well" ever produced by any stage villain.

Then, utter shock. I had gotten a 95, tying for the highest marks in the class with Marita the quiet vegetarian and Angelo. I couldn't hide my smile from Chef Robert, who immediately reverted back to character with a sneer and a cutting comment—"Don't let it go to your head, Meeess Darleeeng. You are a long way from being a chef still." Chef called everyone by their last names, like a prep school instructor, but he added a "Miss" to some of the female students. I couldn't help feeling like it was somehow insulting, as if I was one of those women who asked for special consideration just because I was female, the ones who did girl push-ups in gym class. I was just one of the guys in class—chef first, person second, and female somewhere way down the list. But even that irritating "Miss" couldn't bring me down—I would never have to hear it again after today. I was on top of the world! And Tucker and Ben were right behind me in the rankings with 93s. We were coming into the home stretch, neck and neck, and Level 4 was definitely going to be very interesting.

But before Level 4, there was tonight. I wasn't planning on spending all night with my compatriots—they were going to see the Halloween parade through the West Village, a debauched annual spectacle that I could do without, especially on a school night. But we would begin, as we did almost every afternoon, at Toad Hall. I loved going to Toad with my pals and the chef-instructors—it was fun to mingle with the teachers when they let their hair down. I remembered that long-ago day in June when we had first gone to the bar and were too timid to mingle with the other students or chef-instructors. Now we joked and teased our old instructors and bought drinks—they looked almost normal in their street clothes, and even though they all began by sitting together at one large round table, soon they were in the thick of things, shooting pool, doing shots at the bar, playing quarters at the long back table, or just chatting with the clumps of students filling the dimly lit space. By the time our merry little band walked the few blocks to the bar, the place was already jumping. And with outsiders—people who manifestly were *not* chefs. They were taking up *our* tables, drinking *our* beer, chatting with *our* bartender! *Halloween is so overrated,* I thought to myself, as I pushed my way through the hordes and up to the bar. Five pitchers and two rounds of shots for everyone followed me back to our table.

Soon we expanded our table space to a vacant one nearby and invited our chefs—Paul, Hel, Pierre, Jean, Mark, Tina, and even Cyndee—to join us. After they congratulated us on making it through the level, talk quickly turned to who would be wearing what kind of costume that evening. Chefs are not overburdened by any sense of decorum, and most of the costumes described by the students and the teachers seemed to hinge on a high level of nudity—not enough to get arrested, but enough to turn heads, even in this town. As Ricki described the black rubber halter she was planning on wearing as a goth vampire, Tucker spotted a fresh tattoo on her lower back. I had seen it recently in the locker room, and while some of Ricki's many tattoos seemed excessive, I couldn't help but feel that this one was actually really cool. It was a tattoo of a sauté pan. It seemed to perfectly sum up how chef school had left its mark on all of us.

This was also Ricki's first time back at Toad with all of us in a month. While I hadn't asked why Ricki suddenly started disappearing after school, ditching our now-ritual Friday afternoon drinks at Toad, Imogene had. Since the end of Level 1, it seemed that Ricki had been hitting the kamikaze shots pretty hard, and they had been hitting back. Apparently, after one too many drunken phone calls to her boyfriend back home in Tennessee, Ricki had realized that the partying was getting out of control and had decided to take a break. But here she was again, a drink clutched in her hand like the rest of us. The stress of working in the kitchen was hard on us all, and drinking was an easy way to ease the tensions after a long day. Maybe it was too easy for some of us.

Regardless, Ricki's new tattoo caused a major ripple effect, and soon, all of my classmates were in various stages of undress, showing off their ink and explaining a certain tattoo's significance to the rest of us. I felt like I was at a show-and-tell session at a biker convention. Angelo was secretly covered in tribal tattoos, from his shoulders on down, eventually ending with several wrapped around his meaty calves. Wayne was brilliantly shaded—every square inch from his right shoulder down to the inside of his right wrist was covered in a beautiful collage of tropical flowers and blue waters.

Imogene's tattoo was probably the most awe-inspiring—despite her super stereotypical suburban life inside the Beltway, Imo rode a Harley in her spare time and had an enormous, beautiful tattoo of angel's wings that covered her entire back, from neck to waist, shoulder to shoulder. Chef Tina had a tiny tattoo of a brioche on the inside of her ankle. Even Chef Chris had a large tattoo on his shoulder, a remnant of his college days in a fraternity.

It seemed like I was the only person in class who was not sporting a tat or at least an interesting piercing somewhere unexpected. The tattoo demonstration became even wilder when the bartender sent an extra round of kamikaze shots our way, to congratulate us on moving on to Level 4. Pretty soon, the pool table had been pressed into service as a runway, as chef after chef and student after student jumped up and did a bump-and-grind to the thumping music, stripping off clothing to give everyone a tantalizing peek or full-on gaze at their tattoo. There were tattoos of Asian calligraphy, tribal bands, initials, ankhs, moons, hearts, flowers, naked chicks, and every variation in between. More interesting were the tattoos of chef knives, spoons, even a whisk. There were tattoos of a head of radicchio, a red-ripe tomato, even an elegant rendering of a single stalk of asparagus. I began to fantasize about getting a tiny tattoo of a strawberry on my hip bone, something sexy but culinary. I was definitely feeling left out—even my old partner Tucker, in addition to the names of his wife and kids, had inked "Born to Braise" on his bicep.

Since I had nothing to show off other than the nicks and burns I had acquired in school, and was feeling like a nerd, I decided to head back home. I read the recipes for the upcoming six weeks of classes and wondered which ones would be on our final exam. The streets of SoHo three floors below became more and more noisy as dusk and then darkness fell. I wondered what the other kids from class were up to and scanned the faces in the background of the nine o'clock news story on the parade to see if any of them seemed familiar. None of them did. I hoped they had managed to stay out of trouble and looked forward during class tomorrow to hearing what they had gotten up to.

I didn't have to wait that long, it turned out. At 2:15 in the morning, my cell phone began to ring. It rang over and over again for ten full minutes before I finally gave in and picked up. It was Amanda and Tucker and Jackie and Ravi and Junior and Angelo and about ten more people from class. Tucker and Amanda were trying to lure me out to meet them for one last drink. I toyed with the idea for a brief moment, and asked them where they were while I stalled for time to make up my mind.

"Scores!" Tucker crowed jubilantly. Scores is a well-known strip club on the East Side of Manhattan.

"Really?" I asked, somewhat taken aback. Because Scores is considered pretty high end, for a strip club, it was extremely expensive, way out of range for most of my classmates—all but a few of us were fiscally overburdened by the enormous weight of our student loans. "Really?" I said again, unable to picture that motley collection of almost-chefs making it past the gargantuan bouncers at the front door.

"I gotta go," Tucker said, practically shouting into the phone. "Jackie bought me a lap dance! You really missed out, Darling. We wish you were here!" With that, the line went dead.

I went back to bed, but it took me a long time to fall asleep. My classmates were getting tattoos and staying out all night partying with strippers. While I wasn't exactly tearful to be missing out on some of the fun—I couldn't afford a lap dance from a stripper in any of the seedy topless bars that line the West Side Highway, let alone one at Scores—I did feel as if maybe I was missing out on something. What was it? Tattoos, piercings, strippers, booze—all my classmates seemed to be consummately badass, just like the best of the bad-boy chefs. I was starting to remind myself of Julia Child—a competent chef, a successful chef, but not really a very sexy chef. Much as I was loath to admit it, sex appeal had become a big factor in the kitchen, as in every other industry. I didn't know how I would stack up.

THE HEART OF THE MATTER

I was lucky enough to begin my final level of school in the pastry kitchen. This meant that I would actually get to go through the pastry rotation twice. Which meant twice the desserts. Chocolate-orange brioche pudding. Coconut and banana crisp. Crème brûlée. Pear tarts. Warm chocolate cake with espresso crème anglaise. Yes, Level 4 was shaping up to be quite delicious.

This would also be the first time I would be working with a full brigade—there would be five of us. This could be good or bad. Working in a smaller group had certainly been harder, but I felt that it had also been more fulfilling. We had weathered many storms in our little group of four and had managed to sail through regardless. Even saddled with the burden of babysitting Penny all the way through Level 3, we had managed. Now, I had a new group— Tommy, Jared, Wayne, Amanda. And, of course, me. I am not a bully, by any stretch of the imagination. But the kitchen is still a man's world, and I wanted to make it very clear who would be wearing the checked chef's pants in this group. We would be the best damn group ever to plate our creations for L'Ecole. And there would be no shenanigans.

I should have known better.

It was only Monday and already we seemed to be running off course. There wasn't enough room for all five of us in the advanced workstation. We were just going to have to squeeze in and learn to work with one another in a space approximately the size of a toaster. This was not a good thing. Jared was at least six and a half feet tall, without his chef's hat. Wayne was a teenager, who seemed to show up to school at least twice a week with the distinctive aroma of herb clinging to his chef's jacket—I had already caught him whittling one of the apples we were supposed to be using for our curriculum dessert (warm brioche bread pudding with apples and caramel) into a makeshift bong. Which was fine, but I wasn't sure how I felt about arming him with ten inches of sharpened carbon steel and turning him loose to chop candied orange peel, approximately an inch from my fingers. Tommy was a sweetheart, but he had the attention span of a hyperactive three-year-old. Amanda was our saving grace—she was patient, smart, and very petite—she could work in a shoe box if she had to. But you just can't squeeze that much flesh and ego into a small confined area without sparks flying.

The heat generated by these sparks wasn't exactly what I had in mind, however. If anything, I thought that Jared and I might have a showdown, as we both seemed to want to lead the team. But like well-behaved children who both want to play on the tire swing, we learned to take turns. No, something other than the massive convection ovens seemed to be heating up the atmosphere in the pastry kitchen.

It started with a small token of affection. It took the form of a morsel of succulent grilled quail, snatched from the *entremétier* station and carefully plated with some mâche and sweet Vidalia onions. Tommy had made Amanda a little snack to ease her hunger pangs until lunch. How sweet, I thought, and snagged a bite when Amanda graciously passed it around to the rest of us to share.

Next came an amuse-bouche of sautéed chanterelle mushrooms on a Parmesan crisp, garnished with a few sprigs of fresh chervil. Tommy had begged the Level 3 garde-manger station to make him an extra. This, too, went to Amanda, as an afternoon snack.

It wasn't until midweek I realized what was happening. Early one morning Tommy stole an entire baguette from the bread kitchen and spread it, still piping hot, with sweet butter. He scrambled eggs and Swiss cheese until they formed soft plump curds in a copper saucepan we were supposed to be using to make caramel. Fresh, juicy plum tomatoes and a slice or two of prosciutto topped off the gargantuan sandwich. It was the most gorgeous love letter I have ever seen, and Amanda's eyes lit up when she saw the sweeping, mute romantic gesture sitting on her cutting board.

There was just one small problem.

Tommy was married. With children.

It couldn't be what it looked like, I told myself. True, Tommy did call Amanda "baby," but he called all the girls in class "baby." It was in keeping with his southern accent and his habit of opening doors and saying "Thank you, ma'am" every time someone corrected his grammar. Tommy was just an easygoing guy from the wrong side of the Florida panhandle, who had big plans for transforming the Creole cuisine he had learned cooking in Louisiana with the classical French techniques he was learning at school. The sun rose and set on his two little girls, and he often went home on the weekends to be with them. Surely he wouldn't really cheat on his wife with Amanda, not now, when we were so close to the end of school, and certainly not when they were both in my brigade!

It was easy to understand the attraction. Amanda was a California girl, with a sunny disposition that seemed to light up everything and everyone around her, even Chef Robert. She had long brown hair that was constantly escaping from the loose bun under her chef's hat. Big brown eyes were always squinting shut with laughter. She was also as small and as perfectly proportioned as a doll—she had to trade in her standard issue ten-inch chef's knife for one with a seven-inch blade, because her hands were too tiny to wield the larger model. For such a small person, she was roundly teased by almost everyone in class for her prodigious appetite. Amanda was always hungry, and she was forever pinching a morsel off one thing or another. If the cream cheese and walnut cake looked as if a mouse had nibbled on one corner, I knew I would find Amanda with her cheeks bulging guiltily.

I told myself that it was a harmless flirtation, a friendship consummated only with consommé and apple tartlets. Some people just express themselves differently—after all, was it really so strange that a chef should express his friendship with mushrooms and quail? It was nothing to worry about, I told myself. Surely I would have noticed an affair right under my nose. However, I hadn't reckoned that Amanda's ravenous appetite was for more than just food.

I admit, I was preoccupied. I had enough to handle in my own romantic situation. Michael and I had decided to get married right after chef school was finished in December. We would have a small wedding (family only) on a remote island in the Caribbean. I would get to wear my gorgeous white silk dress and Michael could wear his flip-flops—everyone was happy. But planning a wedding, even a small one, is stressful, and while I spent my evenings on long-distance calls to florists and caterers, Michael sat around watching the World Poker Tour on television. After I spent a particularly stressful week at school and ran into yet more red tape getting our marriage license from the tiny island's incredible bureaucratic maze, I was feeling particularly down. Sensing this, Michael came home early from work with a present for me. Eagerly anticipating a new silk nightgown or a sexy pair of stilettos, I ripped open the wrapping paper and whipped the lid off the box. Inside was a pair of hot pink rubber chef's clogs. Not at all what I was hoping for. Michael, perhaps seeing the look of chagrin I tried hard to hide, quickly explained. It seemed he had spotted Mario Batali on lower Fifth Avenue, wearing a pair of these rubber chef's clogs in his signature bright orange shade. Knowing I revered Mario, Michael had searched everywhere until he found a pair in pink. It was a very sweet, very thoughtful gesture, Michael's way of supporting me in school. I didn't have the heart to tell him they were definitely not part of the school uniform. I put them on and cooked him dinner instead. My relationship wasn't perfect, but we were trying, and we were happy.

❧

We were in the middle of service, and had just gotten swamped with orders. Part of the joy of the stint spent working in pastry was its streamlined schedule. Once all the crêpes have been flipped, the tarts baked, the cakes iced, the ice cream churned, and the cookies cooled, when the crush of orders do roll in, all that's left is the plating. Perhaps just a quick *brûlée* with a plumber's torch to give tarts and custards a nice browned sugar crust, or a quick swirl of caramel, chocolate, or raspberry puree, and a garnish of fresh mint leaves or candied walnuts, and that's it. But the subtle art of plating desserts is more complicated than it seems. Learning to use the squeeze bottles of chocolate, caramel, and fruit puree was truly an art, and we spent a lot of time practicing our artistic squiggles in chocolate on clean plates. I had finally mastered making a sweeping treble clef design, after many attempts and about a thousand dirtied dessert plates, when we were slammed with the dessert orders from a large party of thirty. We didn't have enough hands to squiggle designs, plate, garnish, and carry out trays—where was everybody? Jared and Wayne were there, as always, but where had Tommy gone? And where was Amanda?

Chef Paul just looked at me and scoffed. "You poor innocent," he said.

Just then, the heavy steel door to the walk-in refrigerator opened and out popped Amanda, followed closely by Tommy. She was rebuttoning her chef's jacket, and he was straightening his chef's hat, which looked as if it had been sat on and then replaced—backward.

They were smiling like two maniacs just released from the asylum.

Shit.

Still, what could I do? It wasn't my affair, literally. The burgeoning complications in the social fabric of my brigade were not enough to dim the other great joy of being in the pastry kitchen—the unrestricted access to all the yummy goodies. There was always an extra cookie, or a tartlet that just wasn't pretty enough to pass muster, or an entire tray of ice cream that would go to waste, all there to be scarfed up by ravenous students. And sometimes not so ravenous—it seemed I could always find room, no matter what I had just eaten, for a slice of cake or just one more tuile. Or leftover crème anglaise.

It was Friday, the last day we would spend in pastry, and I had just finished spooning little pools of espresso crème anglaise on fifteen dessert plates. Amanda was then dotting the pools with warm chocolate, and Wayne was using a toothpick to swirl the chocolate into decorative heart shapes. Jared stood ready to add the warm chocolate cakes, and Tommy added a dash of powdered sugar before running the plates to the waiters. At its best, a brigade works like an assembly line, chefs as a series of automatons built to produce plate after perfect plate of food. I had come to the end of my row, and since these were the last plates of the day, I didn't think twice before scooping up a big spoonful of the heavenly sauce and cramming it into my mouth. Mmmm, delicious. My timing couldn't have been worse. Jacques Pépin, the grandfather of superstar chefs and dean of The Institute, was not doing a surprise inspection, as had happened in the past, but Chef Septimus was.

Chef Septimus was a big, jolly Frenchman who had a terrible temper. But when he wasn't shouting, he was marvelous. He told wonderful stories, often about his weekends spent in the woods, going bow hunting. I always imagined him sneaking through the green underbrush, dressed in immaculate chef's whites, stealthily pushing his considerable stomach before him. It was impossible not to grin. He was also always eager for the students to try all sorts of dried game meats and sausages he made at home and brought in. Sausages were an absolute passion of his. They were always delicious, spicy and sweet with just a hint of that elusive, gamy flavor so prized by Old World chefs.

He bounded into the pastry kitchen, armed with a small plate. I tried not to look guilty.

"Here, try this." He shoved a small, dark, wrinkled morsel at me. I couldn't open my mouth to decline the offer, since it was still full of the illicit cream. Grudgingly, I took the horrid little lump and popped it into my mouth, where it immediately began to swim around in the rapidly congealing pastry cream. It was the worst thing I have ever done. The lump was densely chewy, refusing to yield to the frantic motions of my jaws. Each bite released more of its flavor into the cream, and it was putrid. It tasted like the dead mouse I found in my kitchen cabinet smelled. My eyes teared up. Watching my reaction, Jared asked Chef Septimus what it was before chowing down on his own piece, which he was prodding gingerly with his chef's knife.

"Dried deer heart. I killed it myself!" Chef Septimus said, his face round and happy with pride.

I swallowed. Barely.

I decided that day that matters of the heart, no matter what species they came from, no longer interested me.

Flourless Chocolate Cake

Even my terrible experience hasn't cured me of my sweet tooth, and I still relish making—and eating—crème anglaise. It goes perfectly with this chocolate cake, which is so easy to prepare I often make it when I am away from home, visiting friends. It can be made in almost any kind of container, and never fails to impress.

4 ounces best-quality bittersweet chocolate (the finest you can buy)

8 tablespoons (1 stick) unsalted butter, plus extra for the pan

½ cup granulated sugar

1 tablespoon rum

1 teaspoon vanilla paste

3 large eggs

¾ cup unsweetened cocoa powder

Pinch of ground cinnamon

Pinch of salt

Confectioners' sugar, for garnish

1. Preheat the oven to 375°F. Butter an 8-inch round cake pan, line the bottom with a round of wax paper, and butter the paper.
2. Chop the chocolate into small pieces. In a double boiler, melt the chocolate with the butter, stirring until smooth. (I will occasionally do this in the microwave because it saves time and dishes.) Remove from the heat and gently whisk the granulated sugar into the chocolate mixture. Whisk in the rum and vanilla paste. Separate the eggs, and add the yolks to the chocolate mixture and combine. Whip the egg whites to soft peaks, and gently whisk into the chocolate mixture. Sift the cocoa powder, cinnamon, and salt over the chocolate mixture and whisk until just combined.

3. Pour the batter into the pan and bake in the middle of the oven for about 25 minutes, just until the cake has formed a firm crust.
4. Let the cake cool briefly in the pan on a rack, then invert it onto a serving plate. Remove the wax paper and dust the cake with sifted confectioners' sugar.

NOTE: Sometimes the cake will fall a bit in the center because it is so dense. Don't worry! I always throw a few berries, edible flowers, or even silver dragées on top and it looks gorgeous.

Makes one 8-inch cake, and can be doubled easily

THANKSGIVING

On a fit of temporary dementia, I decided that this would be a good year to celebrate Thanksgiving at my house. School was beginning to get extremely hectic—we were a mere three weeks from graduation, and that meant the final exam was looming. Classes were being held on the Wednesday before Thanksgiving, and while many of my classmates were electing to use our one day of excused absence to travel, I was too nervous about the fast-approaching exam to take a day off. So I invited my parents and brother up to New York for the holiday. I thought that, as an almost full-fledged chef, Thanksgiving couldn't possibly be too arduous a task for me.

Of course, I was wrong. Thanksgiving is a favorite holiday for so many people because of the memories it conjures up of a time long past, a deeply held nostalgia for the Thanksgivings of childhood, against which any attempt to emulate would fall flat. This realization came to me only afterward, of course. That, and doing all the actual cooking, takes a great deal of fun out of things.

I was expecting my parents and brother on the 2:45 train from Washington, D.C. School ended at 3:00 PM, but by the time they had gotten off the train and fought their way downtown through the massive snarl of traffic, I would be at the apartment to meet them. Wednesday morning, gale force winds woke me up. Rain beat on the windows, and forks of lightning were the only light in the sky. I tried not to think of the weather as an omen. As usual, I threw on whatever clothes were handiest, splashed some food in the cat's bowl, kissed the still sleeping Michael (he had no idea what was in store for him), and flew out of the house. I was immediately soaked to the bone, as the storm seemed to intensify the second I opened the apartment house door. Trying not to take this as an omen, either, I rushed down the street to Balthazar for my morning cup of coffee.

Balthazar restaurant and its tiny bakery next door were an anchor for my little corner of the city. On the weekend, it attracted oceans of tourists, who washed up in great waves of humanity that covered the sidewalk and even streamed out into the street in torrents, but at seven-thirty on a dark November morning, it was an oasis of calm—the sharp, comforting smell of espresso and the yeasty scent of freshly baked baguettes were a welcome balm to my frigid senses. Unlike an American bakery, where one's purchase is unceremoniously crammed in a wax paper bag or stuffed willy-nilly into a plain white cardboard box, at a French patisserie, and at Balthazar, one's purchase is nestled in paper, and then a tiny box, the perfect fit for the yummy little treat, is gently folded into place around it. But I wasn't here for a treat, and I had a very long day ahead of me. I placed my order for two coffees—in case the morning was particularly difficult, I wanted to be prepared with an extra boost of caffeine—and headed back into the storm, to make the short walk to The Institute. With the wind whipping the puddles into miniature whirlpools, it turned into more of a quick run.

After changing and heading downstairs to the Level 4 kitchens with my red toolbox and knife kit, I was glad I had gotten to school early. The kitchen was oddly silent, and our class, what remained of it, was already hard at work, trying to cover the gap in manpower. While I couldn't imagine that the restaurant would be particularly busy on a dark day like today, we would have to ensure that everything was just as usual, regardless. Wayne was absent, Amanda was leaving at ten o'clock, and Tommy, while present in body, seemed to be mentally far away, back in Florida with his little girls. Either that, or he was using one of his last opportunities to mentally undress Amanda. I couldn't decide.

This left me with Jared. Jared was a tireless worker, moving methodically from one task to another without pause. He was also a gifted chef, with a good sense of what would go well with what, and a nice steady hand with the seasoning. But Jared was not good at cooking meat, for some reason. He simply could not tell when to flip a tuna steak or remove a chicken from the oven. While most of the rest of us had developed a bit of a sixth sense about these things, prodding a steak with a finger occasionally to check for doneness, but mostly going on instinct, Jared seemed unable to. He would ease a pork medallion into a hot sauté pan, and then stand back, or worse, walk away to start another task, without any sense of when to take the poor hunk of meat off the heat. Unless watched assiduously, Jared would turn out a tray of meat that was alternately deep red and raw and blackened beyond recognition. It was a baffling mystery—how could a chef so talented in every other aspect of the culinary arena be defeated by such a basic task? One memorable day Jared had used my expensive electric thermometer to check the doneness of the *boeuf en croûte* and then left it in the meat as it went back in the oven. Both the thermometer and the ninety-dollar hunk of tenderloin were burned beyond recognition. Jared couldn't even remember the way we had learned back in Level 1 to determine doneness in a piece of meat, using the fleshy part of the hand between thumb and index finger. A pinch of the flesh at the very edge of the hand is what rare meat feels like, while medium rare is the feel of the hand a bit farther in, and medium, medium well, and well are further in toward the firm flesh of the hand.

Since Jared, Tommy, and I were in *saucier,* cooking deep-fried quail with a panoply of small, finicky sides and garnishes, I was hoping I could keep Jared occupied with the vegetables and away from the meat, and I could interest Tommy in frying the quail to keep his mind occupied on the meal, and not on Amanda's imminent departure. Despite the walk-in refrigerator incident, I wasn't sure what was going on with those two. Neither seemed to be making any effort to hide the fact they really, really liked each other, but on the other hand, it was rare to find them actually doing anything more than giving each other long looks or perhaps a very subtle squeeze under the table at Toad. I didn't have the time to waste thinking about what was going to happen to the star-crossed couple on my team, though. I hadn't even begun to plan what we would have for Thanksgiving dinner, and time was definitely running out.

Unlike everyone else in America, my family has never liked turkey at Thanksgiving. We have never liked turkey, period. So while the rest of the nation spends Thanksgiving wrestling a mutant, grotesquely large Butterball around the kitchen, dripping bacteria-laden poultry juice from sink to stove and back again, tying up the oven for seven hours trying to cook the factory-farmed behemoth, my father agitates that this be the year we serve lasagna for dinner. However, we do still have some hidebound notions, mostly from my brother, and poultry of some sort is always on the menu. For several years my mother and I sweated over the creation of that Frankenstein's monster, the turducken—where a chicken is boned and stuffed inside a duck, which is boned and stuffed inside a turkey, each layer generously padded with swathes of stuffing. But the effort seemed too great for a party of only five people, and none of us had ever cared for the turkey portion of the monster, so I thought perhaps this year I might scratch it from the starting lineup, despite my virtuoso abilities now with a boning knife.

I found that butchering meat seemed to be my special talent at chef school. The instructors recognized it, and would often pull me aside to do an extra leg of lamb or chicken or veal shoulder while everyone else did other things. Angelo joked that I was the daughter of a butcher who moonlighted as an enforcer for the mob. While that wasn't true, I was very proud of my ability to break down a carcass. I had been premed in college, and while I hadn't made it to med school, at least I was putting some of my skills to good use.

But I still hadn't decided on the main attraction at Thanksgiving dinner as I prepped the teeny tiny bodies of the quail for their meeting with the deep-fat fryer. For a moment I toyed with the thought of having quail for our special dinner, but I would need a gross of them to sate the appetite of the men in the family. They were delicious, even their delicate bones edible, with a satisfying crunch on their way down, but they were just too small and they cost the earth. *There must be gold hidden in their craws,* I thought, as I neatly impaled a semi-boneless carcass and sank it in the waiting marinade. The side dishes would remain the same as they had every year of my memory, a seemingly endless array of carbohydrates ranging from dressing (southerners never ever call it stuffing) to mashed potatoes to a panful of tiny pearl onions that have been cooked *glacer à brun* (a process I could now perform in my sleep) to my mother's special rolls—great, soft white pillows of warmth, the perfect foil for a pat of butter. Then, of course, there were the pies: apple, pumpkin, pecan, buttermilk, chocolate, and sometimes mincemeat or cranberry-apple Dutch, or peach made from the jars of preserved peaches we canned earlier in the year, during the hottest days of July and August.

Needless to say, I hadn't found time to even think about getting the guest room ready, much less go grocery shopping. In the margins of the recipe I began making lists of all the things I would need from the various grocery stores in our area—from extra plates from Pearl River to a tablecloth from Broadway Panhandler to potatoes, beans, onions, carrots, pounds and pounds of butter, heavy cream, candles, and wine. I wasn't sure I hadn't bitten off more than I could chew with this, and I thought about ordering in Chinese for dinner.

And I *still* hadn't come up with a good idea for the main event. Perhaps inspiration would strike during lunch service, or I would overhear some fantastic idea from another student in the locker room. Lunch was a pretty quiet affair, and even though all the brigades were short on manpower, the wretched weather kept patrons away. If possible, the conditions outside had worsened since my quick run to class that morning. There were reports of flooding around the neighborhood, and hail had been spotted by an excitable

Level 1 student. Not the sort of weather in which to sightsee, and not the sort of weather to schlep sacks and sacks of groceries around in the gloom. I wondered what I was going to do with my family for four whole days. I wondered how I was going to manage to cook Thanksgiving dinner, ensure that no one picked a fight with anyone else, keep my own sanity, and start studying for the final exam. I wondered if the rain was ever going to let up.

It didn't. Not by the time class was over for the holiday, and we packed up our knife kits and red toolboxes. I was taking all of my tools home for the duration of the break—after all, I was going to need all the help I could get. Sure, I felt like a dork, traipsing through the puddles, the heavy plastic toolbox banging painfully into my shins every step or two, but also vaguely powerful, with my knife roll slung over my shoulder. It was only a six-block walk home, but I half hoped that on the way I could accost a mugger, save an old lady from a purse snatcher, or even perform an emergency trache-otomy with my newly sharpened paring knife. This, I thought, as I stepped menacingly into the street, daring a passing cyclist to come too close, or even think about splashing my already soaking wet jeans, was why it was a good idea not to go around with concealed weapons. They gave one a completely false sense of confidence.

Confidence was the last thing I had, and even the good spirits I was carefully keeping dry were dampened a bit when I arrived home and found that the trains had been delayed because of flooding on the tracks and the family wouldn't be in until midevening. They would be tired and hungry and grumpy by the time they finally ar-rived at the apartment, and worse yet, they wouldn't be any help car-rying groceries. I was going to have to do the heavy lifting myself.

I stood at the window, looking out at the gathering dark. While it was only four o'clock, the city had already sunk into an early night, a feeling further enhanced by the heavy dark curtains of rain still falling steadily. This wasn't going to be any fun, I thought, but it wasn't going to get any easier, either. Taking a deep breath and a grocery list that had grown as long as Santa's list of bad boys and girls, I headed out to hit the grocery stores in my neighborhood. I trekked over to Gourmet Garage at its converted warehouse space in lower SoHo. It seemed that everyone else had made the trek as well. I was forced to do battle for a midget-size shopping cart, using a neat ass-bump maneuver I usually used to shut the oven door to edge out a particularly grabby Wall Street type. I was then forced to repeat this same maneuver every two or three feet, avoiding other shoppers who were using their own versions of pushing and shoving in order to get to everything from the onions to the decaffeinated coffee beans. I was quickly worn out. I hadn't even made it over to the meat case yet.

Carried along in the tide of humanity, I eventually found my way there and took a number to wait in line. As I waited, I surveyed the various meats, fish, and poultry laid out like bangles in a jeweler's window. It was then I saw the cockroach. Not really a big deal, I thought. After all, this is a big city, and the cockroaches are everywhere, even if you couldn't always see them. In a grocery store, even a nice one like Gourmet Garage, there were bound to be a few lurking in the dark corners of the storeroom. But this guy wasn't the shy type. There he was, crawling up the glass on the meat case. Check that. He was on the *inside* of the case, in there with the filet mignon at $25 a pound, the $22 wild salmon steaks, and the $30 lobster tails. I fought my way to the head of the line, deaf to the hisses and name-calling behind me, and caught the eye of the counter guy.

"Get in line, lady," he snarled as he turned to help the next customer.

"Wait!" I said, and then, pitched loudly enough so that everyone in line behind me could hear, I said, "There's a cockroach in the meat case! Right there, on the inside of the glass, see?" I pointed to the bug, which was now waving his antennae around, as if greeting his audience of stupefied patrons now staring at him.

"Yeah, all right. I got it," the counter guy said, completely unfazed. I didn't stick around to see how, exactly, he was going to get the cockroach out, I just got my tiny cart full of groceries in line and decided to get my bird (whatever it would be) somewhere else. Let the pushy Wall Street type have *filet de cockroach* for his dinner.

I headed home, almost completely submerged in the eddying grocery bags I had slung around my person. Dropping everything in the lobby of the building, I headed out again, to track down my bird. I ended up at Dom's, a small grocery on my block specializing in high-end Italian imported goods. I hadn't been in that often, because Dom's doesn't carry anything but actual food. Things like paper towels, toilet bowl cleaner, and cat food don't make the cut, so I had been sticking with the more down-market but democratically product-inclusive Associated Supermarket around the corner. Somehow, though, I thought Dom's might be a better choice for bird buying. I wandered up and down the aisles of beautifully arranged artisanal pastas, unusual dried herbs, jars of jewel-colored antipasti. I admired the wheels of cheeses at the immaculately clean cheese counter. I sniffed appreciatively; the trays of prepared foods, from homemade meatballs to chocolate cookies the size of dinner plates, all smelled heavenly.

At last I found myself in front of the meat case, looking at the piles of turkeys, chickens, ducks, and other poultry. Almost all of them had been spoken for, apparently—around each leg was a small tag with a name and a date inscribed on it in small script. Rats. I really had left it too late—I would be lucky to secure a chicken at this rate. Just then, from behind the birds stacked like cordwood, a round face beaming a large, gap-toothed smile hailed me.

"Buona sera, signora."

Caught off guard, I answered, "Bonjour!" My Italian is obviously nonexistent.

Taking a leap of faith, I asked for help and advice from the smiling man behind the counter. Turned out I had gone right to the top.

Franco is the owner of Dom's, and as he listened to my dithering explanations about dinner and chef school and the imminent arrival of my family, he began to go through the birds. At last, he found one that was not previously claimed—an enormous goose. I had never cooked a goose before, and while it definitely looked vaguely bird-like, it was also very alien. Franco packed up the goose and a beautiful pink pork loin for dinner this evening and sent me off into the night, giving me explicit instructions on how to prepare everything "for *la famiglia*" and telling me to come back if I had any problems.

Well, I overcooked the goose, burned the chocolate pie, and the mashed potatoes were cold. I made stock out of the wrong parts of the goose (I didn't know that kidneys would make stock bitter) and was forced to make gravy from store-bought chicken broth. I didn't have enough serving spoons and had forgotten to buy napkins—we had to use paper towels. The candles dripped wax all over the borrowed table, and a bottle of wine carefully smuggled back from our trip to Provence and lovingly stored turned out to be corked. It was not my best day in the kitchen.

But I was with my family, and at dinner my mother told a hysterical story about the two geese that we had on the farm when I was still too young to really remember them. They were awful beasts, pecking my brother and me whenever we ventured outside unattended. At one point, my mother tried to run them over with the old Peugeot, but they escaped, flapping their ungainly bodies up into the safety of the boxwoods. However, they couldn't escape from my grandfather and his razor-sharp hatchet. At Christmas, they were both dispatched and prepared for our festive dinner. Full of pride at the gorgeously brown birds (and vanquishing her enemies at last), my mother proudly brought the roasting pan up the steps to my grandparents' house for the traditional evening meal. She slipped on the ice and dumped the whole thing down the frozen walk. It made me feel vastly better about the charred version I had served—at least it reached the dinner table in one piece! It seemed that fate and DNA combined to ensure I would not be able to cook my own goose.

But I was thankful to Franco for finding me something to serve at my Thanksgiving table. While the dinner itself was not the success I had hoped for, I did end up making a very good friend. Franco has advised me on everything from the right time of year to buy fresh porcini to how to cook ricotta pie, even special-ordering everything from quail to venison for my dinner parties. He even shares his mother's recipes and regales me with stories, including one about a toad omelet he had growing up in Italy. While Franco has not the advanced diplomas or decades of restaurant experience that my chef-instructors had, he has been a wonderful guide through all the things they don't teach you in school. How to grow the best tomatoes for sauce, how to choose the right balance of cheeses for a satisfying cheese plate, how to break down an entire cow carcass for sale—I have never done this last one, but after the extensive tutorial Franco treated me to, complete with graphic gestures and sound effects, I have no doubt I could.

CHRISTMAS PARTY

It was almost over. The hard work, the blood, sweat, tears, and shouting. Levels 1, 2, 3, and now Level 4 had come to a close, almost, and everyone—students and teachers—could feel it. Level 4 had been hard—the most difficult we had ever experienced—but we had begun to turn out plates of food that would not be out of place at the French Laundry. We had come a long way from our first days at school, when peeling and dicing vegetables seemed like a challenge. It was time to celebrate. Of course, it helped that Christmas was only a few weeks away. It was marvelous, really, that we would be finished by Christmas, a wonderful way to end the year—*if* we could all manage to hold it together until then. Every morning, despite the fast-approaching final exam, more and more people in class were absent—working on their final projects or just having had a bit too much holiday cheer the night before. Chef Pierre definitely noticed, and had started making grumpy remarks and adding little black marks to his grade book every morning at roll call. Even roll call and our daily morning meetings in the restaurant smacked of the encroaching holiday—the decorations for L'Ecole had switched from the riotous crimsons and oranges and yellows of fall and Thanksgiving to an even more vibrant display of holly, poinsettias, and the heavenly scented evergreen boughs draped from every surface.

And there were Christmas parties; it seemed like hundreds of them. We often were briefed to be in early to prepare for the horde of fifty old biddies having the prix fixe before their annual cookie swap, or the clutch of businessmen who had read the good reviews in Zagat's and recognized an incredible bargain when they saw one. If the patrons were special favorites, or had impressed someone in authority when planning their party, they would often get a tour through the kitchens and classrooms after dessert. It was touching to see them all file through, usually in a sort of silent awe, as we went about our business. We were often working hard by then, but it was always nice to have a bit of a heads-up from a waiter, just enough time to straighten out uniforms, readjust our hats, and stash anything vaguely unseemly—the rabbits being deboned for a game mousse were definitely still a little too true-to-life and macabre for the uninitiated, especially after a very full lunch. Sometimes, as they were on their way back out again, one or two would stop and say thank you for the wonderful meal. It was thrilling—we had managed to convince these perfect strangers that we were chefs, real chefs! Capable of producing the meal that had given them so much pleasure—it was intoxicating.

Lunch for seventy-five became just another task to be accomplished in a day, and we often had time after the initial, incredibly rushed preparation and service to discuss the dishes with Chef Pierre. We debated the merits of serving the pork tenderloin with the tiny crepe towers stuffed with chestnut puree, and whether or not the osso buco looked better when the rosemary sprig used as garnish was fresh or fried. While the things we prepared were interesting, discussing these tiny nuances with Chef gave them a heightened sense of what foods benefited others and what pairings tasted best together. Thus, we learned that the spicy-sweet Asian-influenced marinade we used on the quail would also complement pork, but not lamb or beef. The simple but powerful red wine reduction we used on the beef could be adjusted with several sprigs of rosemary to nap the leg of lamb or pool around a breast of chicken, but the parsnips accompanying these dishes would then have to be changed, as the sweetness of the root vegetable clashed with the tannins in the wine.

All this talk was Chef's way of pushing us beyond the bounds of the school curriculum, to help us use our experience and our palates to put together new ideas and give us the courage to take a chance and try something different—not at school, of course, but at home, and in the future in our own kitchens. School was still school, and the final exam would not be on theoretical dishes but on the ones we were making every day. It would be similar to the midterm: a quick written exam followed by our practical, where we would be randomly assigned either a fish and dessert combination or an appetizer and main dish. But there the similarities ended—we had come a long way since Level 2, and the complexity of the dishes we regularly prepared reflected that. No longer were dishes accompanied by a few simple tournéed potatoes cooked *à l'anglaise*, but rather by a fricassee of butternut squash, potatoes, sweet potatoes, and parsnips, all diced to the same precise measurement, boiled separately, dried, and then browned together in a steep-sided *sauteuse* over high heat. The fish dishes were garnished with everything from gently poached cucumbers to carefully snipped seaweed, with a few light green leaves from celery hearts for flavor and color. Cooking the meat to the proper degree of doneness, the primary goal of the dishes on our midterm, became just another basic step in the complicated dance of preparation for these final dishes.

I and almost everyone else in class spent almost all our free time huddled together, either studying for the final exam or making plans for what we would do when we graduated. Junior dreamed of cooking for a large cruise line—the thought of hot women and tropical destinations settling like a fog over his person, a fog not even the threat of having to prepare the scallop dish for the final seemed able to burn through. Jackie had more personal things on her mind—her boyfriend had proposed, and she was full of plans for a wedding in the New Year, and toying with the idea of making her own wedding cake. Tucker desperately wanted to return to his family in Michigan and begin his new career as a chef in his town's one posh restaurant. Ravi was taking a trip to India with his extended family for a month, and was full of ideas on marrying French technique with Indian spices and the freshest American ingredients. Ben was hoping to win a full-time job at Blue Hill, where he had been interning for almost four months already. I fervently hoped Mimi was planning on taking a job as a short-order cook in hell, but wasn't holding my breath. What did I want? I didn't know, and that scared me. Why didn't I know? Why didn't I have a plan like all my friends and classmates? Once I did graduate, did I really, really want to go to work in a restaurant kitchen? I wasn't sure, but I knew that I wasn't going to be happy unless I graduated with honors, top honors if I could help it. So when I wasn't working to repay my student loan, I was spending long evenings at my own stove, trying to reproduce everything I had learned so far, memorizing the steps of each recipe, the proper feel of each finished product, the look, the taste of my best efforts.

Which left me little time to enjoy the holiday season, my favorite time of year. I reflected on the past six months; all the spent time, effort, and sheer number of vegetables was mind-boggling. I wanted to do something for the people I had spent so much of my life with, a little thank-you for helping me get through days that sometimes seemed as hard to navigate as the endless mountains of tomato seeds, potato peelings, and chicken carcasses we left in our wake. I also wanted to do something nice for the chef-instructors I had, whose kind words and subtle instruction got through when shouting and threats did not. But I didn't have the money to spend on nice presents, and while I could make something delicious to give, they were all chefs, too, or very nearly, and could whip up something just as nice themselves. I was stymied, unable to think of a suitable way to say thank you, until one evening it hit me. I could throw a Christmas party for all my former teammates and chefs in our new apartment, a last hurrah for us before we had to buckle down for the final and then go our separate ways. A big, friendly dinner, with cocktails before and plenty of wine during and after, some good, warming winter food, and music and laughter and dancing. I could give them a good time that they would remember long after the stress of school and the holidays had passed.

Such an event is easier dreamed up than actually carried out, however. If everyone accepted, I would have almost twenty people for dinner—not an impossible feat if one has all day to prepare and a restaurant-quality kitchen and dining room, but a bit more difficult after a long day spent in class, and the constraints of chairs for ten and plates and glasses for twelve. I persevered, however, and planned stuffed, marinated olives, salted nuts, and the Italian flatbread known as *pane carasau* for nibbling; a big beef stew (no one was a vegetarian) bountiful with carrots, mushrooms, well-browned pearl onions, and pulpy bites of tomato; a green salad; a platter of cheeses; baskets of fresh bread from Balthazar; and a flourless chocolate cake for dessert. The beef stew went into the oven on low the night before and simmered slowly through the night. The cocktail snacks I bought from Franco, my friend, adviser, and grocer, who helped me plan the menu. All I had to do was rush home from school, wash the greens, make a vinaigrette, set out the cheeses to lose their refrigerator chill, mix the cake, and set up the bar and trays of snacks.

It was a good thing, too—while everyone was supposed to come at seven, Tucker and Junior showed up almost an hour early, at a little after six. They had nowhere to go, they said, and were tired of staring up at my building, waiting for the lights to go on. I set them to work opening bottles of wine and folding paper napkins while I threw myself into the shower to wash off stray drips of chocolate cake batter and put on clean clothes. By seven-thirty, the candles were lit, the music was playing, and everyone was happily clustered around the kitchen island, scarfing up olives, swilling down cocktails, and having a marvelous time. Michael was happy to play host with the most; while he sometimes thought my friends from chef school were a little crazy, he couldn't resist spending an evening with them, drinking a case or so of wine and hanging out—talking about food was one of his passions, too.

While Michael kept our crowd of guests well stocked with noshes and well lubricated with another round or two of drinks, I found myself trapped in the kitchen, worrying about plating everything, making certain everyone had enough to eat. But I had forgotten that while everyone was a friend and a guest, I had been through chef school with them all as well. When it was time to serve the stew, I found myself suddenly at the head of a seamless production line of plates and workers, just like a station at the school restaurant. Tucker ladled a serving of steamed baby potatoes on each plate, and then Jared came behind, adding generous dollops of stew, while Jackie added a garnish of pepper and fresh herbs and Junior ran the plates out. It was marvelous. Chef Mark and Chef Paul clapped in appreciation of our team effort, and Chef Tina complimented the swift service. With a dozen chefs at my disposal, it should be. As the plates were slowly wiped clean of food and the salad was served and quickly disposed of, the cheeses passed and passed again, I found myself looking around the table at the clutch of people I had come to know so well in the past months, glad I could share this evening with them, that we would all have a happy memory to mark the end of our time together.

After dessert had been eaten and people wandered away from the table for more wine, more music, more conversation, I looked around at the incredible mess waiting for me to address it at some point. But not now. I, too, got up from the table and ambled off to refill my glass with some more of that lovely Châteauneuf-du-Pape someone had brought and spend a few more minutes with my friends.

Eventually, the music got louder, the conversation more and more jovial, and the night got later. When my downstairs neighbor came up to complain about the wrestling match that had broken out between Wayne and Junior, I knew it was time to break up the party and send everyone home.

Since graduating from chef school, I have thrown many dinner parties, and while they have all been fun, and the food has often been more haute than the simple fare I served that evening, that dinner party will always stand out in my mind as a perfect evening among friends.

Beef Stew for a Crowd

*This master recipe serves twelve and can easily be doubled or even
tripled if needed. You can cook it in the oven, on top of the stove, or
even in a very large slow cooker (cut back on the liquids if you choose
this way). Because it is meant to serve a crowd of people at a party, I just
bring everything together in the pot to brown briefly before adding the
braising liquid and simmering, instead of browning everything in separate
batches. If you are throwing a party, there are better ways to spend your
time than in time-consuming details. Remember, this is hearty, stomach-
pleasing peasant fare, not haute cuisine. Figure on a pound of meat
serving two people.*

1 pound slab bacon, cut into lardons

6 pounds rump pot roast, cut into manageable chunks (roughly bite-size)

2 medium onions, chopped

4 medium carrots, peeled and chopped

4 stalks celery, chopped

10 cloves garlic, chopped

8 medium shallots, quartered

2 pounds white button mushrooms, quartered

8 ounces wild mushrooms, shiitakes, criminis, or baby bellas, quartered

¼ cup all-purpose flour

Salt and freshly ground pepper

1 cup balsamic vinegar

One 14.5-ounce can peeled, crushed tomatoes

2 bay leaves

Handful of fresh thyme sprigs

Two 750-ml bottles red wine

1. In a very large pot (big enough to hold everything!) over medium-high heat, brown the bacon. Once the bacon has begun rendering its fat, add the beef, onions, carrots, celery, garlic, shallots, and mushrooms. Dust with the flour and season liberally with salt and pepper. Cook until the veggies begin to color and soften, about 5 minutes. Add the balsamic vinegar, half of the tomatoes, the bay leaves, thyme, and enough wine to completely cover everything. Cook, covered, over very low heat, adding more wine and crushed tomatoes as things cook down.

2. I have cooked this overnight in the oven (I added all the liquid at once and cooked it in an enormous roasting pan covered with foil), and for 3 to 4 hours on the back of the stove. The stew is ready when the meat is so tender it is just on the verge of falling apart and the liquid is thick enough to coat the back of a spoon.

NOTES: This stew pairs well with buttered baby potatoes (easy to make for a crowd if you aren't bothering to peel them, and you shouldn't) or with wide pasta—egg noodles are good, and even textured ziti or campanelle (bellflower shaped—adorable!) would do nicely. Anything that will trap the glorious sauce is a natural pairing here. Fresh pasta (page 225) would be divine, but don't overexert yourself before your party even starts. It is, after all, your party—enjoy yourself!

This stew is even better the second or third day. If you have the time beforehand (and the space!), make the stew and let it sit in your fridge. Skim the solidified fat off the top before rewarming right before serving.

THE FINAL

There wasn't even time to be nervous, that last day. I was up before dawn, pressing my two uniforms, carefully hanging them inside plastic trash bags to shield them from the rain that was, even then, beating against the windows and holding off the light of day. A few minutes at the kitchen table were spent waiting for the coffee to filter through its tiny basket of highly scented grinds, and going over the notes and photos of the possible dishes again and again and again. I closed my eyes, imagining the rich green color of the herb oil against its backdrop of pale beurre blanc. I felt the spiky brittleness of a fried sage leaf between my fingers as I imagined plating the marinated tuna; saw the rosy color of slices of the salt-crusted beef tenderloin poised next to the alternating orange and green bands of the spinach and carrot flan. I laced my fingers together around a cup of coffee and fervently beseeched whoever the patron saint of chefs is not to land me with one of the meat dishes. Of course, having a garde-manger dish and a *saucier* dish meant that you would be through the exam, through the entire long, drawn-out, painful experience, before at least half of the rest of the class. That fact suddenly seemed important. To be done, to taste the uncluttered, uncomplicated sharp notes of freedom on the tongue, suddenly seemed very important, like a jolt of fresh raspberry coulis against a bland and featureless expanse of *blanc mange* or *coeur à la crème*. I tried not to prefer one dish combination to another, not to set my heart on anything in particular, reluctant to cloud my vision of what was to come.

I left the coffee untouched on the counter, kissed a sleepy

Michael for luck, and headed out into the rain with my clean uniforms hooked over my shoulder, my boots polished, and my well-thumbed notes in my pocket. Too soon I was at the students' entrance. Before I could punch in the code, David swung open the door to let me in. His face was wreathed in smiles, and he gave my hand a squeeze.

"Good luck," he said, his heavy Cuban accent making the words thick and sweet as *dulce de leche*.

Suddenly, words were stuck in my throat, and I couldn't squeeze anything past the lump, big as an orange, that was blocking the way. I didn't have to.

"We're all rooting for you," David continued, giving me a wink. "You always were our favorite."

Another squeeze and he was gone, back to the stacks of provisions behind the counter of the storeroom. I knew all the storeroom guys and dishwashers might be rooting for me, but I also knew they ran a lucrative pool among themselves, betting on which student would win top honors in the final and which ones would self-destruct.

Suddenly I was in the locker room, taking off my street clothes and carefully pulling on my chef's uniform, setting my knife roll down next to my steady ally, the old red toolbox, still dusty with flour from the pastry kitchen. It was too early for the students from the other levels to be in school yet, and I was surrounded only by the soft rustlings of my classmates as we silently prepared for our day. It was too quiet. Jackie was fumbling with the French knots of her chef's jacket, trying and failing to button it properly, and Imogene was sitting on her toolbox, scrambling through her own notes, comparing recipes with photos of the final dish, repeating the garnishes of each dish in a barely audible whisper.

I was trying to focus, to make sure I had everything I needed, to remember to put my meat thermometer in my jacket pocket, tie my neckerchief properly, zip my fly. The tension was almost too much to bear. The door bounced backward on its hinges with the force of the blow directed at it, and shy, quiet Keri barreled into the room. She was quiet no longer.

"Hey, guys!" she shouted at us, at the top of her lungs. "What? Is there a funeral? Cheer up! It's our last day! Then we'll be free! Can you believe it?"

She was in such a good mood, so happy to be almost finished with school, she didn't even seem to care that the next six hours were going to be some of the most grueling we had ever faced in the kitchen.

"Let's just enjoy it! Come on, you look so sad! Let's have some fun!"

Her impression of little Mary Sunshine was infectious. I found myself smiling as I looked in the mirror to check that I had everything on correctly. Imogene had struck up a conversation with Marita, and they were laughing about some dirty joke Angelo had told them in a late-night study session. Soon, we were all dressed and ready to head downstairs. As we clomped down the stairs, swinging our toolboxes and gently joking with one another about what was waiting for us in the kitchens, we lost the nervousness and foreboding that had hung over us in the locker room, like a pall of smoke from an overdone tart in the oven.

We marched down the hallway, not allowed on this day to cut through the Level 2 kitchens to the dining room for our regular morning gathering. When we pushed through the swinging door to the restaurant, the difference in the room was at first frightening. Gone was the usual arrangement of tables and chairs, and in its place were four large judges' tables, already draped in immaculate white tablecloths and set with silver and glasses. In the middle of the room stood Chef Pierre. He was standing four square, his legs rooted to the ground like some ancient olive tree, and his meaty biceps and forearms folded and tucked tightly against his chest. He favored us with one of his rare, gorgeous smiles—eyes squinted almost shut, a few teeth and a lot of healthy gum laced with the glint of medieval European dental work. It was as reassuring as the golden yellow yolk of a fresh, poached egg breaking with glorious abandon over buttered toast. My stomach rumbled. Maybe I should have eaten breakfast. It was too late now.

We took our seats at the tables placed around the room and tried to cram in just a few more pieces of information. Like magic, there was one seat left at a four top where Tucker, Ben, and Junior were drinking coffee and running over the details of each dish.

"Hey, Darling." They greeted me with a few high fives, like every single other day. It was hard to believe that today was our last day together in the kitchens. I sat down and helped myself to a sip from Ben's cup of coffee—like every other day I had snagged a sip, I knew Ben wouldn't mind.

"Quick, Darling! The ingredients for *pâte brisée*!" Tucker barked at me. Easy. I could make piecrust backward, in my sleep.

"*Pâte à choux!*" I shot right back at him. We had forgotten any sense of lingering nervousness in the happy groove of our regular competitive friendship. We had come all the way together, and it was down to how we would perform today. But even though the dishwashers might have been betting on me, I still wasn't too certain that I had what it took to perform better than my classmates and my friends.

After what seemed like an age of cramming, coffee, and a few good-natured insults, we were all present and accounted for. Chef Pierre called roll for the last time and then began to go over the final exam. After the written exam was administered at 8:30, we would draw our numbers from Chef's toque, 1 through 24. This would be the order our dishes would appear in front of the judges—whoever drew number 1 would be the first one on the chopping block, 24 would be the last. I prayed that I wouldn't be the first or the last, but snuggled safely in the middle of the pack. When everyone had been assigned a number, we would then be told which two dishes we would be preparing. Then we would file into the kitchens and find our stations at 8:45, check to make certain that we had been supplied with the correct ingredients, had enough pots and pans and squareboys and bowls, and at 9:00 precisely, Chef Pierre would blow his whistle and we could begin cooking.

The first dishes would go out to the judges at 1:00 PM on the dot, and the last round of desserts would leave the kitchen at 2:45. It was going to be a long day. Chef gave us another one of his dazzling smiles—I wondered if he had been saving them up until today, when we really needed them. The minutes ticked by—8:10, 8:13, 8:22, 8:27. The chatter had died, and even the last-minute scrambling for pencils and pieces of paper had faded to a few rustles and dry coughs. Eight-thirty.

Chef shouted, "Give me the ingredients and procedure for . . . *pâte sucrée* and *pâte à choux*!" This was it: all our studying, all the recipes we had memorized, and we would be asked to write only these two. It was all or nothing—you either knew it or you didn't.

And I knew it. We rushed to write down the proper proportion of ingredients and all the steps to both recipes in the proper order. Soon everyone had turned in their papers and it was time to draw our numbers from Chef's hat. Even though Chef Pierre had only been wearing his Chef's hat for an hour, when he took it off, it left a crease in his thick dark hair. It was odd to see Chef without his toque—a disarmingly informal touch in the middle of all our formal preparations.

One by one we filed to the front and fished out a small piece of paper from the depths. When my name was called, I took a deep breath and made a running start to the head of the room. I rummaged deep in the recesses of Chef's toque, hoping my fingers would guide me to a good number. I finally settled on a piece of paper that seemed to flutter right into my hand. I tried not to take it as a sign, but I felt my heart racing anyway. I fumbled the paper open, praying to see 7, 8, 10, anything from the middle of the pack.

Hell, I would have even taken unlucky 13—anything but 1 or 24. There it was, in Chef Pierre's distinctive scrawl and French numerals: 24. Crap. Crap crap crap crap crap! I would be the last one finished with the exam. My four plates of dessert would go out at 2:45, the very final plates to go out to the judges. Then I would have to do my share of the heavy-duty cleaning in my small area of the kitchen before I was free at last to change into my fresh uniform, wash my face, and prepare to meet the judges and receive critiques on my final dishes. CRAP! The judges would have tasted almost two dozen other dishes before they got to my attempts—even if my dishes were better in comparison to the others, who would feel enthusiasm over their fifth plate of sea bass? I would have slightly more time to work on my dishes, which was a good thing, but suddenly, the only thing I cared about was being done, finished with chef school forever. I was suddenly very, very weary, and we hadn't even begun the final exam.

I stomped back to my seat, not even bothering to tell Chef Pierre what number I had drawn. He had to chase me across the room and I shouted, at the top of my lungs, "Twenty-four, goddamnit!"

Chef cocked his eyebrows at me over his glasses, pursed his lips, and said, "Hush, you. Somebody was going to get it. Today it was you. So?"

"I'm ruined, Chef," I mumbled. "It's a sign." I couldn't believe how superstitious I was being, but still. This was worse than anything I had imagined happening today, the one thing I hadn't thought of and planned for. Total emotional tailspin. Chef Pierre tried one of his molten smiles again, but there was no melting the icy lump of dread that had settled itself firmly in my stomach. Exasperated, Chef slapped me firmly in the rump and said, "Just cook your azz off, you'll do fine."

Tucker, Ben, and Junior tried to cheer me up in their own way. "Sucks for you, Darling" seemed to be the consensus. I knew they were just glad to have dodged being the last one, and I couldn't blame them. I would have been happy to be anywhere else as well, even first. At least then the judges would have had nothing to compare me to—now my efforts were going to be compared against every single other plate that my classmates prepared. I would really have to work hard to impress them. Now I could only pray that the gods would have mercy on me and give me a good pairing of dishes, at least. Once everyone had drawn their number, Chef once again called for our silence while he read out who would be receiving what. I was in for a little bit of luck on that score at least—I had gotten the striped bass with lobster sauce and the molten chocolate cakes with espresso crème anglaise. While these dishes were no cinch to make, they were exactly what I was hoping to get. The lobster sauce was the most labor-intensive aspect of the fish dish, and the molten cakes and crème anglaise needed to be made in advance, and only popped in the oven five minutes before plating. Still, it wasn't going to be easy, and for the next six hours I was going to need to cook my ass off, just like Chef said.

Wordlessly, we gathered up our knife bags and toolboxes and trooped through the double doors into the kitchens. A few whispered *good lucks* were passed back and forth, and then we were in, spread across the Level 3 and 4 kitchen, the Level 2 kitchen, even in the garde-manger and patisserie kitchens. In a corner of the garde-manger station, I found a tray of ingredients marked 24. I guess this was it—away from the bustle of the main kitchen, but not as removed as the few people marooned in the Level 2 kitchen. There was one other setup on the other side of the room, and I crossed my fingers I wouldn't be trapped in this confined space with Mimi or Penny. I was lucky again. Ravi sauntered in, all cool confidence, to take his place at the station set up across from me. Phew. Ravi and I had never worked together outside our week spent in the bread kitchen, but we were very friendly and would be able to work on the same stove without too much competition.

Hours passed in minutes, as Ravi and I worked in silence,

methodically preparing one aspect of our separate dishes after another, keeping an eye on each other's pots boiling on the stove. Periodically, one of the chef-instructors would come orbiting through, clipboard at the ready, poking through the lowboys where we kept our ingredients, sticking a tasting spoon into our pots and pans of sauces, barking an occasional question, making notes, and then moving on. I was determined not to let the occasional appearance of these birds of prey throw me off my game. I was in a rhythm; I could feel it; everything was falling into place for me. My lobster and crab shells had roasted nicely in the oven and I had had the good fortune to flame them with Cognac just as Chef Septimus swung through on his rounds. With the loud "whoof" of a controlled explosion, the Cognac ignited, and a blue flame danced merrily in the pan.

Chef Septimus said, "Bravo, Miss Darling. Your timing is impeccable," before moving on. Things were going so well, I was ticking things off my mental checklist at a gallop. *Sauce américain* prepared, strained, seasoned, tasted, ready. Check. Espresso crème anglaise prepared and resting in an ice bath. Check. Potatoes and celeriac peeled, boiled, mashed, and ready. Check. Bass marinating in olive oil, orange slices, and jalapeños over a tray of ice in the lowboy refrigerator. Check. Chocolate cakes prepared and waiting in the refrigerator in the pastry kitchen. Check. I was way ahead of schedule! I cleaned up my work area in the kitchen, retasted everything, prepared my chervil sprigs to garnish the fish, and took a peek into the main kitchen.

It was while I had my head poked around the corner, watching my classmates cooking frantically, that I began to have an uneasy feeling that I had forgotten something. I still had a half hour before I had to begin plating my fish course—the fish would take only five minutes to sauté. What was I missing? Fish, celeriac puree, *sauce américain*, green herb infusion, chervil sprigs, and what else? I racked my brain. There was something missing, definitely. I took a deep breath, closed my eyes, and tried to envision the finished dish. I thought back to the day we had prepared it in the *poissonnier* station, but all I could remember was showing Wayne how to make a beurre blanc sauce—that was it! I needed a beurre blanc sauce to garnish! The celeriac puree would go in a mound on the middle of the plate, surrounded by a moat of the pink-orange lobster sauce. The herb infusion would be evenly spaced, deep green circles in this sauce. Nestled next to this mossy green was supposed to be a drop of white beurre blanc sauce. A toothpick was then pulled through the two sauces, making a very pretty pattern. The fish would go on top of the celeriac puree, skin side up, with a chervil sprig and, and, and—oh, no! I had forgotten something else! A crisply fried, paper-thin slice of celeriac was supposed to crown each fish fillet. CRAP! How could I have forgotten not one but two things! I was running out of time!

I sliced celeriac like lightning and threw it in the deep fryer, willing it to crisp. I pulled it out before it was perfectly browned—no time, no time!—and flew back to my station to mix the fastest beurre blanc sauce on record. Beurre blanc sauce is made from a series of reductions—shallots are sliced and put in a small pot with white wine vinegar to reduce. When the vinegar has almost completely reduced over a low flame, heavy cream is added. When the heavy cream has been reduced by slightly more than half, then the whole is pulled off the heat and vast quantities of slightly chilled butter are vigorously whisked in. The resulting creamy, velvety sauce is strained and kept warm in a bain-marie until ready for use. A classic beurre blanc sauce does not have heavy cream in it, but this addition was a secret Chef Pierre had taught us—it helped the notoriously unstable sauce stay emulsified during a long service. I reduced, reduced again, the sweat sliding down the back of my neck and congealing somewhere near that frozen lump of dread in my guts that had come back full force.

I started to pray.

Time had run out.

I sautéed my four fillets of bass and began to plate. My hands were shaking so badly, I slopped sauce all over the plates and had to wipe it up with my trusty kitchen towel. I suddenly took comfort in the fact that I was last, and had these few precious seconds to work. Chef Pierre called time, and the Level 3 student in charge of carrying my dishes out swept away with my tray of fish held high. I let out a deep breath. There was nothing I could do about it now, I was halfway through. Time to clean up and move on to dessert. I scrubbed the stove, wiped out the lowboy refrigerator, washed my knives and spoons. I took my last load of dishes to the dishwashers, packed up my bag, and headed into the pastry kitchen.

At some point, I realized, I had burned my wrist badly, and a huge blister had formed. Definite points off for carelessness if any of the chefs noticed it. I pulled the sleeves of my chef's jacket down and soldiered through my last few tasks for dessert. In no time it was 2:42, and my four plates of molten chocolate cakes with espresso crème anglaise had been dusted with a beautiful shower of confectioners' sugar and sent off.

I was through.

But time refused to slow down. Almost immediately, it seemed, we were all back in the kitchens, in fresh uniforms and full of nervous excitement. We were finished! All that remained was hearing our critiques from the judges, receiving our official chef's toques and diplomas from Chef Pierre, and finding out who had graduated with honors. We filed out to sit in front of the judges, promising Chef Pierre we would sit quietly and listen with no backtalk to what the judges—all distinguished members of the New York restaurant world—had to say about our efforts. I cannot remember a single word that was said about either of my dishes, but the overall critique didn't seem too scathing.

Suddenly, there we all were, in the school's auditorium, lined up alphabetically, waiting for Chef to call our names one last time and place the tall chef's toques on our heads—the symbol of our successful transition from student to chef. When my name was called, I waved to my parents and to Michael, barely visible in the crowded auditorium, before turning around so that Chef could place my chef's hat on my head. At last.

Finally, everyone's name had been called, and we ranged across the stage, all of us beaming, tired, and happy. Chef André Soltner gave us all a heartfelt speech about his desire that we would become part of something larger, a growing appreciation of food in this country, and hoped that we would continue to work, create, and build on what we had learned in school, for that was just the beginning of our learning. We would all be chefs for a long time, and were expected to continue to grow and evolve and change the culinary world. A tall order for a bunch of exhausted students, but we could have done anything at that point, so filled were we with exhilaration.

There was just one more thing to be done before the Champagne was popped and we were free to mingle with the audience, eat hors d'oeuvres prepared by the peons in Level 2, and bask in the glow of being actual, real, honest-to-goodness chefs. Six of the twenty-four of us students would be graduating with honors—one by one, Chef Pierre called forward Ben, Jackie, Mimi (the rat), Angelo, Tucker, and me. We stood forward and received a pin to wear on our chef's jackets and a certificate of distinction. And now, there would be one student who would graduate first in the class. As Chef Pierre brought out the beautiful chef's knife to be presented to the winner, I thought of all the times that I had forgotten the salt, burned the puff pastry dough, overcooked eggs, and let soufflés fall. I certainly didn't deserve the honor. I had worked hard, and I was thrilled just to be one of the lucky ones to be awarded distinction. So when Chef Pierre called my name, I was staring off into space, a smile on my face, thinking how glad I was it was over, obviously not listening to a word being said. Chef Paul was forced to poke me sharply from behind. I was floored. I kissed Chef Pierre, Chef Paul, Chef Jean, Chef

Mark, Dean Soltner, Dean Jacques Pépin (I kissed Jacques Pépin! YES!)—even Chef Robert got a peck on the cheek.

And then it was over—the audience applauded us all, and we were free. Soon I was flagging down extra glasses of Champagne and fighting my way to the hors d'oeuvres tray, remembering Chef Paul at orientation, coaxing me to have one and enjoy it before having to make them by the hundred spoiled it for me. Nothing tasted more delicious. But soon, the food had run out, there was no more Champagne being poured, and my fellow alums were leaving to change back into street clothes and celebrate with their families. We all made plans to meet at Toad Hall to raise one more glass (or two or three or four) together, but right now, it was time to go.

As we trundled into the women's locker room one last time, each of us was met with a sign recently posted on her locker. It read "Congratulations, recent graduate. Please remove your belongings from this locker before 5 PM. Thank you." It was 4:52.

The journey was over, and it was time to go home.

EPILOGUE

After graduation, despite our vows to stay in touch, we went our separate ways. Surprisingly, though most of us work with food in some capacity, there are few working chefs among us.

Tucker couldn't wait to return to his wife and little kids in Michigan. He does work as a chef in the posh restaurant in town, and spends his weekends training as a National Guardsman.

Amanda moved to the city permanently to chef full-time, but the long hours and extremely low pay forced her out of the kitchen after a year. To keep up with her student-loan payments she works front-of-house as a restaurant manager on the Upper West Side.

Angelo is still around, working as a sous chef at a three-star hotel in New Jersey. Angelo had resisted our efforts to become a Manhattan transplant, saying that even if he did get a job here, he would commute. I guess you can't take the Jersey out of a "Jersey boy."

After returning home to Virginia, Imo snagged a job at the Pentagon, working as a chef for the top-secret posh dining room. She prepares lunch every day for the country's top brass.

Keri moved back to Utah and decided to get a degree in business. She is happily married and making some gourmet dinners for her growing family.

Penny has dropped out of sight, to no one's surprise. She had managed to alienate almost all of us, especially those of us who had been her teammates. But as I looked over our class as we ranged across the auditorium's stage, I caught sight of Penny. She was clutching the blue linen envelope containing her *grand diplome* in her bird-claw hands and her eyes were wet. I wondered whether she had managed to squeak through the final or whether her envelope contained a blank piece of paper. I hope she made it, and that her dream of being the only real chef in her little midwestern town came true.

Wayne shipped out on a cruise liner to work as a chef for the buffet, and ended up cruising the world while churning out lobster thermidor by the gallon.

Jackie landed a job as a food stylist at the Food Network, her dream job. She had taken courses in food styling before becoming a chef, and now combines the two to make some of the best "food porn" in the business. She spent every free minute planning her wedding and baking her own wedding cake—chocolate, of course.

Mimi, my social nemesis, used family connections to land an internship at Daniel. I heard she didn't last long.

Michael took my parents and me out to dinner at Bouley that night to celebrate. I was beyond exhausted, beyond excited. Everything seemed to have happened so fast—I was one of the only students to graduate without a job already lined up, and suddenly school was over and I was officially unemployed. I couldn't wait to add "graduated first in class" to my résumé. I had accomplished my dream—at last, I was a Chef, with a capital C and a tall toque and a killer set of kitchen skills. I could make elaborate delicacies in my sleep, and no recipe, no matter how complicated, could intimidate me. As I sat at our gorgeous table at the restaurant, enjoying sautéed rockfish (I thought my bass with lobster sauce was just a smidgen better), I thought about the frenetic rush that was certain to be going on a few feet away, behind the scenes. As I munched my way through three more courses, cramming down the last of the petits fours on my way out of the restaurant (someone went to a lot of trouble to make those, as I knew better than anyone. The least I could do would be to eat them all!), I thought I would take my time, see what kinds of jobs I could get, before rushing into something I might not love. Chef Jean's advice for making caramel came back to me again: Good things can't be rushed. Have patience, you will know when it is right.

Well, I knew it was right with Michael, and we were married two weeks after I finished school, on our Caribbean beach at sunset, with just our families around us. That night, we went out to dinner, and it was nice letting someone else cook!

Against all odds, I had done it, beating out all of my very talented friends (and a few bitter rivals) to graduate first in my class. Despite the many mistakes I had made along the way, and the near disaster during the final, somehow I had made it through and had earned my tall toque with its hundred folds. Now I was a chef.

For a moment or two I relived my old fantasy, the one I had had before chef school, of being the next Food Network superstar, with all the shiny kitchen gadgets and the adoring studio audience hanging on my every dash of salt, with a self-titled cookbook and a restaurant earning three stars from Frank Bruni in *The New York Times*. These dreams seemed a little silly to me now, a little naïve. I had dreamed them up without any idea how hard it was to get there. Even now, with months of very hard work behind me and with my diploma in my hand, I was only just beginning to learn all the things I needed to know to be a good chef. It would take lots more cooking, making both mistakes and successes, before an eponymous restaurant (let alone cooking show, line of cookware, and frozen entrées) was a possibility.

Still, with my shiny new accolade on my résumé, I was certain that it wouldn't be long before I would find work in a premier restaurant, polishing my skills and picking up recipes and tricks from a superstar chef. The Institute pretty much guaranteed job placement somewhere after successfully completing a degree, and I was sure that I could get a job without too much trouble.

Trouble was, sometimes chefs didn't want a brand-spanking-new chef just out of school. After weeks of quiet on the job front (it was Christmastime, after all), I met up with a career counselor at The Institute to see how my future was going. Almost everyone else in my class had already been placed in a position (far from the city) or simply gone full-time at the internships they had been working throughout school. My lack of internship experience in a New York City kitchen was a problem, but I hadn't had a choice about that: with my student loan payments due every month, I couldn't afford to work for free. What worked against me even more than my lack of restaurant experience was my GPA—it seemed that many chefs wanted to hire people to work in the kitchen whom they could mold to their own way of doing things, not some greenhorn know-it-all who would insist on doing things "like we did in school." While I protested that that wasn't me, that the school's chef-instructors had done a wonderful job of breaking my spirit and I could easily work under anyone, it didn't do me any good.

Looking over my previous employment history and education, the career counselor recommended that I try for a job at a food magazine. It would fit with my work experience and keep me near the food, the only place I wanted to be. I ended up working in the editorial side of a great cult foodie magazine, and while the closest I was getting to the prep work I had grown used to was helping their test kitchen source arcane ingredients, it was about food, and that was good. Writing the occasional blurb or short piece about ice cream shacks of the East Coast, olive oils from Chile, and honey festivals in rural England combined my love of the written word with my love of food. A food pairing made in heaven, at least for me.

I still love to cook, and do it every day, but after the pressures of school, I knew I was burned out. I no longer have the deep desire to give up the next five years of my life for a spot at the *saucier* station, even at Adour. And that's okay. I have found my passion, combining my love of words with my obsession for food and all things culinary.

*

For now, my chef's toque remains in the kitchen cupboard, next to my black Hawaiian sea salt and a set of wicked sharp garniture tools, waiting. Maybe someday, when I pay off my student loans, I will open a little restaurant, one with mismatched Wedgwood plates, real silver, and no set menu, just whatever I feel like creating from my early-morning trips to the Greenmarket. I'll have a cult following of people devoted not to the next Food Network star, but to great food. I don't think I will be resurrecting my polyester checked chef's pants anytime soon, but maybe I will wear my tall toque on special occasions. Until then, I keep my knives sharp and my skills sharper, scoping out new ingredients from unexpected places, dreaming up new plating ideas, and sometimes whipping up a ridiculously decadent dessert, just because I can. Every time I pull a perfectly risen chocolate soufflé from the oven, its high crown a perfect dome dotted with crispy bits of caramelized sugar, wreathed in a wisp of escaping steam, I think of Chef Mark's patient instructions. Every time I flip a perfect omelet effortlessly from the pan, I see Chef Jean's smile, and I am grateful.

ACKNOWLEDGMENTS

This book would not have been possible without the help and support of the following people:

My wonderful editor, Peter Borland, without whose gentle guidance and insight I would have been lost.

My agent, former boss, and very good friend Faith Hamlin. She believed in this book, and in me, from the very beginning. Indeed, just when things were looking very bleak, Faith found this project the perfect home at Atria. She has my eternal affection and gratitude. Her lovely and supremely competent sidekick, Courtney, has also been a great help.

My family: My brother, Eben, read the manuscript ad nauseam and made helpful suggestions at every turn. My sister-in-law, Jenny, tried all my culinary efforts and was unfailingly supportive. My mom and dad, who started me on this path long ago, have been there every single step of the way. Michael and Annabelle make every day, and every meal, a pleasure. You have all my love and I could never have done this without you.

My teachers, particularly Chef Henri, Chef Pascal, Chef Greg, and Chef John, through whose wisdom and guidance I became a chef myself. My classmates, especially my partner Trevor, Dan, Jeanette, Frank, Melissa, Junior, and Monica, whose antics gave me so much to write about.

INDEX OF RECIPES